Counseling: The Spiritual Dimension

Edited by

Mary Thomas Burke, PhD
Judith G. Miranti, EdD

Counseling the Spiritual Dimension

10 9 8 7 6 5 4 3 2 1

American Counseling Association
5999 Stevenson Avenue
Alexandria, VA 22304

Acquisitions and Development Editor
Carolyn Baker

Production Manager
Michael Comlish

Copyeditor
Heather Jefferson

Cover design by Martha Woolsey

Library of Congress Cataloging-in-Publication Data

Counseling: the spiritual dimension / edited by Mary Thomas Burke, Judith G. Miranti.
    p.   cm.
  Includes bibliographical references.
  ISBN 1-55620-145-1 (alk. paper)
  1. Counseling. 2. Counseling—Religious aspects. 3. Religion and psychology. I. Burke, Mary Thomas. II. Miranti, Judith G.
BF637.C6C6546 1995
158' .3—dc20

                                                  95-5667
                                                    CIP

Dedication

In memory of the deceased ASERVIC leaders
who exemplified spiritual values in their lives

and

our loved ones who influenced our
spiritual values.

Table of Contents

Table of Contents

Foreword

Spirituality is deeply personal. Its meaning seems to escape simple definition. As doctoral students, we were asked to write our theory of personality and its implications for counseling. The psychologist who marked my paper chided me for reference to my spiritual values and beliefs because they were inappropriate to the task! Upon reviewing the articles for this book on spirituality and counseling, I felt a sense of relief and vindication. There are no doubt many reasons why we have come to a point of accepting and even celebrating this very personal yet essential dimension of human existence.

As we recount the statistics on violence, substance abuse, suicide, homelessness, sexual harrassment, racial discrimination, and related symptoms of alienation and antipathy among the people of the wealthiest country in the world, one must wonder, why is there such discouragement, such disregard for the worth and dignity of others? While our form of government is predicated upon values which are to protect "life, liberty, and the pursuit of happiness," we fall far short of these ideals.

Medical science has helped us to prolong life. We have information on how to protect and sustain our physical well-being. In fact, we are living so much longer that the aging of our population is creating a new demographic configuration. Aging is no longer a last stage of life, but rather a process to be studied and better understood. What sustains individuals who experience multiple losses over a life time? How do they seem to not only survive but transcend negative circumstances?

We are not the "melting pot" of the world, as many generations were taught. We are a diverse and increasingly complex nation of cultures, races, and ethnic groups who strive to coexist much as the world populations must coexist in cooperation, compassion, and respect for the others' unique qualities, values, and positive attributes. Those human qualities and conditions which we share in common are what bring us together. Whether it be our search for personal meaning in life or deep religious affiliation and conviction, we share spirituality regardless of our historical roots or heritage.

The following readings have been carefully selected for their usefulness to the exploration of this topic. The editors have been deliberate in attempting to provide both theoretical and practice oriented content. Issues and ethics are introduced related to important areas for consideration by counselors. One author's spiritual journey takes the reader to another level of understanding and, potentially, insight with regard to how one counselor integrates this very personal dimension into his counseling practice without imposing an orthodoxy upon another. Finally, for the researcher, a model based upon data across disciplines provides more questions to be answered, but within a frame of reference which has practical implications for counseling interventions as well.

In short, this work will be useful to neophyte, researcher, and practitioner alike. Adler, Jung, and Maslow are among those who professed that to be human was to include dimensions of spirituality, soul, or peak experiences. Recent authors such as Scott Peck have helped to raise consciousness, not only among counselors, but the public at large to the need for a personal exploration of "the road less traveled." If not out of anything but personal motivation and belief, we need to understand and be ready to assist others in this journey. In so doing, each of us will increase our capacity to be helpful to those whom we teach or counsel. Likewise, we leave open the opportunity to be taught and counseled.

Thomas J. Sweeney, PhD
Professor Emeritus
Ohio University

Preface

Throughout history, each culture, civilization, and nation has adopted practices considered to be sacred and life sustaining. The form that these practices take are expressions of religiosity. The core beliefs are said to be one's individual spirituality.

What is it, then, that lies at the very essence of our being, the core of our belief system? Is spirituality what provides meaning to one's existence? How does one define it, operationalize it, use it to direct one's actions? And how, in times of life's passages, crises, and so forth, can we draw upon our spirituality for the strength and courage to live out our conventions.

Through counseling, clients are empowered to consider all possible futures and to decide which would be most meaningful for them. Counselors, in providing the medium for change, must become adept at entering the client's frame of reference; to access the inner resources of the client. Both are prepared to journey together to explore all aspects leading to physical and mental well-being.

Spirituality, the core of wellness, is a dimension of emerging interest in counseling. However, counselors are reluctant to incorporate the spiritual dimension into the counseling process.

With emphasis on mental wellness and the developmental aspects of counseling, counselors-in-training could be challenged to explore their own spiritual dimension, thus enabling them to facilitate this exploration in their clients.

The purpose in compiling a collection of articles on the spiritual dimension of counseling is to encourage counselors to consider their own spirituality, and to facilitate the enhancement of spiritual wellness for their clients.

About the Editors

Mary Thomas Burke, Ph.D. is a professor and department chairperson of the Department of Human Services at the University of North Carolina at Charlotte. She has served as President of NCACA and NCARVIC and President of ASERVIC. She currently serves as Vice-Chair of the CACREP Board and as ACA and CACREP Liaison to the National Board for Certified Counselors.

Judith G. Miranti, Ed.D., is a professor of counselor education and graduate dean at Our Lady of Holy Cross College in New Orleans, Louisiana. Judy has served on the ACA Governing Council, and has been President of ASERVIC and President of the Louisiana Counseling Association. She is a recipient of the *Gilbert and Kathleen Wrenn Humanitarian and Caring Person Award*. She is married to Vincent Miranti and has one son, Vince.

Spirituality:
An Integral Component of the
Counseling Process

JUDITH MIRANTI
MARY THOMAS BURKE

IF ONE READS the counseling journals, or pages through the current counseling textbooks, one quickly becomes aware that the spiritual dimension of personhood is rarely, if ever, addressed as a topic of serious discussion or as a hypothesis for scientific research. One may argue that the spiritual dimension of personhood is omitted because one can't quantitatively measure the spiritual or prove that it exists. Yet much has been written about psychological constructs even though these are not concrete or measurable (Ingersoll, 1994; Bergin, 1991). So, the argument that we must ignore the spiritual because of lack of proof or concreteness is a moot point. Perhaps the spiritual dimension is ignored because many researchers are afraid to address this phase of personhood, either for fear of reprisals or because spirituality has been considered primarily the domain of religion (Chandler, Holden, & Kolander, 1992). How then should a counselor deal with a client who has questions or concerns in the spiritual domain?

Could one argue that the spiritual dimension of a client's life is equally important as that of a career decision? Is it not feasible that much depression, anger, guilt, or sadness has its origin in a lack of connectedness and meaning in a person's life? This lack of connectedness or meaning creates a vacuum that can only be filled by a depth dimension that is often referred to as spirituality (Worthington, 1989).

If one accepts the premise that there is a depth dimension or a spiritual dimension in each life, why would a counselor refuse to explore spirituality with clients? Is there any other issue a client introduces that a qualified professional counselor would ignore, or even worse, refuse to allow the client to explore? Is it possible that counselors refuse to address this dimension because they often do not know what to do or how to respond?

Counselor education programs rarely mention the spiritual dimension. If it is mentioned, they choose to ignore or relegate it to the reality of nontouchable or to refer it to a minister, pastor, or Rabbi. Counselors must be comfortable with their own spirituality or religious beliefs before they can allow a client's religion to have a place in the counseling process (Pate & Bondi, 1992). Some counselors may argue that they are afraid of imposing their own values on clients (Georgia, 1994). Yet, counselor values including spirituality are implicit in the counseling process (Patterson, 1992). It seems to follow that there may be times when counselors cannot be effective because of their own strong beliefs, or because unresolved spiritual issues in their own personal lives may limit their ability to truly focus on the client (Pate & Bondi, 1992). In such cases it becomes incumbent upon the counselor to acknowledge this limitation, and to refer the client to a professional who has both the skill and the facilitative theoretical model to help the client.

Counselors must be prepared to deal with all issues, including the quality that lies at the very core and essence of the clients' being. That core, which transcends the physical and material aspects of existence, which is untouchable and often times undefinable, is so necessary for an explanation to one's existence (Witmer & Sweeney, 1992). Clients themselves often suggest that spirituality is the sustaining core or essence that keeps them going when all else seems to fail. Conversely, the guilt, anger, and sadness that clients often endure stems from a misinterpretation of the spiritual, thus causing a deep depression and a sense of worthlessness. The inclusion of these issues in the DSM-IV may be a helpful step toward recognition of the importance of spirituality and religious ideals in life's journey.

Clients come to counselors to help them resolve deeply troubling issues in their lives. It is incumbent upon the counselor to be prepared to deal with these issues that transcend the immediate domain of the present reality (Smith, 1993). As with all issues, clients have the resources within them to resolve these conflicts provided that the counseling environment is facilitative and empathetic. For many clients, in times of transition and crises, the spiritual domain is their solace, comfort, and a major sustaining power. Take, for example, the person who has lost a loved one in death and is overcome by grief. If the person's spiritual belief recognizes a transcendent power, then this person will be helped by an exploration of these beliefs. The counselor must explore what exists in life for clients, and how they can commune with their loved ones who may be separated from their physical bodies (Ingersoll, 1994).

A recognition of the importance of spirituality and religion seems to be gaining some credibility in the fields of psychology and counseling. The fourth edition of the *Diagnostic and Statistical Manual for Mental Disorders* (American Psychiatric Association, 1994) has added religious and spiritual difficulties as a distinct mental disorder deserving treatment. Examples include distressing experiences that involve loss or questioning of faith, problems associated with conversion to a new faith, or questioning of other spiritual values that may not necessarily be related to an organized church or religious institution. Pate and Bondi (1992) assert that spirituality and religious beliefs should be included in the counselor education curriculum to the same extent as cultural diversity, because spirituality is unique to each client, and counselors need the skill and sensitivity to deal with these areas of the client's life.

This suggestion seems most appropriate when one considers that the United States is a decalog nation that is rooted in a deeply spiritual belief system. Kroll and Sheehan (1989) reported that as many as 90% of the general public profess a belief in God. Many of our ancestors came to the United States to escape religious oppression and in search of religious freedom. Is it possible that the refusal to allow clients to explore their spiritual/religious beliefs may be construed as a type of religious oppression? By neglecting to draw on the spiritual values that clients hold may deprive them of a singular sense of strength and support in times of great need. This is particularly true as persons grow older and they seem to exhibit a greater desire to explore religious/spiritual issues (Smith, 1993). These clients need counselors who are not afraid to address their spiritual needs and who are comfortable with their own spiritual selves. Counselors need to be nonjudgmental and open to their clients in these times of great importance and momentous decision making, thereby providing an invaluable source of strength for their clients.

For counselors, the challenge is not whether the issue of spirituality should be addressed, but how it can best be addressed by well-prepared and sensitive professionals.

REFERENCES

American Psychiatric Association. (1994). *Diagnostic and statistical manual of mental disorders* (4th ed.). Washington, DC: Author.

Barret, R. L. (1988). The spiritual journey: Explorations and implications for counselors. *Journal of Humanistic Education and Development, 26,* 155-162.

Bergin, A. E. (1991). Values and religious issues in psychotherapy and mental health. *American Psychologist, 46,* 394-403.

Chandler, C., Holden, J., & Kolander, C. (1992). Counseling for spiritual wellness: Theory and practice. *Journal of Counseling and Development, 71*(2), 168-175.

Georgia, R. T. (1994). Preparing to counsel clients of different religious backgrounds: A phenomenological approach. *Journal of Counseling and Values, 38,* 143-151.

Kroll, J., & Sheehan, W. (1989). Religious beliefs and practices among fifty-two psychiatric inpatients in Minnesota. *American Journal of Psychiatry, 67-72,* 146.

Ingersoll, R. E., (1994). Spirituality, religion and counseling: Dimension and relationships. *Journal of Counseling and Values, 38,* 98-111.

Pate, R. H., & Bondi, A. M. (1992). Religious beliefs and practice: An integral aspect of multicultural awareness. *Counselor Education and Supervision, 32,* 108-115.

Patterson, C. H. (1992). Values in counseling and psychotherapy. *Counseling and Values, 10,* 67-78.

Smith, D. C. (1993). Exploring the religious—spiritual needs of the dying. *Journal of Counseling and Values, 37,* 71-77.

Witmer, J., & Sweeney, T. (1992). A holister model for wellness and prevention over the life span. *Journal of Counseling and Development, 71*(2), 140-149.

Worthington, E. L., Jr. (1989). Religious faith across the life span: Implications for counseling and research. *The Counseling Psychologist, 146,* 167-172.

Spirituality, Religion, and Counseling: Dimensions and Relationships

R. ELLIOTT INGERSOLL

ALTHOUGH SPIRITUALITY HAS been noted by some authors to be a vital aspect of the counselor-client relationship and of human development (Fowler, 1981; Westerhoff, 1976), generally spirituality has been slighted in therapeutic literature (Barnhouse, 1979; Torrey, 1986). When the spiritual component of the helping relationship is discussed, it is often in the context of a particular religious worldview (Banks, 1980; Canda, 1988). The concept of spirituality is rarely described beyond generalization (Ellis, 1992) and when specific dimensions of spirituality are noted, they are too few in number to address the breadth of the construct (Moberg, 1984).

A COUNSELING ISSUE?

Research on spirituality in the social sciences has become more common in the last two decades, beginning with the inclusion of spiritual well-being in the social indicators movement (Ellison, 1983). According to Moberg (1971), one reason for the dearth of research is the confusion of spirituality with religiosity, and concern over church-state separation in institutions receiving federal funds. Ellison (1983) stated that for scientific investigation to occur, there must be consensus on the meaning of the phenomenon or construct to be studied. Ellison claimed that difficulty in operationalizing terms like "spiritual" has contributed to behavioral scientists' disdain for the topic.

Treatment of "spirituality" as a construct in the social sciences has been correlated with the appearance of works discussing the relativity of constructs and scientific paradigms in general (Kuhn, 1970). Despite this, counselor training rarely includes instruction on working with clients in areas of spirituality (Collins, Hurst, & Jacobson, 1987). A review of The Council for Accreditation of Counseling and Related Educational Programs (CACREP) recommended areas for counselor education shows no explicit reference to human spirituality (CACREP, 1988). It is only recently that the construct has received increased attention under the heading of "wellness" (Chandler, Holden, & Kolander, 1992; Witmer & Sweeney, 1992).

From "Spirituality, Religion, and Counseling: Dimensions and Relationships," by R.E. Ingersoll, 1994, *Counseling and Values*, 38, 98–111.

Many express the opinion that spiritual issues should be addressed exclusively in the religious arena, the domain of the pastoral counselor or ordained clergy. Critics disagree, noting that organized religion is often grounded in social stratification and reflects an external locus of control (Fox, 1991; Fromm, 1950; Schaef, 1992; Spong, 1992; Watts, 1971). In addition, the boundaries drawn by some denominations of the world's religions (e.g., Islamic Jihad and Christian fundamentalism) may act to preclude helpful dialogue with those who don't share the expressions of that particular community of faith. Schaef (1992) noted that when helping professionals deny the existence of a spiritual force greater than the self, they fail to account for how nonphysical things like values and ideas actually affect the physical world.

The aims of this article are threefold: (a) to suggest an expanded, seven dimensional model of spirituality for counselors to use in their work with clients, (b) to discuss spirituality as an organismic construct distinct from religion, and (c) to explore case examples utilizing the suggested model. These three aims are integrated to form a new conceptualization of spirituality and its place in human development and the therapeutic encounter.

SEVEN DIMENSIONS OF SPIRITUALITY

What is spirituality? In a day of New Age movements, cult practices, and continuing revisions and variations of mainstream religions, the word is the center of more and more attention (Canda, 1988; Chandler, Holden, & Kolander, 1992; Wallace, 1992). Even the Association for Religious and Value Issues in Counseling has incorporated a name change to include the word "spirituality" (McGowan, 1991).

Sheldrake (1992) noted that the common use of the word "spirituality" has a surprisingly short history. Sheldrake felt that human knowledge and historical-cultural events continually affect people's perceptions of the divine and their worship experience, and that each generation is required to define what spirituality is meant to encompass.

"Spirit" is taken from the Latin *spiritus* meaning breath, courage, vigor, or life. The adjective spiritual comes from the Latin *spiritualis* meaning simply "of the spirit." Sheldrake (1992) stated that both the latter are attempts to translate the corresponding Greek noun (pneuma) and adjective (pnuematikos) as they are used in the Pauline letters. Both Sheldrake and Lapsley (1990) were quick to stress that in Pauline theology, spirit and matter are not contrasted with physical and material, contrary to many popular interpretations. Lapsley stated that this understanding is clearly an error in translation that must be avoided when describing what spirituality is.

Delbane and Montgomery (1981) discussed the Hebrew word for spirit, which is *ruach*. They noted that the Hebrew definition is threefold, meaning wind, breath, and spirit. The Greek word for spirit (pneuma) also means breath (Roth, 1990). "Spirituality" is defined as being of a spiritual character, quality, or nature, the suffix "ity" referring to the state or characteristic this article attempts to describe.

The Latin, Hebrew, and Greek roots of spirituality do not point clearly to explicable dimensions but employ metaphors to point to the nonobservable dimension of the human spirit. The method of metaphor is clarified through examination of Polanyi's (1946) description of "the spiritual reality." Polanyi described the spiritual reality as "the reality of emergent meaning and truth" (p. 17). Polanyi's (1966) theory of tacit knowing essentially stated that all inquiry (scientific or otherwise) proceeds from something observable in the environment, to something nonobservable in the inquirer. The observable points to truth that is ever unfolding, but the observable is not Spirituality and Religion the full embodiment of this truth. Spirituality, like many constructs, must be understood as having observable and non-observable elements. The observable elements can point to, but never fully explicate, the nonobservable elements. As this article explores the meaning of spirituality, the term *description* is used in lieu of *definition* to avoid the illusion of full explication.

Recent descriptions of spirituality include communication with God (Fox, 1983) and one's journey toward union with God (Magill & McGreal, 1988). Tillich (1959) wrote that spirituality encompassed human beings' ultimate concerns and is the "meaning giving" substance of culture. Witmer (1989) referred to spirituality as a belief in a force or thing greater than oneself. Bollinger (1969) described spiritual needs as the deepest needs of the self that, when met, move the individual toward meaningful identity and purpose. Booth (1992) said spirituality is an "inner attitude that emphasizes energy, creative choice, and a powerful force for living" and emphasized that it was a partnership with a power greater than the individual, a "co-creatorship with God" (p. 25). May (1988) stated that human spirit "is the source of our yearning as well as our very life" (p. 65). Schaef (1992) has equated spirituality with "sobriety" and "living in process," which translates as going where our life, our process, directs us (p. 112).

Because of the failing of words to fully describe spirituality, Ellison (1983) noted that it may be alluded to by studying states it directly affects and said spiritual well-being functioned as one of those states. Spiritual well-being may be understood as a measurement of the state of one's spirituality or one's spiritual health. Ellison noted that spiritual well-being is an expression of spiritual health much like one's blood pressure is an expression of physical health. Ellison wrote that such a conception of spiritual well-being was composed of many dimensions just as there may be many dimensions to physical health. As there are many dimensions to our physicality, it should be equally assumed that there are numerous dimensions to our spirituality. Although researchers on spiritual well-being note that spirituality must be understood as multidimensional (Ellison, 1983; Moberg, 1984), little work has identified those dimensions.

Spirituality is described below within the seven dimensions of meaning, conception of divinity, relationship, mystery, experience, play, and an integrative dimension.

Meaning

Although broad, descriptions like those presented begin to identify initial dimensions of spirituality like meaning and conceptions of divinity. Although meaning is impossible to define in a general way, it can be thought of as that which the individual experiences as making life worth living (Frankl, 1948). Frankl (1958) also noted that human beings have an innate will to meaning that manifests itself as a searching for an ultimate meaning for the individual life. Although Frankl viewed the human as mind, body, and spirit, he noted that the key was the spirit, which he referred to as *noos* (his own expansion of the Greek for "mind") (Gould, 1993).

In addition, Franks (1955) found that the problem of meaning can overwhelm a person and is apt to arise more frequently (but not exclusively) in times of crisis. Meaning is also experienced in aesthetic appreciation. This is akin to the Kantian notion of beauty (Allen, 1957), which claims the appreciation of beauty is disinterested in purpose, so meaning (rather than purpose) is derived from beauty. This experience of beauty is included in what Fox called "natural" or "creation ecstasies" (1981, p. 45). Fox noted that such experiences allow people to forget or "get outside of" themselves, and thus are renewing.

Conception of Divinity

How an individual conceptualizes divinity may be as diverse as individuals themselves but may be categorized under the four areas of theistic, atheistic, pantheistic, or panentheistic. Theistically, individuals relate to a primarily transcendent force or being. Atheistically, individuals refute or resist conceptions of divinity they are aware of. In a pantheistic relationship, individuals relate to an absolute force or being that resides in all things, including the individual. In a panentheistic relationship, the force or being flows through all things and paradoxically transcends all things (Fox, 1983).

Beyond categorizing an individual's conception of divinity, counselors must recognize that the conceptions may also vary according to gender, demeanor, temperament, and degree of personal relationship.

Relationship

One of the aims of all mythologies (which include religious systems) is to address relationship (Campbell, 1990; Canda, 1988). Relationship encompasses how individuals relate to their conception of divinity (if any) and to others. Sheldrake (1992) postulated that spirituality "does not so much concern itself with defining perfection as with surveying the complex mystery of human growth in the context of a living relationship with the Absolute" (p. 50). Nelson (1988) stated "by spirituality I mean the ways and patterns by which the person—intellectually, emotionally, and physically—relates to that which is ultimately real and worthful for him or her" (p. 21).

Burns (1989) further developed the notion of relationship in spirituality by defining it as a striving for and infusion with the reality of the interconnectedness among self, other people, and the Infinite/Divine. Burns pointed out that this relationship occurs during a depth experience and results in a life change and further noted the relationship increases one's sense of connectedness to that considered Divine and also to all other living beings.

Mystery

Many attempts to describe spirituality allude to the mystery or ambiguity of the spiritual. Banks (1980) elaborated on this aspect noting that spirituality is typically perceived as unknown, hazy, or ineffable. This reflects the difficulty mentioned earlier in explicating spirituality. Whenever people speak of transcendent forces, the phenomenological experience of meaning, or awareness of tacit realms like the interconnectedness of individuals, they are at the boundary of the ineffable and the mysterious. Mystery, and a tolerance for it, are a part of all spiritual traditions. Any description of spirituality must provide some vocabulary that recognizes the mysterious and must also provide people with a way to talk about it.

One way to include this element is to define the manner in which individuals experience mystery. Toward this end, the phrase "negative capability" can be used. This phrase was suggested by poet John Keats who described it as the ability to be in mystery or doubt without any irritable reaching after fact or reason (Barnett, 1960). Keats maintained that people in Western culture, anxious for "black and white" solutions, did little to cultivate negative capability because it required cessation of activity and tolerance of ambiguity. This assertion is supported by other commentaries on Western culture (Capra, 1982; Deikmann, 1971; Schaef, 1992; Smith, 1990).

Play

Play is best described by Fox's (1981) notion of "natural ecstasies." In forgetting oneself in play (which can include sexual play) individuals give themselves to something greater than themselves, a giving that is simultaneously pleasurable. The idea behind the spiritual dimension of play is akin to that described as "aesthetic" under the dimension of meaning. To play for a purpose (such as winning a game or using one's sexuality to control) is not play at all but simply more purposeful work that exacerbates the very things play would refresh.

Why include a dimension of play when conceptualizing spirituality? Schaef (1992) and Schor (1991) described an American culture in which there is precious little value of "quality leisure" let alone much empirical support that emphasizes its necessity. The play dimension is an attempt to balance Western "seriousness" with "sincerity" (Watts, 1964) and precludes an understanding that spirituality is "work" or another "duty" that must be attended to (Fox, 1991).

One of the few psychometric measurements of playfulness is the "play" scale on the Personality Research Form (Jackson, 1989). Descriptions of someone who enjoys play are light-hearted, easy-going, laughter-loving, merry, care-free, and frivolous. Many of the latter are used pejoratively in American "workaholic" society and many times "play" is actually aggression masquerading as play (for example violent sports like football or a focus on winning over playing).

Experience

Once a conception of the Infinite, a sense of meaning, the dynamic of relationship, and the dimension of mystery have been outlined, it is necessary to describe how these are manifested within individual experience. Campbell (in Cousineau, 1990) emphasized the importance of spiritual experience stating that "People talk about looking for the meaning of life; what (they're) really looking for is an experience of life" (p. 20). Campbell felt that meaning was derived from experience. Furthermore, Moberg (1971) noted that spirituality is often related to a vibrant experience of being alive and can underlie some of the most ecstatic human experiences like sexual orgasm and aesthetic thrill.

Certainly these latter understandings of experience are similar to what Maslow (1971) called peak experiences. Maslow stated that the spiritual elements of peak experiences influenced values in the secular realm and the yearning for meaning (Maslow, 1970). In a discussion of a precipitating event or experience, Burns (1989) also alluded to a Maslovian notion of peak experiences.

Although Campbell (1988) stated that the function of all mythologies is to help the individual cultivate an experience of being alive, this does not have to be strictly understood as peak experience. An adequate description of spirituality must refer not only to peak experiences, but also to the ordinary experiences of everyday living and their behavioral correlates. In Zen Buddhism, the ordinary is seen with all its sacred ramifications (Suzuki, 1949; Watts, 1957) and, although often isolated in the mainstream practice of Christianity, the sacred aspects of the ordinary (meaning that which is in our daily life) are also the pillars upon which incarnational theology is built (Thompsett, 1990; Watts, 1947).

In most organized mythic systems, there is provision to cultivate and receive peak experiences (the Islamic Hajj or a charismatic Christian conversion) as well as a daily rhythm for individuals' spirituality (the Islamic Salah or the Anglican Daily Office). The religions usually prescribe ritualistic behaviors aimed at cultivating these experiences.

Dimensional Integration

It should be noted that all seven dimensions discussed earlier function as an integrated, synergistic entity. They are complementary, not exclusive categories. Sheldrake (1992) emphasized that spirituality ". . . seeks an integration of all aspects of human life and experience" (p. 50). Moberg (1984) also noted that the spiritual pervades every aspect of a person's life.

Building on the aforementioned discussion, it then seems logically to follow that spirituality can be described as synergistically utilizing all of the seven dimensions.

1. One's conception of the divine, absolute, or "force" greater than one's self.
2. One's sense of meaning or what is beautiful, worthwhile.
3. One's relationship with Divinity and other beings.
4. One's tolerance or negative capability for mystery.
5. Peak and ordinary experiences engaged to enhance spirituality (may include rituals or spiritual disciplines).
6. Spirituality as play.
7. Spirituality as a systemic force that acts to integrate all the dimensions of one's life.

RELIGION AND SPIRITUALITY

If spirituality may be better understood through the seven dimensions, what then is the relationship between spirituality and religion? "Religion" comes from the Latin root *religio,* which means a bond between humanity and the gods. The Latin term is a transformation of the word *religare,* which means "to bind back or bind together." When these roots are studied in relation to the commonly accepted definition of religion as an expression of beliefs in conduct and ritual, the basis for a medium of organized worship and fellowship becomes apparent.

According to Marty (1991), contemporary understandings of religion are as broad as those of spirituality. Marty wrote that religion is related to what

11

ultimately concerns people; provides them with personal and social identity; and leads adherents to prefer myth, symbol, rite, and ceremony over other forms of expression. He added that religion tends to allude to a cosmic or metaphysical backdrop as well as stipulate particular behavioral correlates. Marty's definition parallels the aforementioned seven dimensions of spirituality in noting ultimate concerns such as meaning and the nature of divinity, alluding to a notion of Divinity, provision of a personal identity and actions adherents engage to relate to the divine and other living beings.

From Marty's definition, two distinctions can be drawn between spirituality and religion. First, religion's provision of a social identity may not necessarily be provided in a personal spirituality. Second, due to the corporate nature of religion there may be fewer variations in its stipulated behavioral correlates than those found in personal spiritualities.

Paralleling Moberg's (1971) statement that all things religious may not be spiritual, Coles (1990) noted that there is a clear distinction between a spiritual life and a religious life. Citing examples from the New Testament writings of Paul and quotations of Jesus, Coles distinguished between the "letter" and "spirit" of the law and applied the distinction to children's spiritual metaphors that indicate their own awareness of the difference. Regarding an 8-year-old client, Coles wrote "Most important, she let me know that her religious life was far more many-sided than I had been prepared to admit—and that there was a personal, spiritual life in her that was by no means to be equated with her religious life" (p. 14).

Perhaps one way to differentiate between spirituality and religion is to view spirituality as an organismic construct endemic to human beings. Haase, Britt, Coward, Leidy, and Penn (1992) noted that spirituality is a quality inherent in all human beings. The authors stated that the individual expression of spirituality is one's spiritual perspective. This phrase could be used synonymously with "spirituality."

From this perspective, religion is conceptualized as a variety of frameworks through which spirituality is expressed. These frameworks would be viewed as heavily influenced by the culture in which they originate (Campbell, 1969; Frobenius, 1921). Through this conceptualization, spirituality becomes an organismic, developmental dimension and religion, a "culturally flavored" framework that helps develop the organismic spiritual potential.

SPIRITUALITY IN THE COUNSELING SESSION

In applying the latter understandings of spirituality and religion to work with clients, the counselor's cultural sensitivity is crucial. To use these conceptualizations with clients will require a comfort with the idea that there is a diversity of spiritualities expressed by the many diverse peoples in the world (Pate, 1992). Barring destructive, unhealthy practices (an ethical judgment) all expressions have some validity. Polanyi and Prosch (1975) noted that this understanding is rooted in philosopher John Locke's notion that we can never be so sure of the truth in matters of religion or spirituality to impose our views on others. It is important to remember that this does not rule out working with clients who hold rigid definitions of what is acceptable religious practice.

A personal experience of the latter is a client of mine who identified with being an "Evangelical Christian." In this intervention and for the purposes of this article, Evangelical generally refers to beliefs in the historicity and inerrancy of the bible, the exclusive divinity of Jesus, and a Calvinian emphasis on personal conversion (Watt, 1991). The client was originally seen at a public agency for financial counseling, and subsequently referred to me for apparent anxiety.

After three sessions with little progress, the client noted that she usually only spoke to her pastor about the "demons" causing her anxious feelings. In discussing at length her view of the anxiety (via religious imagery) and her attempt to alleviate it through prayer, I aimed to enter her world without necessarily adopting her worldview. I made attempts to use the client's vocabulary and imagery when discussing the problematic symptoms. I also expressed comfort consulting with the client's pastor.

Although the client attempted to "convert" me on several occasions, she was willing to engage in desensitization exercises to treat symptoms of anxiety that prayer was not alleviating. By affirming (but not converting to) the client's faith, I recognized that some of her spiritual development was being promoted by her religion. In openly recognizing and addressing this, enough rapport was established for a working therapeutic alliance.

Although conceptualizing spirituality as an organismic construct is not incongruent with the Latin definition of religion, there are three inherent Western biases of modernism (Marty, 1991), which might limit the conceptualization. First, the differentiation reflects secular rationality in that it attempts to explicate with reason the existence of a social institution ordained of God (the church) and thus subjugate it to the individual. Second, the conceptualization is highly individualistic, subjugating the social institutions of religion to the preference or orientation of the individual in the assumption that what is "spiritual" flows forth from the individual to the religion and not the opposite. Third and last, the conceptualization implies religious tolerance with what Marty suggested as "accompanying tendencies toward relativism" (p. vii). If spirituality is organismic, one may express and develop it equally through one of many religions. As Marty noted, these three modern biases are usually unacceptable to groups defined as "fundamentalist."

Despite the limitations, there are numerous recommendations in the literature that seemingly warrant the development of an inclusive model for working with client spirituality in helping relationships (Banks, 1990; Canda, 1988; Moberg, 1984). Conceptualizing spirituality as an organismic construct may address the concerns of many authors who have called on counselors to convey a respect for individual differences in spirituality. The counselor's understanding of spirituality as an organismic construct allows for nonspecific advocation in a way that can be unique to and meaningful for the client.

Counselors working with clients committed to a particular spiritual or religious expression can enhance the counseling process in the following ways. First, affirm the importance of the clients' spirituality in their lives. Second, attempt to enter client worldviews with congruent vocabulary and imagery in conceptualizing problems and treatments. Last, counselors need to be willing to consult with other "healers" in clients' lives, meaning people identified as everything from ordained clergy to folk healers. In the latter guidelines, counselors must adhere to the ethical standards of their profession, keeping alert to unhealthy uses of spiritual practices such as those described by Allport (1950) and Arterburn and Felton (1991).

Regarding unhealthy uses of religion, Arterburn et al. (1991) defined and discussed the concept of "religious addiction" as a system that sets the follower apart from the rest of humanity, possesses a dictatorial leadership, is typically at enmity with the dominant culture, and is punitive and highly legalistic in nature. The systems described by the authors would inhibit growth in the seven spiritual dimensions outlined herein by encouraging distorted images of divinity, modeling unhealthy relationships, offering certainty, discounting mystery, and particularly overemphasizing work while devaluing play.

An example of the aforementioned is a court-ordered client I worked with who insisted on justifying physically abusing his spouse as "part of God's divine orders." The client supported his destructive behavior through an almost systematic misinterpretation of certain Judeo-Christian scriptures. All the exegesis in the world to the contrary, the client persisted in his beliefs and was encouraged by a man who led a local "bible study." It is sad that when the client's court order expired, he left counseling still clinging to his belief system.

On the opposite end of the therapeutic continuum, counselors working with clients who are seeking to understand and develop their spirituality in a healthy manner can assist the client by engaging in exploration of the seven dimensions of spirituality. Counselors must explore what is in the client's life that makes it worth living. Counselors can explore how (if at all) clients conceptualize the "absolute" or "divine." Counselors can deepen their understanding of how the client relates to their image of divinity as well as others in the client's life. Counselors may explore how the client deals with uncertainty or mystery and, if appropriate, help the client enhance their ability to live with ambiguity. Counselors may also explore their client's level of playfulness. Last, counselors may support and empower clients in their exploration of practices and rituals that are helpful in spiritual development. The latter tasks must be conducted with the understanding that in order to be successful, they must meaningfully interrelate with the clients' experience of their own spirituality and its hoped for development.

Counselors may also benefit from familiarity with resources that describe various spiritual traditions, their beliefs, and practices. Common resources may include, but are not limited to, the comparative works of Campbell (1959, 1962, 1964, 1968), Smith (1990), and Watts (1962); lexicons of spiritual traditions including Jacquet (1990) and Mayer (1961); scholarly exegesis such as Laymon (1991); and lay exegesis of specific traditions such as Spong (1991) and Theiring (1992).

CONCLUSION

In his classic work *The Decline of the West,* Spengler (1926) noted that Western civilization was quickly approaching a "second religiousness" wherein spirituality would be released from exclusive expression in cultural forms. Spengler seemed to describe this as a developmental inevitability. Campbell (in Larsen & Larsen, 1991) believed that in this "second religiousness," people would begin to explore a personal spirituality that took them beyond the forms of religion to a meeting with that which animates all forms and escapes all symbolic description. If this hypothesis is valid, and spirituality grows into popular understanding as a construct of human development, counselors may truly be on the "cutting edge," helping people to engage in what is no less than a developmental revolution.

REFERENCES

Allen, E. L. (1957). Guide book to western thought. London, England: The English University Press.

Allport, G. (1950). *The individual and his religion.* New York: Macmillan & Co.

Arterburn, S., & Felton, J. (1991). *Toxic faith: Understanding and overcoming religious addiction.* Nashville, TN: Oliver Nelson.

Banks, R. (1980). Health and the spiritual dimension: Relationships and implications for professional preparation programs. *Journal of School Health, 50,* 195-202.

Barnett, B. (1960). *A dictionary of literary terms.* Boston: Little Brown.

Barnhouse, R.T. (1979). Spiritual direction and psychotherapy. *Journal of Pastoral Care, 33*(3), 149-163.

Berthold, S. M. (1989). Spiritism as a form of psychotherapy: Implications for social work practice. *Social Casework: The Journal of Contemporary Social Work, 3,* 502-509.

Bettelheim, B. (1983). *Freud and man's soul.* New York: Alfred Knopf.

Bollinger. T. E. (1969). *The spiritual needs of the aging: In need of a specific ministry.* New York: Alfred Knopf.

Booth, L. (1992). The stages of religious addiction. *Creation Spirituality, 8*(4), 22-25.

Burns, P. (1989). *The experience of spirituality in the well adult: A phenomenological study.* Unpublished doctoral dissertation, Texas Women's University, Denton, Texas.

Campbell, J. (1959). *The masks of god: Primitive mythology.* New York: Viking.

Campbell, J. (1962). *The masks of god: Oriental mythology.* New York: Viking.

Campbell, J. (1964). *The masks of god: Occidental mythology.* New York: Viking.

Campbell, J. (1968). *The masks of god: Creative mythology*. New York: Viking.

Campbell, J. (1969). *The flight of the wild gander: Explorations in the mythological dimensions of fairy tales, legends, and symbols*. New York: Viking.

Campbell, J. (1988). *The power of myth*. New York: Doubleday.

Campbell, J. (1990). *The transformations of myth through time*. New York: Harper & Row.

Canda, E. R. (1988). Spirituality, religion, diversity, and social work practice. *Social Casework: The Journal of Contemporary Social Work, 6*, 238-247.

Capra, F. (1982). *The turning point: Science, society, and the rising culture*. New York: Bantam.

Chandler, C. K., Holden, J. M., & Kolander, C. A. (1992). Counseling for spiritual wellness: Theory and practice. *Journal of Counseling & Development, 71*(2), 168-176.

Coles, R. (1990). *The spiritual life of children*. Boston Houghton Mifflin.

Collins, J. R., Hurst, J. C., & Jacobson, J. K. (1987). The blind spot extended: Spirituality. *Journal of College Student Personnel, 28*(3), 274-276.

Council for Accreditation of Counseling and Related Educational Programs. (1988). *Accreditation and procedures manual and application*. Alexandria, VA: American Counseling Association.

Cousineau, P. (Ed.). (1990). *The hero's journey: Joseph Campbell on his life and work*. San Francisco: Harper.

Deikmann, A. (1971). Bimodal consciousness. *Archives of General Psychiatry, 25*, 481-489.

Deikmann, A. (1976). *A guide to implementing the receptive mode*. Washington, DC: National Park Service.

Delbane, R., & Montgomery, H. (1981). *The breath of life: Discovering your breath prayer*. San Francisco: Harper & Row.

Edwards, T. (1980). *Spiritual friend: Reclaiming the gift of spiritual direction*. New York: Paulist Press.

Ellis, A. (Speaker). (1992). *Introduction to rational emotive therapy*. Baltimore MD: American Association for Counseling and Development National Convention.

Ellison, C. W. (1983). Spiritual well being: Conceptualization and measurement. *Journal of Psychology and Theology, 11*(4), 330-340.

Fowler J. W. (1981). *Stages of faith: The psychology of human development and the quest for meaning*. San Francisco Harper.

Fox, M. (1981). *Whee! we, wee all the way home: A guide to sensual, prophetic spirituality*. Santa Fe: Bear & Co.

Fox, M. (1983). *Original blessing*. Santa Fe Bear & Company.

Fox, M. (1991). *Living in an ecological era*. Speech given at St. John's Episcopal Church, Shaker Heights, OH.

Frankl, V. E. (1945). *Man's search for meaning*. New York: Beacon Press.

Frankl, V. E. (1957). *The doctor and the soul: An introduction to logotherapy*. New York: Alfred Knopf.

Frankl, V. E. (1958). The will to meaning. *Journal of Pastoral Care, 12*, 82-88.

Fromm, E. (1950). *Psychoanalysis and religion*. London: Yale University Press.

Gould, W. B. (1993). *Frankl: Life with meaning*. Pacific Grove, CA: Brooks/Cole.

Haase, J. E., Britt, T., Coward, D. D., Kline, N., & Penn, P. E. (1992). Simultaneous analysis of spiritual perspective, hope, acceptance and self-transcendence. *Images, 24*(2), 141-147.

Isbister, J. N. (1985). *Freud: An introduction to his life and work*. Cambridge: Polity Press.

Jacquet C. H. (1990). *Yearbook of American and Canadian churches*. Nashville, TN: Abingdon.

Jones, A. (1982). *Exploring spiritual direction: An essay on Christian friendship*. Chicago: The Seabury Press.

Kelsey, M. (1989). *Companions on the inner way*. New York: Crossroads.

Klukas, A. W. (1993). *Anglican spirituality*. Speech given at Pilgrims on the Way Retreat, Painesville, OH.

Kuhn, T. S. (1970). *The structure of scientific revolutions*. Chicago: University of Chicago Press.

Lapsley, J. N. (1990). Spirit and self. *Pastoral Psychology, 38*(3), 135-146.

Larsen, S., & Larsen, R. (1991). *A fire in the mind: The life of Joseph Campbell*. New York: Doubleday.

Laymon, C. M. (Ed.). (1991). *The interpreter's one volume commentary on the bible: Including the apocrypha and general articles*. Nashville, TN: Abingdon Press.

Marty, M., & Appleby, R. S. (Eds.). (1991). *Fundamentalisms observed*. Chicago: University of Chicago Press.

Maslow, A. H. (1970). *Religions, values, and peak experiences*. New York: Penguin.

Maslow, A. H. (1971). *The farther reaches of human nature*. New York: Penguin.

May, G. G. (1982). *Care of mind, care of spirit: Psychiatric dimensions of spiritual direction*. San Francisco: Harper & Row.

May, G. G. (1988). *Addiction and grace: Love and spirituality in the healing of addictions*. San Francisco: Harper.

Mayer, F. E. (1961). *The religious bodies of America* (4th ed.). St. Louis, MO: Concordia Publishing.

McGill, F. N., & McGreal, I. P. (Eds.). (1988). *Christian spirituality: The essential guide to the most influential spiritual writings of the Christian tradition*. San Francisco: Harper & Row.

McGowan, S. (1991). ARVIC to consider name change. *Guidepost, Nov. 13*.

Meissner, W. W. (1984). *Psychoanalysis and religious experience*. London: Yale University Press.

Moberg, D. O. (1971). *Spiritual well being: Background*. Washington, DC: White House Conference on Aging.

Moberg, D. O. (1984). Subjective measures of spiritual well being. *Review of Religious Research, 25*(4), 351-364.

Nelson, J. B. (1988). *The intimate connection: Male sexuality, masculine spirituality*. Philadelphia: The Westminster Press.

Pate, R. H., & Bondi, A.M. (1992). Religious beliefs and practice: An integral aspect of multicultural awareness. *Counselor Education and Supervision, 32*(2), 108-116.

Polanyi, M. (1946). *Science, faith, and society: A searching examination of the meaning and nature of scientific inquiry*. Chicago: University of Chicago Press.

Polanyi, M. (1966). *The tacit dimension*. Gloucester, MA: Peter Smith.

Polanyi, M., & Prosch, R. (1975). *Meaning*. Chicago: University of Chicago Press.

Roth, N. (1990). *The breath of God: An approach to prayer*. Cambridge: Cowley Publications.

Schaef, A. W. (1992). *Beyond therapy, beyond science: A new model for healing the whole person*. San Francisco: Harper Collins.

Schor, J. B. (1991). *The overworked American: The unexpected decline of leisure*. New York: Basic Books.

Sheldrake, P. (1992). *Spirituality and history: Questions of interpretation and method*. New York: Crossroad.

Smith, H. (1991). *The worlds religions*. San Francisco: Harper.

Smith, M. L. (1989). *The word is very near you*. Cambridge: Cowley.

Smith, M. L. (1991). *A season for the spirit*. Cambridge: Cowley.

Spengler, O. (1926). *The decline of the west*. New York: Alfred Knopf.

Spong, J. S. (1991). *Rescuing the bible from fundamentalism: A bishop rethinks the meaning of scripture*. San Francisco: Harper & Row.

Spong, J. S. (1992). *Sexual ethics and biblical truth in the twenty-first century*. Unpublished lecture given at St. Luke's Church, Toledo, OH.

Suzuki, D. T. (1949). *Essays in zen buddhism*. New York: Grove Press.

Theiring, B. (1992). *Jesus and the riddle of the dead sea scrolls: Unlocking the secrets of his life story*. San Francisco: Harper.

Thompsett, F. (1990). *Incarnational theology*. Kenyon Conference, Gambier, OH.

Tillich, P. (1959). *Theology of culture*. New York: Oxford University Press.

Torrey, E. F. (1986). *Witch doctors and psychiatrists: The common roots of psychotherapy and its future*. New York: Harper & Row.

Wallace, A. M. (1992). ARVIC + spirituality = Interaction. *Newsletter of the Association for Religious and Value Issues in Counseling, 18*(6), 1.

Watt, D. H. (1991). *A transforming faith: Explorations of twentieth century American evangelicalism*. New Brunswick, NJ: Rutgers University Press.

Watts, A. L. (1947). *Behold the spirit: A study in the necessity of mystical religion*. New York: Vintage.

Watts, A. W. (1957). The way of zen. New York: Vintage.

Watts, A. W. (1962). *The two hands of god: The myths of polarity*. New York: George Braziller.

Watts, A. W. (1964). *Beyond theology: The art of godsmanship*. New York: Vintage.

Watts, A. W. (1971). *In my own way*. New York: Vintage.

Westerhoff, J. (1976). *Will our children have faith?* New York: The Seabury Press.

Witmer, I. M. (1989). *Reaching toward wholeness: An integrated approach to well being over the life span*. In T. J. Sweeney (Ed.), *Adlerian counseling: A practical approach for a new decade*. Muncie, IN: Accelerated Press.

Witmer, J. M., & Sweeney, T. J. (1992). A holistic model for wellness and prevention over the life span. *Journal of Counseling & Development, 71*(2), 140-149.

A Holistic Model for
Wellness and Prevention
Over the Life Span

J. MELVIN WITMER
THOMAS J. SWEENEY

THERE IS A growing body of research and related literature to support the concept that our society would do well to reassess our model for human development and health services. With the primary attention being given to "sickness" and "dysfunction," we have committed ourselves and our re-sources almost exclusively to remediating problems. More than a decade ago, the United States Public Health Service (USPHS, 1979) reported that at least 53% of the deaths in the United States are caused by life-style and self-destructive and negligent behavior.

Recently, Health and Human Services Secretary Dr. Louis W. Sullivan released the *Healthy People 2000* report, setting the nation's health promo-tion and disease prevention goals for the next decade (U.S. Department of Health and Human Services, 1990). The report makes a call to all U.S. resi-dents for healthier living. Noted is the fact that the federal government spends more than 75% of its health care dollars caring for people with chronic diseases, such as heart disease, strokes, and cancer. At the same time, less than one half of 1% is spent to prevent these same diseases from occurring.

Over the last decade, however, the concept of wellness has been devel-oped in several disciplines to describe the "total person" approach for im-proving the quality of life in proactive and positive ways. In this approach, life-styles are looked at in view of creating high-level wellness. As early as 1947, the World Health Organization defined health as "physical, mental, and social well-being, not merely the absence of disease or infirmity" (World Health Organization, 1958). Recently "spiritual well-being" was added to this definition.

What is the origin and nature of this wellness frequently referred to as wholeness? Adler (1954), in his writing about individual psychology, ob-served that the final purpose of the psychic life "is to guarantee the contin-ued existence on this earth of the human organism, and to enable him to securely accomplish his development" (p. 28). Maslow (1970) in his study of

From "A Holistic Model for Wellness and Prevention Over the Life Span," by J.M. Witmer and T.J. Sweeney, 1992, *Journal of Counseling & Development, 71*, 140–148.

the characteristics of healthy persons, noted that growth, self-actualization, and the pursuit toward health must now be accepted as a widespread and perhaps universal human tendency. Jung (1958) observed that the human psyche seeks integration, that there is an instinctual drive toward wholeness and health.

We are proposing a model of wellness and prevention over the life span that incorporates theoretical concepts from psychology, anthropology, sociology, religion, and education. Experimental and applied research data are integrated from personality, social, clinical, and health psychology. Stress management and behavioral medicine research are seminal sources for a wellness paradigm. For the application of our knowledge on wellness we propose a "global village" ecology and a cosmic consciousness that emphasizes the interconnectedness of all things. The major themes relate to wholeness in mind, body, spirit, and community. As individuals and families strive to meet their daily responsibilities in work, friendship, and love relationships, there is a need to maintain a perspective not only on what is adequate health and what is normal but also what is necessary and desirable for optimum health and functioning.

FIGURE 1
Wheel of Wellness and Prevention

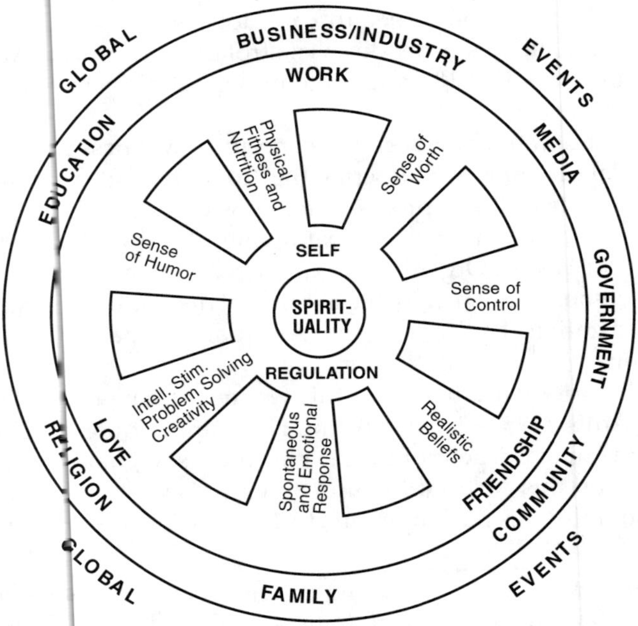

The characteristics of the healthy person over the life span are described under five life tasks, which are likened to a wheel of wholeness (see Figure 1). The characteristics of wellness are expressed through the five life tasks of spirituality, self-regulation, work, love, and friendship. These life tasks dynamically interact with the life forces of family, community, religion, education, government, media, and business/industry. Global events, both natural and human, have an impact on and are affected by the life forces and life tasks. As a member of the human community, we engage in these life tasks as identified and suggested by Adler in our striving for well-being (Dreikurs, 1953; Mosak & Dreikurs, 1967). At the center of wholeness is spirituality (e.g., oneness, purposiveness, optimism, and values). Self-regulation is the second life task, which includes such characteristics as sense of worth; sense of control; realistic beliefs; spontaneous and emotional responsiveness; intellectual stimulation, problem solving, and creativity; sense of humor; and physical fitness and nutrition. Work as a third life task not only affords economic sustenance but also serves psychological and social functions. The fourth life task of friendship enables us to connect with the human community. Wellness is enhanced by the fifth life task of love, in which our health is nurtured in marriage or intimate relationships through trust, caring, and companionship.

Our model is an effort to demonstrate the interconnectedness of the characteristics of the healthy person, the life tasks, and the life forces. All of these components interact for the well-being or detriment of the person. If we understand these dynamics, our counseling and human development services will be more holistic for growth and learning over the life span.

LIFE TASK 1: SPIRITUALITY

Throughout history including contemporary times, every civilization, culture, or nation has expressed and practiced religious beliefs that represent values that reflect what is considered sacred and essential for the sustenance of life. For some groups, religious practices have focused on nature worship, and for others, a divine being who knows about and intervenes in human activities. Still others seek an inner or higher consciousness that is in harmony with the forces of the cosmos.

These spiritual beliefs are translated into ethical, moral, and legal codes, all of which in part are intended to protect and sustain the sacredness of life. Individual character and the life-style are developed in a way that is thought to nurture the soul while at the same time be acceptable or harmonious with the supreme being-force of the universe.

A basic code of human behavior common to humankind is noted by Buscaglia (1978) in his sketch of seven of the world's great religions and philosophies. Little dissonance is seen among the systems in what it means to live in full humanness. Their commonality seems to be summarized in the proverbial Golden Rule, "Do unto others as you would have them do unto you." Spirituality for our purpose assumes certain life-enhancing beliefs about human dignity, human rights, and reverence for life.

Oneness and the Inner Life

Through nature and the world of thought, the individual is in awe of the universe and desires to experience the universe as a single significant whole (Einstein, 1954/1984; Harman, 1988). Both Eastern and Western religions tend to recognize the oneness of the person and the desire to attain an inner peace and sense of wholeness, free from inner conflict and fragmentation. Universal sisterhood and brotherhood are seen as part of this unity. Sources of spirituality probably come from within as well as outside the person. Inner voices, inner wisdom, higher consciousness, or the Spirit of God are all forms of the spiritual side of wholeness. Traditionally religion and spirituality have sought peace, guidance, and contact with the universal force through meditation, prayer, worship, contemplation, or introspection. Elements of religion and science have been combined by Benson (with Proctor; 1984) to create a meditative relaxation response, eliciting a mind-body quieting that enhances health and well-being.

Purposiveness, Optimism, and Values

Other dimensions of spirituality to be mentioned are purposiveness or meaning in life, hope or optimism in anticipation of future events, and values for guiding us in human relationships and decision making. Longevity and stress research support the importance of meaningfulness for coping with stress and for enhancing one's own health and wellness. In stress research, Kobasa (1979) found that psychological hardiness could decrease chances of becoming ill by as much as 50%. Contributing to this was the commitment factor of hardiness described by Kobasa as the tendency to involve oneself in whatever one is, does, or encounters.

Optimism is another dimension of spirituality. As such, it is an expression of hope that with a certain degree of confidence, one can either expect the best possible outcome or dwell on the most hopeful aspects of the situation. Tiger (1979), an anthropologist, developed a strong argument that optimism is a biological phenomenon and that religion is deeply intertwined with optimism. Witmer, Rich, Barcikowski, and Mague (1983) studied a nonclinical, general population for psychosocial characteristics associated with the stress response. Optimism was found to be one of the prime variables that characterized the good copers who had less anxiety and fewer physical symptoms. A follow-up study confirmed the initial findings (Witmer & Rich, 1991).

Values important to the spiritual self are those that are moral in nature. Moral values are those that guide our behavior in acting for our own well-being and demonstrating respect and compassion for the good of others (Young & Witmer, 1985). Maslow (1968) emphasized, "The human being needs a framework of values, a philosophy of life, a religion or religion-surrogate to live by and understand by in about the same sense that he needs sunlight, calcium or love" (p. 206). Valuelessness is the ultimate disease of our time and leads to value illnesses, illustrated by Maslow (1959, 1968) as apathy, alienation, hopelessness, and cynicism. Such conditions can become physical illnesses as well as lead to psychological and social ills. Healthy (self-actualized) people in Maslow's (1968) research were strongly ethical with definite moral standards. Their values tended to be universal in nature, transcending time and culture, with the ability to distinguish between means and ends.

LIFE TASK 2: SELF-REGULATION

The life task of self-regulation is used in this chapter to include a majority of the characteristics of the healthy person: sense of worth; sense of control: realistic beliefs; spontaneity and emotional responsiveness; intellectual stimulation, problem solving, and creativity; sense of humor; and physical fitness and health habits. More generic than self-esteem and self-efficacy, self-regulation is the process involved in how an individual coordinates relatively long-term patterns of goal-directed behavior (Bandura, 1986; Heppner & Krauskopf, 1987; Mischel, 1981). Through this life task, the individual is able to direct, control, and manage the self in ways that are self-enhancing, but within norms as prescribed by the larger society.

What are the healthy traits that enable the individual to regulate the self successfully on the pathways to wholeness? In this section, we briefly sketch each characteristic and cite support from the health and wellness literature.

Sense of Worth

Although separate headings are being used for sense of worth and sense of control, they constitute what is frequently cited in the literature as self-esteem. Self-esteem is the greatest single factor that affects individual growth and behavior (Frey & Carlock, 1989; Witmer, 1985). Adler (1954) referred to this as striving for superiority or significance. The healthy individuals of Maslow's (1970) research had a strong acceptance of themselves and their own nature. They accepted their own weaknesses and imperfections without being upset or disturbed. In a national study by Campbell (1981), 12 domains of life were considered for their contribution to satisfaction with life. Satisfaction with self, which included a sense of worth and control, had the strongest relationship to feelings of well-being.

Self-esteem was significantly related to physical and mental health in a large survey conducted by the California Department of Mental Health (1979). Those who had high self-esteem reported having better mental and physical health. Low self-esteem also went along with more self-reported physical illness and with disturbances such as insomnia, anxiety, and depression. Low self-esteem was also related to higher frequencies of marital problems, financial problems, emotional problems about illness, and problems with self. Persons who sensed that they had a high degree of control over their lives were more likely to feel good about themselves mentally and physically, and reported fewer ailments. A recent study commissioned by the California State Legislature revealed that self-esteem is the likeliest candidate for a *social vaccine* to empower us to live responsibly and inoculate us against the personal and social ills plaguing our society (California State Department of Education, 1990).

Sense of Control

Beliefs about personal control have to do with feelings about mastery and confidence. Any understanding about control needs to include the literature on competence, locus of control, or self-efficacy.

Control is sometimes defined as a sense of competence as in the research by Witmer et al. (1983). One factor that described the good copers was competence, which included items on optimism, control, and perceived overall ability to cope with stress. Those who had perceived life as manageable had less anxiety and fewer physical symptoms.

Control along with challenge and commitment made up the three dimensions that Kobasa (1979) found to characterize hardiness in her study of several hundred telephone company executives. *Control* was defined as the opposite of powerlessness—more in control of events; expressed as a tendency to feel and act as if one is influential (rather than helpless) in the face of varied contingencies of life; and perception of oneself as having a definite influence through the exercise of imagination, knowledge, skill, and choice.

Those with internal locus of control believe that events are contingent upon their own actions and as such yield more effort and persistence in achievement situations (Lazarus & Folkman, 1984). An external locus of control refers to the belief that events are contingent on luck, chance, fate, or powers beyond their control. Persons with a sense of inner control are more likely to collect information about disease and health maintenance, take action to improve their health habits, and engage in preventive care (Strickland, 1978).

Realistic Beliefs

Healthy people have a keen perception of reality, seeing reality more as it is, not as one might want or desire it to be. They recognize that which is rational and logical as well as that which is distorted or wishful thinking. The superiority in the perception of reality leads to a superior ability to perceive the truth, come to conclusions, and be logical and cognitively efficient (Maslow, 1968).

Private logic is the Adlerian conceptualization of personal beliefs that guide the feelings and behavior of individuals (Sweeney, 1989). It is a "biased apperception" about self, life, and others. The greater the discrepancy between one's private logic and reality, the greater the probability for inappropriate behavior in response to life events.

Unhealthy persons who have mood disturbances are not emotionally sick, but cognitively wrong. That is, they are thinking irrational thoughts, doing faulty reasoning, or living by maladaptive rules made up of unrealistic or inappropriate "shoulds" and "oughts" or "do's" and "don'ts." Research and clinical evidence have documented that negative thoughts that cause emotional turmoil nearly always contain gross distortions or unrealistic expectations (Beck, 1976, 1984; Ellis, 1962).

In addition, research by Witmer et al. (1983) indicated that those persons with a more positive outlook and those who scored lowest on five of Ellis's irrational beliefs were less anxious and had fewer physical symptoms. The five irrational beliefs contributing to stress were the following: (a) The past continues to influence me so much that it is hard for me to change or prevent bad things from happening; (b) I can't help getting down on myself when I fail at something or when something goes wrong; (c) it is very important for me to be liked and loved by almost everyone I meet; (d) I must be perfectly competent, adequate, and achieving in all that I do to consider myself worthwhile; and (e) I have little control over my moods, which are caused mostly by events outside myself.

Spontaneity and Emotional Responsiveness

Maslow (1970) described "self-actualizing" people as relatively spontaneous in behavior and far more spontaneous than others in their inner life, thoughts, impulses, emotions, desires, and opinions. A childlike simplicity and authenticity are in their responsiveness to events. Their relationships are essentially free of defensiveness and deceptiveness. They are sensitive to the predicaments of others. They appreciate their own positive circumstances and approach life with a continuing freshness and wonderment about life. They experience and willingly share their emotions with others in a spontaneous way.

If we look to the young child for traits in this area, Montagu's (1981) list includes a sense of wonder, playfulness, joyfulness, laughter and tears, and dance and song. These traits that naturally unfold with the growing child will continue into adulthood when they are nurtured and there is no severe deprivation in the environment.

Behavioral medicine, psychosomatic medicine, and psychoneuro-immunology have established a relationship between thoughts, feelings, and illness (Benson with Proctor, 1984; Borysenko, 1987; Locke & Colligan, 1986; Rossi, 1986; Siegel, 1986). When negative emotions become chronic or are suppressed, they can become destructive to our well-being.

Ornstein and Sobel (1987), in reviewing the literature, found that hostility seems to be the most likely characteristic that contributes to high blood pressure, coronary artery disease, and death among those who have the competitive, hard-driving Type A personality. Researchers have gathered a wealth of data suggesting that chronic anger is so damaging to the body that it ranks with cigarette smoking, obesity, and a high-fat diet as a powerful risk factor for early death (Williams, 1990). He reported that people who scored high on a hostility scale as teenagers were much more likely than were their more cheerful peers to have elevated cholesterol levels as adults.

In another study, Julius (1990), an epidemiologist at the University of Michigan, analyzed the effects of chronic anger on women older than 18 years of age. She found that women who had obvious signs of long-term suppressed anger were three times more likely to have died during the study than were women who did not harbor such hostile feelings. Research findings also suggest that anxiety, loneliness, and depression are associated with suppressing the immune system, thus increasing the chance for illness to occur (Locke et al., 1984).

By contrast, relaxation and positive emotional states seem to strengthen immune function (Dillon, Minchoff, & Baker, 1985; Kiecolt-Glaser et al., 1984; McClelland, Ross, & Patel, 1985). Indeed, responses to daily events influence internal bodily functions. Not only does a negative mood result in lower antibody response but a positive mood is associated with a higher antibody response (Stone, Cox, Valdimarsdottir, Jandorf, & Neale, 1987).

Disclosing our feelings to another person who is nonjudgmental can be therapeutic. Using writing as a means of disclosure of innermost thoughts (some may call it confession) can measurably improve physical and mental health. Pennebaker (1990), in more than a decade of research, has demonstrated that keeping a journal of your innermost feelings can improve your health, but mood, immune functioning, and health are improved only if *facts and feelings* are disclosed.

Intellectual Stimulation, Problem Solving, and Creativity

When reduced to its basic elements, thinking is primarily a problem-solving process (Montagu, 1981). According to Montagu, the need to think soundly is accompanied by a cluster of traits characteristic of the developing child. These traits include the need to know, the need to learn, the need to organize, curiosity, and a sense of wonder. Explorativeness, experimental-mindedness, flexibility, open-mindedness, imagination, and creativity are additional intellectual conditions and characteristics that enable the person to master the environment and pursue mental, artistic, and productive activities that challenge thinking and produce satisfaction.

Maslow found that creativity was a universal characteristic of the self-actualizing people whom he studied. They demonstrated a special kind of creativeness, originality, and inventiveness. These characteristics have commonly been observed in children; researchers and personnel working with older persons, however, have noted how involving them in intellectually stimulating and creative tasks has the effects of regeneration and rejuvenation. Being mentally active and creative enriches the quality of life along with the longevity (Pelletier, 1981).

Sense of Humor

Humor, particularly when it is accompanied by laughter, promotes physiological, psychological, and social change. The skeletal muscles become more relaxed, breathing changes, and the brain is believed to release certain chemicals that are positive to our well-being, serving as an analgesic, a relaxant, or energizer. Humor creates an open flexibility for problem solving, reduces defensiveness, and improves communication while neutralizing stress (Cousins, 1979; Loehr & McLaughlin, 1986; Moody, 1978). Psychologically, the right kind of humor overrides negative emotions associated with "unsound" thinking, dissipating such thoughts at least for a time, and opens the possibility to changes in perception (Mosak, 1987).

Vaillant (1977) found a positive correlation between physical and psychological health of more than 200 Harvard graduates followed up over 30 years. Among the results, those graduates with the best adjustment used more humor than did those with poorer adjustment. Humor was seen as an antidote for distress because it allowed both the idea and the affect to coexist in consciousness.

Adler (1954) believed that in addition to specific training, therapists should have "a jovial attitude...blessed with cheerfulness and good humor..." (p. 201). Mosak (1987) and Fry and Salameh (1987) have described the benefits of humor in counseling and psychotherapy. Humor is seen as being useful in establishing a relationship, making assessments, turning the client around, and acting as a criterion in termination.

Physical Fitness and Health Habits

A landmark study that showed the significant relationship between health habits, health, and life expectancy was conducted with approximately 7,000 adults in Alameda County, California (Belloc, 1973; Belloc & Breslow, 1972). Seven factors were found to be significantly related to health and life expectancy:

1. Three meals a day at regular times and no snacking
2. Breakfast every day
3. Moderate exercise two or three times a week
4. Adequate sleep (7 or 8 hours a night)
5. No smoking
6. Moderate weight
7. No alcohol or only in moderation

Exercise. The benefits of exercise were summarized early in the 1980s by Cooper (1982), nationally known for his research in revolutionizing U.S. residents' exercise habits with his aerobics program specifically designed to strengthen the heart and lungs. Exercise according to Cooper contributes to our well-being through such benefits as the following: more personal energy, greater ability to handle domestic and job-related stress, less depression and "free-floating" anxiety, fewer physical complaints, better self-image and more self-confidence, bones of greater strength, slowing of the aging process, more restful sleep, and better concentration at work and greater perseverance in all daily tasks.

A large, definitive follow-up study of 17,000 Harvard alumni was conducted by Paffenbarger, Hyde, Wing, and Hsieh (1986). They studied the exercise habits of these men, whose ages ranged from 35 to 74 years of age, for more than a decade and concluded that mortality rates were significantly lower among the physically active. Based on the Harvard alumni study, a middle-age man can expect to live an extra 2 hours for every hour of exercise.

Mental functioning and mood are improved with regular, proper exercise (Doan & Scherman, 1987). Although the physiological pathways are not yet understood Sime (1984), in his review of the research, noted that the association between exercise and a state of mind show the following:

1. A positive relationship with mental well-being
2. A decrease in state and trait anxiety
3. A decrease in mild to moderate depression
4. A decrease in muscular tension along with anxiety

A majority of the studies using self-concept measures show an improvement by increased feelings of self-worth and competence. The beneficial emotional effects of exercise tend to hold up across all ages and both sexes.

Likewise, the antidepressant effect of exercise is likely to be greater if combined with traditional counseling and psychotherapy.

Nutrition. Nutritional research has demonstrated that there is a relationship between what we eat, our health, our moods, and our performance (Wurtman, 1986). Five nutrients are necessary for good health—proteins, carbohydrates, fats, vitamins, and minerals. Water is the sixth substance essential for life sustenance. Nutritional scientists agree that a balanced diet is the most important rule. In eating a variety of foods to get the full variety of more than 40 nutrients, one should select foods low in fat, low in sugar, and high in fiber.

Dietary Guidelines for Americans, a booklet published by the U.S. Department of Agriculture and U.S. Department of Health and Human Services (1990), provides sensible guidelines for nutrition and health:

1. Eat a variety of foods.
2. Maintain healthy weight.
3. Choose a diet low in fat, saturated fat, and cholesterol.
4. Choose a diet with plenty of vegetables, fruits, and grain products.
5. Use sugars only in moderation.
6. Use salt and sodium only in moderation.
7. If you drink alcoholic beverages, do so in moderation.

Eating habits and food preferences have ethnic, religious, and cultural origins. Eating habits are established early in life and consequently become difficult to change with increasing age. When serious deficiencies or imbalances occur in any of the basic nutrients, optimal health is sacrificed and diseases are likely to occur. Two diseases that have dietary components are heart attacks and cancer. What we eat affects our health, mood, and performance.

LIFE TASK 3: WORK

Work as a Life-Span Task

Work is a fundamental life task that provides economic, psychological, and social benefits to the well-being of the individual and to others. Those who are unable to engage in work activities struggle psychologically and economically for survival. Persons unwilling to work usually are discouraged persons who have given up on achieving life satisfaction through this life task. The inability to fulfill this life task was regarded by Dreikurs (1953) as a serious symptom of illness.

The definition of work broadly encompasses everything we do to sustain ourselves and contribute to the sustenance of others (Adler, 1954). This includes not only gainful employment but also childrearing, home-making, volunteer services, educational endeavors, and innumerable other activities that engage individuals in activities meaningful to themselves and others. We wish to include the play of children and many leisure-time activities of adults as an extension of Adler's concept of work as a life task.

Psychological, Social, and Economic Benefits

The different purposes that work can serve have been summarized by Herr and Cramer (1988). Psychological purposes include self-esteem, self-efficacy (control), identity, a feeling of mastery or competence, and commitment (meaning in life). Social benefits include a place to meet people, a feeling of being valued or needed by others, social status, and potential friendships. Economic purposes include the obvious resources to purchase goods and services, evidence of success, and assets to purchase leisure or free time.

Work as a significant life domain has been well documented through research (Campbell, 1981). Work was one of several major domains that contributed to the overall quality of life. Job satisfaction has been found to have a significant, beneficial relationship with such factors as hardiness—commitment, challenge, change (Kobasa, 1982), less stress, less anxiety, fewer physical symptom, meaning in life (Witmer et al., 1983), longevity (Danner & Dunning, 1978; Palmore, 1969; Pelletier, 1981), and greater productivity (Pelletier, 1984). One of the best predictors of longevity is satisfaction with one's work.

Another measure of the importance of work can be derived by examining the effects of unemployment. Pelletier (1984) reported, "During periods of economic slump there is a marked increase in murder, suicide, mental illness, heart disease, alcoholism, divorce, domestic violence, family fights, and childhood abuse" (p. 129). Although unemployment may not be the direct cause of disease and mental illness, it undoubtedly exacerbates the factors that trigger such conditions.

LIFE TASK 4: FRIENDSHIP

Social Interest and Connectedness

The fourth life task of friendship is used to describe all those social relationships that involve connection with others either individually or in community, but do not have a marital, sexual, or familial commitment. Relationships that are formed on the basis of a commitment to one another and involve emotional intimacy, sexual intimacy, or both, including a family, are discussed under the fifth life task of love. Differences between the two life tasks are defined according to the nature of the relationship, the level of emotional attachment, and the extent of self-disclosure.

What begins as behaviors to satisfy physical needs soon evolves into satisfaction of emotional needs through interaction with others. Adler (1954) considered "social interest" or "social feeling" as innate to human nature (i.e., we are born with the capacity and need to be connected with each other and in a cosmic relationship). Therefore, the broad meaning of social interest is a "sense of fellowship in the human community" (p. 38). Empathy and altruism are manifestations of social interest. Montagu (1955) has applied the concept of social interest in support of his own view that "life is social and man is born to be social, that is cooperative—an interdependent part of a whole"- (p. 185). The healthy persons in Maslow's (1970) research had deep feeling, sympathy, and affection for human beings in general as well as deep, profound interpersonal relationships.

Social Support, Interpersonal Relations, and Health

Three functions are served through social support (Schaefer, Coyne, & Lazarus, 1982). These consist of (a) emotional support—attachment, reassurance, being able to rely upon and confide in a person; (b) tangible support—involving direct aid such as loans, gifts, and services (e.g., doing a chore or caring for someone who is ill); and (c) informational support—providing information or advice and feedback.

Satisfaction with life has been found to be related to the presence of friendships (Campbell, 1981; Flanagan, 1978). Berkman and Syme (1979), two epidemiologists, found through a 9-year study of 7,000 persons that single persons, widowed persons, persons with few friends or family, and persons who did not participate in community organizations died at a rate two to five times greater than those with more extensive ties. This was true regardless of income, sex, race, or ethnic background, age, and selected life-style factors.

A 10-year study of 2,754 adults in Michigan revealed that those persons with the least social contacts had two to four times the mortality rate of the better socially connected persons (House, Robbins, & Metzner, 1982). The social support findings were independent of the traditional risk factors such as smoking, abusing alcohol, not exercising, and being obese. They also found that doing volunteer work dramatically increased longevity. Men who did no volunteer work were $2\,^1/_2$ times as likely to die during the study as were men who volunteered at least once a week.

Loneliness, an enduring condition of estrangement or rejection, is associated with such variables as depression, suicide, alcohol abuse, anxiety, adolescent delinquency, poor self-concept, and increased mortality (McWhirter, 1990). Loneliness as well as mild upsets are associated with decreased activity of certain cells in the immune system. Kiecolt-Glaser and her colleagues (1984) compared 38 married women with an equal number of women who were separated or divorced. They found that married women had better immune function than did unmarried women, and women who reported they were happily married had the healthiest immune system of all the groups. Weiss (1988), in his article on loneliness, reported, "Among both students and psychiatric inpatients, the lonely have been shown to be more likely to have impaired immune system functioning: they definitely catch more colds and are probably more vulnerable to every sort of illness" (p. 5).

Sharing sorrow with someone protects people from the stress of life. Siegel (1986) summarized the work of Pennebaker at Southern Methodist University when he found that "those who bore their grief alone had a much higher than average rate of illness, while those who could talk over their troubles with someone else had no increase in health problems" (p. 187).

In summarizing the research between social support and various health dimensions, Cohen (1988) noted the potential connections between social support and health behaviors, positive and negative affect, self-esteem and personal control, neuroendocrine response, and the immune system. In the absence of friendships, illness, a shorter life expectancy, and less satisfaction in life are likely companions to those individuals who fail to master the opportunities and responsibilities of friendships.

LIFE TASK 5: LOVE

The life task of love tends to be intimate, trusting, self-disclosing, cooperative, and long-term in commitment and often includes sexual relations. In quality of life research directed by Flanagan (1978), spouse, children, and friends were found to be the top three contributors to overall satisfaction of life for women and men. Well-being research by Campbell (1981) in a national survey affirmed that marriage and friends significantly contributed to satisfaction with life. In their study of sources of satisfaction in long-term relationships, Argyle and Furnham (1983) found age and sex differences. Women derive more satisfaction in the emotional support area and from friends and family; men get more satisfaction from spouses and work superiors. Older people derive more satisfaction from family and neighbors, younger people from friends and work associates.

In early adolescence, the sexual drive awakens, reaches its peak in early adulthood, and continues throughout adulthood, with a gradual decline occurring in the older years. For most persons, the fulfillment of the life task of love includes the desire for sexual satisfaction, procreation, and the continuation of life through children. No one dies, however, from lack of sex because individual survival does not depend on it, although survival of the species does. The extent to which sexual satisfaction contributes to longevity and wellness is unknown.

Research reported by USA Today ("A wife adds," 1988) noted the added satisfaction and health for men in marriage relationships. Married men were almost twice as likely to outlive never-married men and were three times more likely to live longer than divorced men. Husbands had a lower depression rate than did people of any other marital status. The mental health of men improves unbelievably when they marry, according to University of Michigan sociologist Ronald Kessler, who completed a study of 1,000 Detroit-area couples. Men consistently gave higher ratings to their marriages than did wives, and men were much more affected than women if the marriage ended.

Major studies by Berkman and Syme (1979) and Lynch (1977) confirmed the health benefits of intimate relationships. Nonmarried persons always had higher death rates, sometimes as much as five times higher than did those of married individuals. Not only was this true for heart disease, but this was true for all causes of death. The U.S. mortality rates are consistently higher for divorced, single, and widowed individuals of both sexes and all races.

Vaillant (1977) examined the linkage between loving and health in following 200 Harvard graduates for 30 years. The healthier men reflected a friendlier disposition and closer relationships with their children and were happily married over time and revealed better sexual adjustment. He concluded that being able to love one's friends, wife, parents, and children were predictors of good mental health. He also found that altruistic behavior was associated with better mental health, especially so during times of stress in people's lives. This study and the others reported support the position that trust, intimacy, caring, companionship, compassion, and similar qualities of a loving relationship promote good health and longevity.

LIFE FORCES

Development and performance of the five life tasks are influenced by forces from within the individual and from outside in the way societal institutions function to achieve their purposes. The outer band of the model as illustrated in Figure 1 represents the life forces as major societal institutions that impinge on the health and well-being of each individual. Each of them is mentioned only briefly, because their exposition is beyond the purpose of this article.

Family

In national studies of strong families, certain characteristics emerge despite political, cultural, and language differences. Strong families share six major qualities (Stinnett & DeFrain, 1985):

1. Commitment to each other's welfare and happiness
2. Appreciation that is shown for one another
3. Communication skills and time spent talking with each other

4. Time spent with one another both in quality and quantity
5. Spiritual wellness, which recognizes a greater good or power in life, a source of strength and purpose
6. Coping ability that views stress or crises as an opportunity to grow

These six qualities that strong families have in common deserve top priority.

Religion

Religions that have weathered the test of time in their recognition of a higher power and reverence for human life are a well-spring for hope, values, and meaning in life. Although U.S. residents seem to be religious when polled, probably no more than half the population has made a long-term commitment to the beliefs and life-style exemplified in the religion. In certain cultural groups, the young people have largely abandoned not only the religion of their parents but also the values inherent in the religion. The role of religion in functioning as a primary source for inner peace, values, and social harmony merits exposition.

Education

Education has unlimited potential for creating a community in which the characteristics of the healthy person can be nurtured. Growth is both incidental and intentional. When implementing a holistic approach to education, the most effective method is modeling a life-style of holistic health and wellness. With an educational climate that is encouraging, striving for wellness becomes a process that is likely to extend over the life span.

Community

With the breakup of the extended family, industrialization, urbanization, and social mobility, has come the fragmentation of a sense of community in American (in this article *American* refers to the United States) life. The interdependence built into the small town and rural social structure of earlier years seems unnecessary at an economic level but is essential today for fulfilling our needs at a social level. The ingredients of community building need to be identified, then built into the social fabric of our cities, towns, and rural areas. Support groups, church groups, and work groups should all nurture a feeling of connectedness and a belief that our destiny is intertwined, yet, as individuals, retaining a healthy degree of independence.

Media

Shaped by the norms of society, the media also shape our individual values and public policies. Because it has the power to mold our attitudes, beliefs, and desires, the media must be considered for the potential they have for positive influence as well as negative. Given the fact that children watch on average 25 to 30 hours of commercial television a week with little or no supervision, one must consider its potential for harm as well as good. An overwhelming majority of the studies on the relationship between TV and violence in children conclude that children who watch television violence are more prone to use physical aggression than are those who do not watch so much.

Government

Three underlying values promulgated in the Declaration of Independence are life, liberty, and the pursuit of happiness. Government policies and practices do have an impact on human behavior and change attitudes. With a vision of wellness and prevention, the government, through farsighted leadership, can promote policies that have the possibility of influencing every American (e.g., by lowering the death rate of children and extending the longevity of adults). One very current example is the just-released report on *Healthy People 2000* (USDHHS, 1990) that sets the nation's health promotion and disease prevention goals for the next decade.

Business/Industry

Although the workplace exists primarily as an economic force for the production of goods and services, it can be designed in a way that elements of the wellness and prevention model will contribute to its own financial health. Healthier people are more productive, creative, cooperative, competent, and committed; miss fewer workdays; and have fewer illnesses. The relationship between health and worker productivity is being recognized by the business community (Naisbitt, 1982; Pelletier, 1984). Many of the larger industries have not only started Employee Assistance Programs but also have initiated wellness programs that include such components as smoking cessation, control of alcohol and substance abuse, means of coping with stress, good nutrition, exercise, effective communication, noise reduction, and control of toxic substances.

GLOBAL EVENTS AND COSMIC CONSCIOUSNESS

Beyond the life forces are global events that have an impact on our everyday living and the quality of our lives. Wars, hunger, disease, poverty, environmental pollution, overpopulation, violation of human rights, economic exploitation, unemployment, and competition for limited resources are heavy clouds across the international sky. All are part of the ecology of living in a "global village" on the Planet Earth. We cannot afford to ignore these events if we wish to build a "neighborhood village" that is committed to a life-style of wellness and prevention.

In conclusion, the model of wellness and prevention we have proposed is based on findings from the social, psychological, medical, and behavioral sciences. Characteristics of healthy persons have been described to include spiritual values; sense of worth; sense of control; realistic beliefs; spontaneous and emotional responsiveness; intellectual stimulation, problem solving, and creativity; sense of humor; physical fitness and nutrition; success in the work task; satisfying friendships and a social network; and satisfaction in marriage or other intimate relationships. These characteristics can be used as indicators of wellness in assessing the health of students and clients. Educational learnings, personal growth, treatment plans, and progress can be based on the use of these 11 dimensions of a healthy person. We hope that the model will engender discussion, debate, research, and clinical application. On a larger scale, we envision its potential as a paradigm for advocacy and public policy making.

REFERENCES

A wife adds satisfaction to man's life. (1988, February 29). *USA Today*, p. 10.

Adler, A. (1954). *Understanding human nature* (W. B. Wolf, Trans.). New York: Fawcett Premier. (Original work published 1927)

Argyle, M., & Furnham, A. (1983). Sources of satisfaction and conflict in long-term relationships. *Journal of Marriage and the Family, 45*, 481-493.

Bandura. A. (1986). *Social foundations of thought and action: A social cognitive theory*. Englewood Cliffs, NJ: Prentice-Hall.

Beck, A. T. (1976). *Cognitive therapy and the emotional disorders*. New York: New American Library.

Beck, A. T. (1984). Cognitive approaches to stress. In R. L. Woolfolk & P. M. Lehrer (Eds.), *Principles and practice of stress management* (pp. 255-305). New York: Guilford Press.

Belloc, N. B. (1973). Relationship of health practices and mortality. *Preventive Medicine, 2*, 67-81.

Belloc, N. B., & Breslow, L. (1972). Relationship of physical health status and health practices. *Preventive Medicine, 1*, 409-421.

Benson, H., with Proctor, W. (1984). *Beyond the relaxation response*. New York: Times Books.

Berkman, L., & Syme, S. L. (1979). Social networks, host resistance, and mortality: A nine-year study of Alameda County residents. *American Journal of Epidemiology, 109*, 186-204.

Borysenko, J. Z. (1987). Healing motives: An interview with David McClelland. *Advances, 2*, 29-41.

Buscaglia, L. F. (1978). *Personhood: The art of being fully human.* New York: Fawcett Columbine.

California Department of Mental Health, Office of Prevention. (1979). *In pursuit of wellness* (Vol. 1, No. 1). San Francisco: 2340 Irving Street, Suite 108. Copies are available from the California Department of Mental Health at the Irving Street address.

California State Department of Education. (1990). *Toward a state of esteem.* Sacramento. CA: Bureau of Publications.

Campbell, A. (1981). *The sense of well-being in America: Recent patterns and trends.* New York: McGraw-Hill.

Cohen, S. (1988). Psychosocial models of the role of social support in the etiology of physical disease. *Health Psychology, 7,* 269-297.

Cooper, K. B. (1982). *The aerobics program for total well-being.* New York: Bantam.

Cousins, N. (1979). *Anatomy of an illness as perceived by the patient.* New York: Norton.

Danner, S., & Dunning, A. (1978, January 23). Spared allusion, they've lived past 90. *Medical World News,* p. 42.

Dillon, K. M., Minchoff, B., & Baker, K. H. (1985). Positive emotional states and enhancement of the immune system. *International Journal of Psychiatry in Medicine, 15,* 13-17.

Doan, R. E., & Scherman, A. (1987). The therapeutic effect of physical fitness on measures of personality: A literature review. *Journal of Counseling and Development, 66,* 28-36.

Dreikurs, R. (1953). *Fundamentals of Adlerian psychology.* Chicago: Alfred Adler Institute.

Einstein, A. (1984). Ideas and opinions (selected excerpts). In K. Wilber (Ed.), *Quantum questions: Mystical writings of the world's great physicists* (pp. 100-104). Boston: New Science Library. (Original work published 1954)

Ellis, A. (1962). *Reason and emotion in psychotherapy.* New York: Lyle-Stuart.

Flanagan, J. (1978). A research approach to improving our quality of life. *American Psychologist, 33,* 138-147.

Frey, D., & Carlock, C. J. (1989). *Enhancing self esteem* (2nd ed.). Muncie, IN: Accelerated Development.

Fry, W. F., & Salameh, W. A. (Eds.). (1987). *Handbook of humor and psychotherapy.* Sarasota, FL: Professional Resource Exchange.

Harman, W. W. (1988). *Global mind change: The promise of the last years of the twentieth century.* Indianapolis, IN: Knowledge Systems.

Heppner, P. P., & Krauskopf, C. J. (1987). An information processing approach to personal problem solving. *The Counseling Psychologist, 15,* 371-447.

Herr, E. L., & Cramer, S. H. (1988). *Career guidance and counseling through the life span* (3rd ed.). Boston: Little, Brown.

House, J. S., Robbins, C., & Metzner, H. L. (1982). The association of social relationships and activities with mortality. *American Journal of Epidemiology, 116,* 123-140.

Julius, M. (1990). *The effects of chronic anger on women over 18 years* (Paper presented at the Gerontological Society of America meeting at the University of Michigan).

Jung, C. G. (1958). *The undiscovered self* (R. F. C. Hall, Trans.). New York: Mentor Books.

Kiecolt-Glaser, J. K., Garner, W., Speicher, C., Penn, G. M., Holliday, J., & Glaser, R. (1984). *Psychosomatic Medicine, 46,* 7-14.

Kobasa, S. C. (1979). Stressful life events, personality and health: An inquiry into hardiness. *Journal of Personality and Social Psychology, 37,* 1-11.

Kobasa, S. C. (1982). The hardy personality: Toward a social psychology of stress and health. In G. S. Sanders & J. Suls (Eds.), *Social psychology of health and illness.* Hillsdale, NJ: Erlbaum.

Lazarus, R. S ., & Folkman, S. (1984). *Stress, appraisal, and coping.* New York: Springer.

Locke, S., & Colligan, D. (1986). *The healer within: The new medicine of mind and body.* New York: New American Library.

Locke, S. E., Kraus, L., Leserman, J., Hurst, M. W., Heisel, J. S., & Williams, R. M. (1984). Life change stress, psychiatric symptoms, and natural killer cell activity. *Psychosomatic Medicine, 46*, 441-453.

Loehr, J. E., & McLaughlin, P. J. (1986). *Mentally tough: The principles of winning at sports applied to winning in business*. New York: M. Evans.

Lynch, J. J. (1977). *The broken heart: The medical consequences of loneliness*. New York: Basic Books.

Maslow, A. H. (Ed.). (1959). *New knowledge in human values* (Gateway edition published by Harper & Row, 1970). Chicago: Henry Regnery Company.

Maslow, A. H. (1968). *Toward a psychology of being* (2nd ed.). New York: D. Van Nostrand.

Maslow, A. H. (1970). *Motivation and personality* (2nd ed.). New York: Harper & Row.

McClelland, D. C., Ross, G., & Patel, V. (1985). The effect of an academic examination on salivary norepinephrine and immunoglobulin levels. *Journal of Human Stress, 11*, 52-59.

McWhirter, B. T. (1990). Loneliness: A review of current literature, with implications for counseling and research. *Journal of Counseling & Development, 68*, 417-422.

Mischel, W. (1981). A cognitive-social learning approach to assessment. In T. V Merluzzi, C. R. Glass, & M. Genest (Eds.), *Cognitive assessment* (pp. 479-502). New York: Guilford Press.

Montagu, A. (1955). *The direction of human development: Biological and social bases*. New York: Harper.

Montagu, A. (1981). *Growing young*. New York: McGraw-Hill.

Moody, R. A. (1978). *Laugh after laugh: The healing power of humor*. Jacksonville, FL: Headwaters Press.

Mosak, H. H. (1987). *Ha, ha and aha: The role of humor in psychotherapy*. Muncie, IN: Accelerated Development

Mosak, H. H., & Dreikurs, R. (1967). The life tasks III, the fifth life task. *Individual Psychology, 5*(1), 16-22.

Naisbitt, J. (1982) *Megatrends: Ten new directions transforming our lives*. New York: Warner Books.

Ornstein, R., & Sobel, D. (1987). *The healing brain*. New York: Simon & Schuster.

Paffenbarger, R. S., Jr., Hyde, R. T., Wing, A. L., & Hsieh, C. (1986). [Title not available.] *New England Journal of Medicine, 314*, 605-613.

Palmore, E. B. (1969). Physical, mental and social factors in predicting longevity. *Gerontologist, 9*(2), 103-108.

Pelletier, K. R. (1981). *Longevity: Fulfilling our biological potential*. New York: Delacorte Press/Seymour Lawrence.

Pelletier, K. R. (1984). *Healthy people in unhealthy places: Stress and fitness at work*. New York: Dell.

Pennebaker, J. W. (1990). *Opening up: The healing power of confiding in others*. New York: William Morrow.

Rossi, E. W. (1986). *The psychobiology of mind–body healing: New concepts of therapeutic hypnosis*. New York: Norton.

Schaefer, C., Coyne, J. C., & Lazarus, R. S. (1982). The health-related functions of social support. *Journal of Behavioral Medicine, 4*, 381–406.

Siegel, B. S. (1986) *Love, medicine and miracles*. New York: Harper & Row.

Sime, W. E. (1984). *Psychological benefits of exercise*. Advances, *1*(4), 15-29.

Stinnett, N., & DeFrain, J. (1985). *Secrets of strong families*. New York: Berkley Books.

Stone, A. A., Cox, D. S., Valdimarsdottir, H., Jandorf, L., & Neale, J.M. (1987). Evidence that IgA antibody is associated with daily mood. *Journal of Personality and Social Psychology, 52*, 988-993.

Strickland, B. R. (1978). Internal-external expectancies and health-related behaviors. *Journal of Consulting and Clinical Psychology, 46*, 1192-1211.

Sweeney, T. J. (1989). *Adlerian counseling* (3rd ed.). Muncie, IN: Accelerated Development.

Tiger, L. (1979). *Optimism: The biology of hope.* New York: Simon & Schuster.

U.S. Department of Agriculture and U.S. Department of Health and Human Services. (1990). Dietary guidelines for Americans (3rd ed.). *Home and Garden Bulletin, No. 232.*

U.S. Department of Health and Human Services, Public Health Service. (1990). *Healthy people 2000: National health promotion and disease prevention objectives.* Washington, DC: Superintendent of Documents, Government Printing Office.

U.S. Public Health Service. (1979). *Smoking and health: A report of the Surgeon General* (DHEW Publication No. (PHS) 79-50066). Washington, DC: U.S. Government Printing Office.

Vaillant, G. E. (1977). *Adaptation to life.* Boston: Little, Brown.

Weiss, R. S. (1988). Loneliness. *The Harvard Medical School Mental Health Letter,* 4(12), 4–6.

Williams, R. (1990). *Hostility as a risk factor for early death* (Paper presented at the American Heart Society Meeting at Duke University Medical Center).

Witmer, J. M. (1985). *Pathways to personal growth.* Muncie, IN: Accelerated Development.

Witmer, J.M., & Rich, C. (1991). *Optimism as a mediating variable in coping with stress.* Unpublished manuscript.

Witmer, J. M., Rich, C., Barcikowski, R., & Mague, J. C. (1983). Psychosocial characteristics mediating the stress response: An exploratory study. *The Personnel and Guidance Journal, 62,* 73-77.

World Health Organization. (1958). *Constitution of the World Health Organization, Annex 1. In the first ten years of the World Health Organization.* Geneva, Switzerland: World Health Organization.

Wurtman, J. (1986). *Managing your mind and mood through food.* New York: Rawson.

Young, M. E., & Witmer, J. M. (1985). Values: Our internal guidance system. In J. M. Witmer (co-author), *Pathways to personal growth* (pp. 275-289). Muncie, IN: Accelerated Development.

Counseling for Spiritual Wellness: Theory and Practice

CYNTHIA K. CHANDLER
JANICE MINER HOLDEN
CHERYL A. KOLANDER

WELLNESS CAN BE conceptualized as consisting of six major dimensions: intellectual, emotional, physical, social, occupational, and spiritual (Hettler, 1979, 1991). Spiritual wellness is an element of emerging interest in health education and in counseling, but relative to the other five dimensions, it continues to lack clarity in definition and application. Health education has focused primarily on physical wellness, whereas counseling has focused primarily on emotional, social, and occupational wellness.

> The development of the profession should include an expansion of efforts.... An elemental weakness, at this point, is the area of spiritual health. It is unexplored territory that the profession has so far avoided for lack of a clear conceptual definition of the construct. This area needs further development and integration.... (Allen & Yarian, 1981, p.5)

Thus far, spiritual wellness has been defined as "a continuing search for meaning and purpose in life: an appreciation for depth of life, the expanse of the universe, and natural forces which operate: a personal belief system" (Myers, 1990, p. 11). Spiritual wellness is evident in the following:

> ...the willingness to seek meaning and purpose in human existence, to question everything, and to appreciate the intangibles which cannot be explained or understood readily. A spiritually well person seeks harmony between that which lies within the individual and the forces that come from outside the individual. (Opatz, 1986, p. 61)

These definitions provide some initial guidelines for understanding the spiritual dimension of wellness; theories that include concepts of spiritual health and events and techniques that stimulate spiritual growth (Assagioli, 1965; Grof, 1985), however, seem to have enjoyed only limited recognition. Spiritual health is often viewed as intangible or unteachable, or even as an inappropriate domain for health educators and counselors. This may be, at least in part, because spirituality has been considered primarily the domain of religion. It is our contention that spirituality is a natural part of being human and can be conceptualized in an understandable and practical fashion.

From "Counseling for Spiritual Wellness: Theory and Practice," by C.K. Chandler, J.M. Holden, and C.A. Kolander, 1992, *Journal of Counseling & Development*, 7, 168–175.

To encourage greater familiarity with and use of the spiritual dimension by counselors and health educators, it is necessary to define more clearly the concept of spiritual health and to describe ways to use spontaneous events and deliberate techniques to facilitate spiritual growth. The purposes of this article will be the following:

1. To provide a clearer conceptual definition of spiritual wellness based in psychological theory
2. To discuss the interactional relationship between spiritual health and the other dimensions of wellness
3. To describe spontaneous events and intentional activities that can contribute to enhanced spiritual awareness and spiritual growth

THE NATURE OF SPIRITUALITY

Several psychological models include spirituality in their concepts of the nature of persons. Maslow (1971) contended that "the spiritual life (the contemplative, 'religious,' philosophical, or value life) is…part of the human essence…a defining characteristic of human nature…" (p. 325). In his study of optimally functioning people, he labeled those at the top of his hierarchy "transcendent self-actualizers." In comparison to "mere" self-actualizers, transcenders demonstrated the following characteristics, or proportionately more of these characteristics: a more holistic perspective about the world; a natural tendency toward synergy (cooperative action)—intrapsychic, interpersonal, intracultural, and international; much more consciously and deliberately metamotivated behavior (i.e., by truth, goodness, unity); more responsiveness to beauty; a greater appreciation for peak experiences: nonpower-seeking attitude over others; the ability to speak naturally and easily—the language of "Being"; the ability not only to be aware of their self-identity but the capability of going beyond the ego self; attitudes that were more lovable and awe-inspiring; and more cognizance of the sacredness of every person and of every living thing.

Assagioli's (1965) approach, psychosynthesis, included the hypothesized construct of a "higher unconscious" or "superconscious" in all humans, a region of the psyche from which we "receive our higher intuitions and aspirations—artistic, philosophical, or scientific, ethical ' imperatives' and urges to humanitarian and heroic action…the source of higher feelings, such as altruistic love, of genius and of the states of contemplation, illumination, and ecstasy" (p. 17). He clarified that "'spiritual' refers not only to experiences traditionally considered religious but to *all* the states of awareness, all the human functions and activities which have as their common denominator the possession of values higher than average" (1989, p. 30). He further asserted that "spiritual drives or spiritual urges are…real, basic and fundamental…" (1965, p. 194).

Grof's (1976, 1985, 1988) psychospiritual model grew out of observation of thousands of LSD (lysergic acid diethylamide) psychedelic and psycholytic sessions of both psychiatric patient and nonpatient populations. He found that at some point in the course of repeated LSD sessions, those being studied would inevitably experience an existential crisis provoked by "the shattering encounter with...critical aspects of human existence [such as biological birth, physical pain and agony aging, disease and decrepitude, and dying and death] and the deep realization of the frailty and impermanence of man as a biological creature" (1976, p. 95). This existential crisis, in turn, provoked the following:

> ...opening up of areas of spiritual and religious experiences that appear to be an intrinsic part of the human personality and are independent of the individual's cultural and religious background and programming...everyone who has reached these levels develops convincing insights into the utmost relevance of the spiritual and religious dimensions in the universal scheme of things. Even hard-core materialists, positivistically oriented scientists, skeptics and cynics, and uncompromising atheists and antireligious crusaders such as the Marxist philosophers suddenly become interested in a spiritual search after they [have] confronted these levels in themselves. (1976, p. 95-96)

Grof's implication that spiritual motivation is intrinsic to, but often lies dormant in, human nature finds agreement with the other two theorists. Maslow (1971) believed that motivation at the lowest level of the hierarchy of needs is relatively strong, but that as one achieves each subsequent level, motivation to achieve the next highest level is relatively weaker. In particular, he thought motivation to achieve the metaneeds (self-actualization and self-transcendence) to be "less urgent or demanding, weaker (than) the basic needs" (Maslow, 1980, p. 125). Assagioli (1965), too, contended that in the realm of the superconscious "are *latent* [italics added] the higher psychic functions and spiritual energies" (p. 17).

The concept of the intrinsic but sometimes dormant nature of spirituality in humans is further supported by research on near-death experiences (NDEs: Ring, 1984) and near-death-like experiences (Holden & Guest, 1990), which seem to be catalysts for spiritual growth. Reminiscent of Grof's findings, Ring (1984) found that NDErs' beliefs prior to the experience ran the gamut from hard-core atheists to the devoutly religious. The fact that the NDE flew in the face of the worldview of atheists did not prevent them from having a substantially identical experience as frequently, and being as profoundly and permanently affected by it, as were religious and spiritual believers.

Specifically, what Ring conceptualized as spiritual transformation included personality changes such as greater authenticity, actualization of inner potentials, and positive self-concept; value changes such as increased appreciation of life, concern for others, and quest for meaning in life; decreased concern with impressing others and with materialism; and specifically spiritual changes such as a tendency to characterize oneself as spiritual rather than religious, a feeling of being inwardly close to God, a conviction that there is life after death, and a belief in the essential underlying unity of all religions. To supplement this profile, Moody (1975) found that many NDErs independently reported having learned the twofold purpose of life during their experiences in the presence of an all-knowing, all-loving "being of light" (p. 65): to acquire knowledge and grow in the capacity to love.

That spiritual awakening can sometimes be violent and profoundly disorienting is illustrated by the phenomenon of spiritual emergency, a concept that has been gaining momentum in recent psychological literature (Bragdon, 1988, 1990; Grof & Grof, 1989c). Spiritual emergency can take many forms including, for example, ego inflation or the aftermath of an NDE. Beneath the various manifestations is apparently an influx of spiritual energy in an amount too great or form too foreign for the limited personality to integrate smoothly. For this reason, spiritual emergency is indeed well represented by the Chinese pictogram for crisis, which includes symbols of both "danger" and "opportunity" (Grof & Grof, 1989b, p. 7).

DEFINING SPIRITUALITY

Webster's dictionary (Guralnik, 1984) defines "spiritual" as "(1). of the spirit or the soul (2). of or consisting of spirit; not corporeal (3). religious; sacred" (p. 576). We find this definition to be too restrictive to account for the varieties of spiritual experiences. Such phenomena as NDEs, past life experiences, and the practice of meditation often seem to foster similar developmental changes as do religious conversion and the experience of oneness with the universe. Some of these experiences occur outside the context of the human institution of organized religion; others do not explicitly include a subjective sense of "spirit," "soul," or "noncorporeality."

Based on an incorporation of the material cited previously, we propose the following definition:

Spiritual: Pertaining to the innate capacity to, and tendency to seek to, transcend one's current locus of centricity, which transcendence involves increased knowledge and love.

This definition includes many implications that we wish to make explicit.

1. "Innate capacity" is not meant to imply a capacity found *only* in humans—a point of debate that exceeds the scope of this article. The phrase *is* meant to imply a capacity *found in all humans, albeit realized to different degrees by different people at different times.*
2. "Tendency" implies internal motivation toward spirituality that may be demonstrated on a continuum from totally repressed (Haronian, 1972) at one end to a central preoccupation in one's life (Grof & Grof, 1989c) at the other.
3. "To seek" implies that one cannot cause experiences of a spiritual nature to occur; one can only create certain conditions in which spiritual

44

experiences are more likely to occur. This is similar to the concept of "passive volition" in biofeedback.

4. "One's current locus of centricity" refers to the psychological position from which one experiences and evaluates life events, for example, egocentricity (how life events impinge upon my personal wants and goals).

5. "Transcend" is meant to imply a "moving beyond" in a direction of higher or broader scope, for example, someone whose current functioning is characterized by unhealthy egocentricity (self-centered or narcissistic) experiencing healthy egocentricity (enlightened self-interest in which one gleans personal satisfaction through contribution to the greater good), humanicentricity (centered in humanity), geocentricity (centered in the planet), and cosmicentricity (centered in the cosmos). The concept of subsequent levels of transcendence is meant to imply that spirituality is a process to be conceptualized on a continuum, not conceptualized as an either-or proposition; indeed, the identification of discrete stages is recognized as an arbitrary delineation along the continuum (Wilber, Engler, & Brown, 1986).

6. "Greater knowledge" is meant to imply a higher or broader worldview that includes but also transcends the worldview of the previous stage (Wilber, 1980). Greater knowledge involves conceptualization that is increasingly inclusive and focused on commonality and unity, and decreasingly exclusive and focused on difference and duality.

7. "Greater capacity to love" is meant to imply the paradoxical combination of benevolent acceptance of what is, and a motivation to bring about change that results in the greater good. Together with greater knowledge, this implies an evolving sense of life purpose with its increasingly comprehensive and constructive systems of ethics and values.

Compared to a dictionary definition, the one proposed herein can include a sense of spirit, soul, noncorporeality, and sacredness. These components, though extremely common in spiritual experiences, however, are not requisite by our definition. In addition, our definition allows for the experience of relationship to a higher power, as well as the experience of "no-thingness" considered to be the epitome of enlightenment in some Eastern traditions. And finally, we define "spirituality" independently of "religion"; that is, spirituality can occur in or out of the context of the institution of organized religion, and not all aspects of religion are assumed to be spiritual.

We define spiritual experience as an acute experience of a spiritual nature. The term *spiritual experience* tends to conjure up images of the profound phenomena characterized by ineffability, noetic quality, transiency, passivity, unity, and positive affect (Noble, 1987), such as the NDE or experiencing a visitation by a divine presence (Sample, 1984). By our definition, *any* experience of transcendence of one's former frame of reference that results in greater knowledge and love is a spiritual experience. This includes, for example, a husband who, by virtue of coming to understand his wife's behavior in a new way, is able to respond more lovingly toward her, or a client whose contemplation of some existential question seems to facilitate her recovery from an eating disorder. The term *acute* is not meant necessarily to imply "short-lived." Although many and perhaps most spiritual experiences are transient, some advanced practitioners of Eastern spiritual disciplines claim to be living in an almost constant state of spiritual experience. Acute is meant to imply "unmistakably noticeable."

We consider the term *spiritual development* to be the process of incorporating spiritual experience that results ultimately in spiritual transformation. The occurrence of spiritual experiences does not guarantee spiritual development (Grof & Grof, 1989c). Although more intense experiences may press more relentlessly for resolution and integration, they may nevertheless go unresolved for years. The term *ultimately* reflects that spiritual development can involve such episodes or periods of upheaval. At the other extreme, less profound experiences may result in only transient change and not in the achievement of a new level or stage that would characterize development.

This concept of achievement of a new level or stage that would characterize development is exactly what is implied in the term *spiritual transformation*. Transformation is demonstrated by the stable expression of a new mode of functioning that is characterized by a broader locus of centrism and by greater knowledge and love.

Finally, we consider the term *spiritual wellness* to be a balanced openness to or pursuit of spiritual development. "Openness to or pursuit of" is meant to imply that spiritual wellness may be, but is not necessarily, a conscious undertaking. The term *openness to* addresses especially the concept of "repression of the sublime" (Haronian, 1972), in which one denies or defies the spiritual tendency within oneself. This concept includes that of "desacrilization" (Maslow, 1971, p. 49), whereby denial of the reality or importance of higher values defends one against the pain of disillusionment. "Balanced" refers to two dimensions of spiritual wellness. The first is the horizontal dimension, characterized by a continuum with repression of the sublime at one end, and spiritual emergency (Bragdon, 1988, 1990; Grof & Grof, 1989c) at the other. In spiritual emergency, one is overwhelmed by or preoccupied with spirituality, to the detriment of the other dimensions of wellness. Spiritual wellness, then, is conceptualized as a position at or near the midpoint of this continuum (see Figure 1).

In Figure 1, note that at any point in spiritual development, one may shift between a position of wellness and one of either repression or emergency-preoccupation (horizontal dimension). At a position of spiritual wellness, one may demonstrate any stage along a continuum of spiritual development (vertical dimension). Whereas the first meaning of "balance" refers to this horizontal dimension, a second meaning refers to the vertical dimension. To remain at the horizontal position of balance and yet progress

46

FIGURE 1
Model for Spiritual Wellness and Classes of Techniques

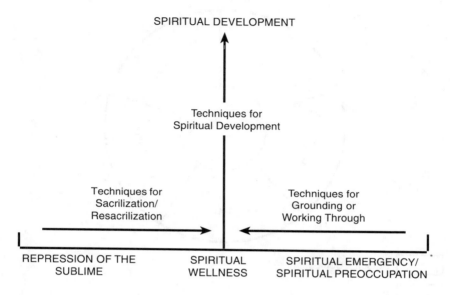

to ever higher stages of spirituality, one must progress relatively gradually and generally in sequence (Assagioli, 1965; Maslow, 1971; Wilber et al., 1986).

Confrontation with life events that, because of one's current locus of centricity, one is unable to incorporate can foster a shift in the direction of either spiritual emergency or repression of the sublime. Examples of such life events include existential events such as death of a loved one, imprisonment in a concentration camp (Frankl, 1959), and lack of fulfillment upon having achieved those goals valued by one's culture, as well as spiritual experiences such as the NDE and near-death-like experiences.

ACHIEVING OPTIMUM WELLNESS

We suggest that spiritual health not be conceptualized as just one of the six dimensions of wellness. Spiritual health should be considered as a component present, along with a personal component, within each of the interrelated and interactive dimensions of wellness (i.e., social, physical, emotional, intellectual, and occupational; see Figure 2). Note in Figure 2 that this model is interrelated and interactive, with personal and spiritual components. Optimum wellness exists when each of these five dimensions has a balanced and developed potential in both the spiritual and personal realm. Working to achieve high-level wellness necessitates the development of the

FIGURE 2
Holistic Wellness Model

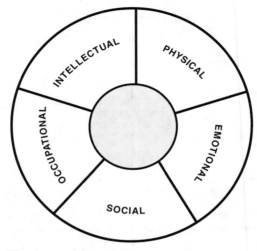

Personal Component

Spiritual Component

spiritual component in each of the five dimensions of wellness. Without attention to spiritual health in each dimension, the individual remains incomplete.

Observable behavioral change that is not accompanied by spiritual development may be especially vulnerable to recidivism. Behavior change that is manifested outwardly is a cue that personal changes are occurring for the individual. Without accompanying spiritual changes, however, the maintenance of these behavioral changes is difficult at best. Consider, for example, the obese person who loses weight only to gain it back when the diet ends, the ex-smoker who continues to fight the urge to have another cigarette, and the workaholic who continually struggles against taking on more and more tasks. We suggest that attention to spiritual health plays a major role in helping individuals maintain positive change. The dieter must internalize the new self as healthy and at the appropriate weight. The ex-smoker must internalize the new self as a nonsmoker. The workaholic must internalize the new self as a balanced individual. Spiritual health provides an avenue through which the individual can create the new and more complete self. Attending to both personal and spiritual modalities for transformation contributes to greater balance and will more likely lead to transformation of the self with its accompanying opportunity to achieve higher level wellness.

We believe that the capacity to develop in both the spiritual and personal realms is present from birth (or perhaps before). Cultures that emphasize the development of the spiritual component in each wellness dimension from early in a person's life may be less likely to produce individuals who experience a spiritual crisis from sudden spiritual awakening. Also, a culture that fosters the development of the spiritual component as well as the personal component contributes to the likelihood that its members can achieve higher levels of wellness in all dimensions than if just one or the other of these two components is emphasized.

COUNSELING AND SPIRITUAL WELLNESS

The practice of incorporating the spiritual dimension into psychotherapy was introduced into Western psychology by Jung (Laszlo, 1954). His ideas influenced Assagioli (1965), who presaged several implications of our model of spiritual wellness for the practice of counseling. He viewed personal and spiritual development as essentially unique and sequential yet predominantly overlapping and interactive, each potentially contributing to the other. He recommended that the therapist introduce spiritual ideas and experiences in a form and with a frequency commensurate with the client's level of personal development and wellness, so as to neither collude with the self in any defense against spirituality (a collusion that would foster repression of the sublime) nor overwhelm the self (an overwhelming that could precipitate spiritual emergency). A more detailed exposition of the stages of spiritual development by Wilber et al. (1986) reflected a similar philosophy about the counselor's role in the process. Both of these approaches suggested two facets of the counselor's role: assessment and intervention.

Assessment

At this time there is no known objective measure of spiritual development. Most existing assessment is based on the clinical interview, including some history gathering, and interactions with the client. Assessment of spiritual wellness involves attention to the following:

1. The client's current personal development (age and maturation level) and degree of health within that stage of development (including the level of functioning in each of the dimensions of wellness [i.e., emotional, occupational, physical, intellectual, and social]).
2. The client's spiritual wellness in relation to spiritual repression versus spiritual preoccupation (see Figure 1, horizontal axis).
3. The client's level of spiritual development (see Figure 1, vertical axis).

Client status on one directional dimension frequently may be found to be related to status on the other directional dimension, but this is not always the case (Assagioli, 1965; Grof & Grof, 1989c; Maslow, 1971). For example, someone may be at a very high level of spiritual development but be thrust into spiritual emergency-preoccupation because of some unexpected occurrence, such as a near-death experience. Someone else may not be as highly developed spiritually but could be in a state of spiritual wellness. Spiritual wellness is a balance, the middle point between a repression of one's spirituality and a preoccupation with one's spirituality. The ultimate goal is to work toward maintaining or regaining balance in a state of spiritual wellness while also striving to develop spiritually to higher levels.

Differential diagnosis of spiritual emergency versus, for example, psychosis is not yet fully refined, in our opinion. Assagioli (1965) offered:

> These various manifestations of the crisis [of spiritual awakening] bear a close relationship to some of the symptoms regarded as characteristic of psychoneuroses and borderline schizophrenic states.... The differential diagnosis is generally not difficult. The symptoms observed isolatedly may be identical; but an accurate analysis of their genesis, and a consideration of the patient's personality in its entirety and (most important of all) the recognition of his actual existential problem, reveal the difference in nature and level of the pathogenic conflicts. (p. 42)

Lukoff (1985) offered some guidelines to differentiate a psychotic episode with mystical features from a mystical experience with psychotic features. To summarize Lukoff's recommendations, if a clinician can confirm all of the following sequential determinants, then the client is experiencing a mystical experience with psychotic features:

1. The client meets a *Diagnostic and Statistical Manual of Mental Disorders* revised edition criterion (*DSM-III-R:* American Psychiatric Association, 1987) for psychosis.
2. The client's symptoms overlap with a mystical experience.
3. With this client, a positive outcome is likely.
4. With this client, there is low risk.

A single no response to any one of criteria 2 to 5 would, instead, potentially result in a more serious primary diagnosis of psychosis. Grof and Grof (1989b) encouraged mental health practitioners to be open to the possibility that a given functional psychosis (a class of disorders that currently have no known medical cause) may have its roots in neither the client's medical history nor the client's biographical history, but in the transpersonal realm.

Intervention

Growth in the spiritual dimension can be stimulated by both spontaneous events and intentional activity. An expanded sense of spiritual being often occurs in the aftermath of near-death experiences (Ring, 1984) and near-death-like experiences (Holden & Guest, 1990). Likewise, persons who work consciously and deliberately with meditation, creative visualization, rhythmic breathing, and other similar techniques often experience effects that reflect enhanced spiritual awareness and movement toward greater spiritual wellness (Gawain, 1978; Hendricks & Weinhold, 1982; Vaughan, 1979).

In determining the most appropriate intervention with regard to counseling for spiritual wellness, several issues must be taken into consideration. Spiritual interventions should be geared to the client's stage of personal development and degree of health (Assagioli, 1965; Wilber et al., 1986). For example, someone functioning minimally well who is 5 years of age or older might benefit from a visualization of rising progressively upward and viewing oneself from the perspective of the clouds (S. Waterman, personal communication, September, 1990). Such a visualization would most likely be contraindicated for a chronic schizophrenic person (Wilber et al., 1986). Certain other visualizations may require more sophisticated cognitive abilities and would, therefore, be inappropriate for young children but potentially appropriate for persons in their teens or older.

Proposed classes of interventions are identified in Figure 1. Note that the function of any technique is to help the client move horizontally toward a position of spiritual wellness and to move vertically toward more advanced stages of spiritual development. If the client is in spiritual emergency, techniques exist for grounding or working through (Grof & Grof, 1989a). *Grounding* refers to slowing down the process of spiritual emergence. This renders spiritual experiences more capable of being assimilated and, therefore, more likely to result in spiritual development; failure to help a client become grounded may result in a chronic state of upheaval characterized by no development. To this end Kornfield (1989) suggested that one do the following:

> Take showers, do a lot of jogging, walking or tai chi, dig in the garden, do anything that connects with the earth. Inwardly, bring the attention down through the body, visualize the earth, get some good bodywork or massage, or use whatever movements help...acupuncture can work...change the diet and eat heavy foods, grains and meats... Do the kinds of activities that slow and bring one back down. (p. 159)

In a similar vein, Ram Dass (1989) asserted that when he encounters someone preoccupied with spiritual pursuits, "(he) feel(s) like saying, 'Come on, get your act together, learn your zip code, go get a job' " (p. 182). In his own humorous way, he is exemplifying the value of spiritual pursuit that is in balance with the other, personal dimensions of wellness.

By contrast, techniques designed to help the client work through spiritual emergency include helping the client "stay with" the crisis to facilitate its potential for transformation. Recommendations for counseling NDErs (Greyson & Harris, 1987) and others in spiritual emergency (Bragdon, 1988, 1990; Grof & Grof, 1989a; Prevatt & Park, 1989) include skills and processes that, like the emergencies themselves, go beyond traditional counseling. In addition to expressing the core conditions of counseling and using basic counseling skills, spiritual emergency counselors must believe in the validity and transformative potential of spiritual emergency. Counselors are further charged with being well informed about altered states of consciousness and spiritual emergency to conceptualize, and thoroughly and accurately inform clients about, their experiences. Spiritual emergency counselors should also be skilled in the use of experiential techniques and should be willing to deviate from traditional clinical roles (but not ethical guidelines) to respond flexibly to the sometimes unconventional needs of these clients. This includes flexibility in the length, frequency, and content of counseling sessions, as well as a willingness to persevere. Whenever possible, the counselor is also charged with helping the client to establish a support system among family and friends.

If a client is spiritually well, techniques exist for promoting spiritual development. If a client is repressing the sublime (consciously or unconsciously), techniques exist for *sacrilization* (sensitizing to the spiritual those who have no conscious experience of the spiritual) or *resacrilization* (resensitize those who have been spiritually well but have moved, consciously or unconsciously, toward repression). Hundreds of books and articles exist on various techniques for spiritual development or sensitizing to the spiritual. Although an exhaustive review of these sources is beyond the scope of this article, we can suggest a few selections from among our favorites. Meditation instruction and practice is a common technique used to foster spiritual development (Gawain, 1986; Hendricks & Weinhold, 1982; LeShan, 1974; Mahesh Yogi, 1963; Novak, 1989; Tan, 1990). Meditation can facilitate feelings of personal balance and harmony (centeredness), relaxation, and increased awareness of oneself and one's environment. Meditation practice can also assist with the development of intuition, self-insight, and greater self-trust. An expansion of consciousness often occurs from meditation that replaces feelings of isolation, provides greater personal security, and creates a sensation of being in communion with the universe.

Gawain (1986) described a beginning-level meditation exercise that is briefly summarized with the following steps:

1. Ask the client to lie in a comfortable position with eyes closed and breath deeply, relaxing the mind and body.
2. Instruct the client to imagine a very powerful presence within and all around that is totally loving, strong, and wise and that is nurturing, protecting, and guiding.
3. Have the client relax and enjoy the feeling that he or she is being totally taken care of by the universe.
4. Conclude the meditation with the following affirmation: "I feel and trust the presence of the universe in my life" (p. 9).

Gawain (1986) referred repeatedly to a meditation that involves a "wise presence" from whom one can solicit guidance. This type of meditation encourages individuals to turn within, to the spiritual realm, for intuitive insight and creative ideas.

Meditation can be a guided exercise or can take the form of completely blanking one's mind to allow for spontaneous imagery or insight. Meditations designed for healing purposes may involve a focus on the body and its healing mechanisms. Healing meditation may be more abstract such as to visualize a swim in healing waters (Highstein, 1985) or to be showered by a colorful rainbow that symbolically represents the chakras, hypothetically the main energy centers in the body. Yoga and Tai Chi are used as meditations of "movement" that simultaneously align the body with mind and spirit.

Novak (1989) reviewed a variety of additional schools or types of meditation. The meditation of contemplation is essentially learning to look at something actively and alertly but without words, and as if feeling it but without actually touching it. The meditation of "breath counting" is a focus on one's own exhalations—to have the whole attention involved in the counting with the goal of eliminating personal distraction that may interfere with the discipline of focus. The meditation of the "safe harbour" is a guided meditation directing all of the areas of the body and mind into a feeling of safety. Meditation on universal symbols, such as the "thousand-petaled lotus flower," is a symbolic rendition that everything is connected to everything else. Meditation with mantras, such as positive phrase repetition, "All is one," or "I am one with God," is believed to have beneficial effects because of the content.

The meditation of "who am I?" (Novak, 1989) is a rigorous form of self-inquiry and is usually practiced by more experienced meditators. During this meditation, the meditator asks a series of questions, beginning with "who am I?," and answers each question with another question that requires deeper inquiry. For examples if "who am I?" is responded to in one's mind with a name, then one follows with the response, "No, this is a name I have given myself. Who is the I who I gave that name to?" Should the next response be something like an image of oneself, then the response would be, "No, this is an image I have of myself. Who is the I that gave me this image?" This meditation process continues for a while until one obtains a deeper understanding of oneself. This meditation is similar to Assagioli's (1965) exercise of disidentification where the ultimate goal is the experience of pure consciousness.

What are the specific values that meditational procedures can bring to psychotherapy? LeShan (1974) answered this question with the following ideas:

1. Many meditations bring about an increase in ego strength.
2. Meditations can be applied to special problem areas; they can be used to help explore a specific area and help "loosen" client defenses.

3. Mediation assists with "centering"; the quality of feeling at ease with oneself and with one's environment.
4. Mediations facilitate growth by teaching the individual to regard his or her being as something of real value and to pay serious attention to the totality of being.
5. Meditation assists with growing beyond the ability to function in everyday life and being relatively "pain-free." (pp. 115–116)

Relaxation (Charlesworth & Nathan, 1984; Curtis & Detert, 1981), rhythmic breathwork (Grof, 1988; Hendricks & Weinhold, 1982), creative visualization (Gawain, 1978), imagery (Witmer & Young, 1985), and awareness exercises (Small, 1982; Vaughan, 1979) are frequently used interventions in counseling and therapy that can foster personal as well as spiritual development. Creative visualization can be conceptualized as a form of meditation that involves the imagining of what I want out of life, mentally rehearsing it, and believing in my creative potential to bring it about. Incorporating the practice of daily positive affirmations into therapeutic homework may facilitate both personal and spiritual growth (Chandler & Kolander, 1988; Gawain, 1988). A sample affirmation for someone with poor self-esteem might be, "I am confident and strong." For someone who fears failure an appropriate affirmation might be, "I have the courage to strive for my goals." It is not necessary that the client already believe these affirmations. The purpose is that, through daily repetition, the individual can reprogram the subconscious or unconscious to be more positive and self-affirming. The individual eventually comes to believe in these affirmations and acts upon them in a way that brings about positive change. From this perspective, daily affirmations may be considered a form of miniature meditation or mantra.

Dream-level therapy is a practiced art in counseling to enhance personal and spiritual growth (Faraday, 1972; Headrick, 1985; LaBerge, 1985; Tholey, 1983; Ullman & Ullman, 1979). The psychotherapeutic approach of psychosynthesis offers several techniques for spiritual growth (Assagioli, 1965; Brown, 1983; Ferrucci, 1982; Yeomans, 1989). The existential-phenomenological perspectives in psychology provide an additional framework for conceptualizing and intervening with persons regarding the less observable-quantifiable and more spiritual concerns (Valle & Halling, 1989). Additional resources that consider a spiritual component in the context of counseling and psychotherapy include the following periodicals: *Journal of Transpersonal Psychology*, *Journal of Humanistic Psychology*, *Common Boundary*, and *Meditation*. Another potentially valuable resource for working with a client in spiritual emergency is the Spiritual Emergence Network in Menlo Park, California. Substantial overlap exists between counseling for spiritual emergency, for sacrilization-resacrilization, and for spiritual development; that is, certain techniques could serve more than one (or all) of these purposes.

At least three concerns deserve mention regarding counselor use of the interventions identified earlier: ethical considerations, legal ramifications, and personal-spiritual development. Professional ethics prohibit the use of techniques for which the counselor has not been adequately trained (American Association for Counseling and Development, 1988). Counselors increase their malpractice liability by using approaches not substantiated by tradition or the current literature (Picchioni & Bernstein, 1989); many of the techniques described herein have not been researched well, if at all. An axiom exists in the realm of spiritual development that one cannot help another past one's own level of development (Assagioli, 1989). This axiom refers to the necessity that counselors themselves must have practiced the techniques and reached some level of proficiency prior to teaching or demonstrating these techniques. An example of this can be borrowed from biofeedback therapy, which requires that biofeedback therapists themselves be able to demonstrate proficiency at self-regulation and relaxation using the biofeedback instruments they apply in practice with their clients.

CONCLUSION

Counseling for spiritual wellness includes attention to the spiritual component of each dimension of wellness. It also involves helping an individual move toward spiritual wellness through sacrilization or resacrilization (following repression of the sublime) or through grounding or working through (following spiritual emergency or preoccupation). An individual who is in a state of spiritual wellness can also be assisted in counseling to achieve further spiritual development.

"Psychotherapy, if it is to provide substantial assistance to the process of mental and spiritual growth, is not a quick or simple procedure" (Peck, 1978, p. 12). One does not have to belong to any particular theoretical orientation to attend to the spiritual component of wellness with clients; one does need, however, an understanding, appropriate training, and, of course, a willingness to work with the spiritual dimension.

"Awareness is wider and deeper than anyone had guessed; intention, more powerful. Clearly, human beings have not begun to exploit their potential for change" (Ferguson, 1980, p. 154). Let this statement be a challenge to counselors to pursue spiritual wellness and development for themselves and for their clients in the decade of the 1990s and beyond. We believe spirituality is innate within all humans. Choosing to ignore the spiritual component of wellness out of fear or ignorance is somewhat irresponsible of those in health service fields. Spiritual wellness is not an undefinable, unworkable construct. It is a part of the human being that needs to be attended to and fostered as much as do the mind and the body. Counselors, by virtue of their professional description as promoters of human development, are likely facilitators for the enhancement of spiritual wellness.

REFERENCES

Allen, R. J., & Yarian, R. A. (1981). The domain of health. *Health Education, 12*(4), 3-5.

American Association for Counseling and Development. (1988). *Ethical standards of the American Association for Counseling and Development.* Alexandria, VA: Author.

American Psychiatric Association. (1987). *Diagnostic and statistical manual of mental disorders* (3rd ed., rev.). Washington, DC: Author.

Assagioli, R. (1965). *Psychosynthesis: A manual of principles and techniques.* New York: Viking Penguin.

Assagioli, R. (1989). Self-realization and psychological disturbances. In S. Grof & C. Grof (Eds.), *Spiritual emergency: When personal transformation becomes a crisis* (pp. 27-48). Los Angeles: Jeremy P. Tarcher.

Bragdon, E. (1988). *A sourcebook for helping people in spiritual emergency.* Los Altos, CA: Lightening Up Press.

Bragdon, E. (1990). *The call of spiritual emergency: From personal crisis to personal transformation.* San Francisco: Harper & Row.

Brown, M. Y. (1983). The unfolding self: Psychosynthesis and counseling. Los Angeles: Psychosynthesis Press.

Chandler, C.K., & Kolander, C. A. (1988). Stop the negative, accentuate the positive. *Journal of School Health, 58*(7), 295-297.

Charlesworth, E. A., & Nathan, R. G. (1984). *Stress management: A comprehensive guide to wellness.* New York: Ballantine.

Curtis, J. D., & Detert, R. A. (1981). *How to relax: A holistic approach to stress management.* Mountainview, CA: Mayfield.

Faraday, A. (1972). *Dream power.* New York: Berkeley.

Ferguson, M. (1980). *The aquarian conspiracy: Personal and social transformation in the 1980s.* Los Angeles: Jeremy P. Tarcher.

Ferrucci, P. (1982). *What we may be: Techniques for psychological and spiritual growth through psychosynthesis.* Los Angeles: Jeremy P. Tarcher.

Frankl, V. (1959). *Man's search for meaning.* New York: Washington Square.

Gawain, S. (1978). *Creative visualization.* New York: Bantam Books.

Gawain, S. (1986). *Living in the light.* Mill Valley, CA: Whatever Publishing.

Gawain, S . (1988) *Reflections in the light: Daily thoughts and affirmations.* San Rafael, CA: New World.

Greyson, B., & Harris, B. (1987). Clinical approaches to the near-death experiencer. *Journal of Near-Death Studies, 6*(1), 41-52.

Grof, S. (1976). *Realms of the human unconscious: Observations from LSD research.* New York: E. P. Dutton.

Grof, S. (1985). *Beyond the brain.* Albany, NY: State University of New York.

Grof, S. (1988). *Adventure of self-discovery: Dimensions of consciousness and new perspectives in psychotherapy and inner exploration.* Albany, NY: State University of New York.

Grof, S., & Grof, C. (1989a). Assistance in spiritual emergency. In S. Grof & C. Grof (Eds.), *Spiritual emergency: When personal transformation becomes a crisis* (pp. 191-198). Los Angeles: Jeremy P. Tarcher.

Grof, S., & Grof, C. (1989b). Spiritual emergency: Understanding evolutionary crisis. In S. Grof & C. Grof (Eds.), *Spiritual emergency: When personal transformation becomes a crisis* (pp. 1-26). Los Angeles: Jeremy P. Tarcher.

Grof, S., & Grof, C. (Eds.). (1989c). *Spiritual emergency: When personal transformation becomes a crisis.* Los Angeles: Jeremy P. Tarcher.

Guralnik, D. B. (Ed.). (1984). *Webster's new world dictionary of the American language*. New York: Warner Books.

Haronian, F. (1972). *Repression of the sublime*. New York: Psychosynthesis Research Foundation. (Available through Psychosynthesis Distribution, 2561 Tioga Way, San Jose, CA 95124).

Headrick, M. F. (1985). Dream-level therapy: Of bees and tigers. *Journal of Counseling and Development, 64*(3), 191-194.

Hendricks, G., & Weinhold, B. (1982). *Transpersonal approaches to counseling and psychotherapy*. Denver: Love Publishing.

Hettler, W. (1979). *Six dimensions of wellness*. Stevens Point, WI: National Wellness Institute. University of Wisconsin.

Hettler, W. (1991, May). Hettler urges counselors to set example for society. *Guidepost*, pp. 17-18.

Highstein, M. (1985). *The healing waterfall*. Los Angeles: Inner Directions.

Holden, J. M., & Guest, C. (1990). Life review in a non-near-death episode: A comparison with near-death experiences. *Journal of Transpersonal Psychology, 22*(1), 1-16.

Kornfield, J. (1989). Obstacles and vicissitudes in spiritual practice. In S. Grof & C. Grof (Eds.), *Spiritual emergency: When personal transformation becomes a crisis* (pp. 137-170). Los Angeles: Jeremy P. Tarcher.

LaBerge, S. (1985). *Lucid dreaming*. Los Angeles: Jeremy P. Tarcher.

Laszlo, V. S . (Ed.). (1954). *The basic writings of C. G. Jung*. New York: Random House.

LeShan, L. (1974). *How to meditate*. New York: Bantam.

Lukoff, D. (1985). The diagnosis of mystical experiences with psychotic features. *Journal of Transpersonal Psychology, 17*(2), 155-181.

Mahesh Yogi, M. (1963). *Transcendental meditation*. New York: Signet.

Maslow, A. (1971). *Farther reaches of human nature*. New York: Viking.

Maslow, A. (1980). A theory of metamotivation: The biological rooting of the value-life. In R. N. Walsh & F. Vaughan (Eds.), *Beyond ego: Transpersonal dimensions in psychology*. New York: Jeremy P. Tarcher.

Moody, R. A. (1975). *Life after life*. New York: Bantam.

Myers, J. E. (1990, May). Wellness throughout the lifespan. *Guidepost*, p. 11.

Noble, K. D. (1987). Psychological health and the experience of transcendence. *The Counseling Psychologist, 15*(4), 601–614.

Novak, J. (1989). *How to meditate*. Nevada City, CA: Crystal Clarity.

Opatz, J. P. (1986). Stevens Point: A longstanding program for students at a midwestern university. *American Journal of Health Promotion, 1*(1), 60-67.

Peck, M. S. (1978). *The road less traveled: A new psychology of love, traditional values and spiritual growth*. New York: Touchstone.

Picchioni, A., & Bernstein, B. (Producers & Directors). (1989). *Risk management for mental health professionals* [Film]. Austin, TX: Texas Association for Counseling and Development.

Prevatt, J., & Park, R. (1989). The spiritual emergence network (SEN). In S. Grof & C. Grof (Eds.), *Spiritual emergency: When personal transformation becomes a crisis* (pp. 225-230). Los Angeles: Jeremy P. Tarcher.

Ram Dass, (1989). Promises and pitfalls of the spiritual path. In S. Grof & C. Grof (Eds.), *Spiritual emergency: When personal transformation becomes a crisis* (pp. 171-187). Los Angeles: Jeremy P. Tarcher.

Ring, K. (1984). *Heading toward omega: In search of the meaning of the near-death experiences*. New York: William Morrow.

Sample, A. R. (1984). *Racehoss: Big Emma's boy*. New York: Ballantine.

Small, J. (1982). *Personal transformation: The way through*. Marina del Rey, CA: DeVorss.

Tart, C. T. (1990). Adapting Eastern spiritual teachings to Western culture. *Journal of Transpersonal Psychology, 22*(2), 149-166.

Tholey, P. (1983). Techniques for inducing and manipulating lucid dreams. *Perceptual and Motor Skills, 57,* 79-90.

Ullman, M., & Ullman, N. (1979). *Working with dreams.* Los Angeles: Jeremy P. Tarcher.

Valle, R. S., & Hailing, S. (1989). *Existential-phenomenological perspectives in psychology.* New York: Plenum.

Vaughan, F. E. (1979). *Awakening intuition.* New York: Anchor.

Wilber, K. (1980). A developmental model of consciousness. In R. N. Walsh & F. Vaughan (Eds.), *Beyond ego: Transpersonal dimensions in psychology* (pp. 99-114). Los Angeles: J. P. Tarcher.

Wilber, K., Engler, J., & Brown, D. P. (1986). *Transformations of consciousness.* Boston: New Science Library.

Witmer, J. M., & Young, M. E. (1985). The silent partner: Uses of imagery in counseling. *Journal of Counseling and Development, 64*(3), 187-190.

Yeomans, T. (1989). *Psychosynthesis practice: Vol. I. Psychosynthesis exercises for personal and spiritual growth.* (Available from Psychosynthesis Distribution,. 2561 Tioga Way, San Jose, CA 95124.)

Religious Values as Cross-Cultural Issues in Counseling

D. RUSSELL BISHOP

THIS ARTICLE GIVES counselors specific guidelines that will increase their therapeutic effectiveness in working with clients' religious values as part of the counseling process. Counselors are challenged to consider client religious values from the same perspective that they consider the client's ethnicity or culture.

The first section focuses on a definition of culture and an explanation of how religious values are a part of this definition. The second section is a brief discussion of values as a part of the general counseling and therapy process; research on the counseling process and the impact of client and counselor value similarity is also reviewed. Specific guidelines are provided in the third section to help counselors enhance their ability to deal with religious values as part of the counseling process. The conclusion provides recommendations for additional work integrating religious values and counseling.

DEFINING CULTURE AND RELIGIOUS VALUES

The advances in the study of cross-cultural issues in psychology have been significant, although a comprehensive approach to the integration of cross-cultural issues remains to be developed. The current paradigm of theory, research, and practice is oriented toward a reductionistic approach that analyzes specific elements of differences among cultures (e.g., nonverbal behaviors, child-rearing practices, or use of English language; Sue, 1981). This approach falls short when applied to some cultural issues, however, because cultural issues are far more global than is sometimes reflected by cross-cultural study in psychology. Vontress (1987) suggested that effective cross-cultural therapy focuses on anxiety, death, authenticity, meaning, and responsibility. These are existential issues that are common throughout all cultures. Religious ideology is also common across cultures. Every culture has some sort of religious or moral value system. Prohibitions against murder and incest, for example, have near-universal acceptance throughout the world.

Consideration of formal definitions of *culture* provides additional insight into elements common across cultures. Some of the general elements of

From "Religious Values as Cross-Cultural Issues in Counseling," by D. R. Bishop, 1992, *Counseling and Values, 36*, 179-191.

culture were identified from an anthropological perspective by Linton (1945) who defined culture as "the configuration of learned behavior and results of behavior whose component elements are shared and transmitted by the members of a particular society" (p. 32). Kroeber and Kluckhohn (1952) offered a slightly expanded definition of culture:

[Cultures are] patterns, explicit and implicit, of and for behavior acquired and transmitted by symbols, constituting the distinctive achievement of human groups, including their embodiments in artifacts; the essential core of culture consists of traditional (i.e., historically derived and selected) ideas and especially attached values. (p. 81)

The common elements in these two definitions of culture include shared behavior patterns, ideas, and values.

Cultures also differ in a wide variety of ways. In order for counselors to place clients' values in cultural context, they must know some specific information about the client's culture (Pedersen, 1987; Sue, 1981). According to Sue (1988) there is a dearth of "therapists who can communicate and can understand the values, life-styles, and backgrounds of these clients" (p. 302), "these clients" meaning people from diverse cultural backgrounds. Education about particular aspects of specific cultures is one way to prepare counselors to work with these clients (Ridley, 1985).

Information about specific religious values is an important part of preparing counselors to work with these issues in counseling. Two specific examples of religious value issues are presented in the next subsections. Counselors are encouraged to learn more about other similar issues.

Mental Health and the Counseling Process

To be able to establish goals for counseling, counselors need to understand the client's views on what constitutes healthy functioning, and how healthy functioning is promoted or achieved. The Jehovah's Witness religious group believes that health is in the purview of God's providence and workings. Members of this particular religious orientation resist human intervention in the healing process, and may even refuse potentially life-saving medical intervention. As another example, members of different Hispanic subgroups rely in varying degrees on the powers of religious faith healers to promote health (Padilla & De Snyder, 1987). Therapeutic resistance of a particular Hispanic client may be due in part to value conflicts whereby the client discounts the therapist's interventions, or may find specific suggestions completely at odds with his or her religious practices.

The Role of Religious Community in Promoting Healthy Psychological Functioning

Organized religious communities are the largest untapped resources for aiding the therapeutic process with religious clients. Clinebell (1965) suggested that religious communities provide unique contributions to psychological development and maintenance of healthy functioning: (a) they provide for a periodic renewal of basic trust, (b) they develop a feeling of both horizontal and vertical belonging, (c) they provide a viable philosophy of life, (d) they help the person transcend himself or herself, (e) they provide procedures for dealing with many of the developmental and accidental crises of living, and (f) they foster personal growth and social change. Different types of religious communities provide these contributions in varying amounts. It would behoove the counselor to ascertain the relative contributions of the client's church environment. Long-term therapeutic interventions can easily be oriented toward getting the client to increase his or her involvement in church programming that would enhance positive coping skills. Depressed clients who greatly value evangelism, for example, could be encouraged to become involved in a church outreach program that would increase positive social contacts and interactions, while at the same time allowing the client to express his or her evangelistic value.

From a psychological perspective, Triandis (1987) suggested that major dimensions of cultural variation were attributable to differences in perceptual selectivity, information-processing strategies, cognitive strategies, and habits. He went on to describe how differences in belief systems (values) must be considered to make therapeutic interventions effective.

> Religion is a crucial attribute in Muslim cultures and very important in some segments of the population in Christian and Jewish subcultures . . . If the therapist knows nothing about the client's religion the client's behavior may appear bizarre. (p. 26)

Although religious values are a part of the global elements of culture, and are an important aspect of a person's psychological development and functioning, they are often not assessed or considered important from a psychological perspective (Russo, 1984; Sperry, 1988; Spilka, 1987; Theodore, 1984). Many counselors are quick to explain that they separate and exclude religious values from counseling, and discuss them only when the client is the initiator. Counselors who fail to directly assess the client's religious values run the risk of overlooking potentially important aspects of the client's cultural background and current cultural experience. Even counselors who are sensitive to other aspects of cultural differences are hesitant to explore clients' religious values. Some reasons for counselor hesitance to integrate religious values in counseling are discussed in the next section.

RELIGIOUS VALUES IN COUNSELING

In a seminal article, Bergin (1980) described the conflict between psychology and counseling and religious values in reference to the therapeutic process. He identified the tensions that perpetuate the alienation of religious values from counseling and therapy. He proposed six theses for the purposes of broadening the scope of counseling theory, research, and practice, to include stronger considerations of religious values. Bergin's theses 1, 4, and 5 are of particular relevance to this article and they are discussed further.

At the core of Thesis 1 is the notion that divergent values on the part of the counselor and client may likely lead to difficulties in the establishment of criteria for measuring therapeutic change (Beutler & Bergan, 1991). For example, a fundamentalist Christian client who wishes to become more self-sacrificing in her relationship to her husband risks a values clash in therapy. The current prevailing Western view of healthy marital relationships places an emphasis on spousal equality, and would likely lead the therapist to consider a treatment approach that promoted empowerment and assertiveness to help the client balance out the marital relationship. Which therapeutic goal is correct? Counselors who are unfamiliar with, or who are unwilling to accept the client's religious values, risk disrupting the client's value system and risk working toward unreasonable therapeutic goals. Such an approach will inevitably lead to conflict in the therapeutic relationship, and borders on ethical malpractice (cf. Woody, 1988).

Client and Counselor Value Dissimilarity

In concluding his comments on Thesis 4, Bergin (1980) stated that

> . . . the beliefs of mental health professionals are not very harmonious with those of the subcultures with which they deal, especially as they pertain to definitions of moral behavior and the relevance of moral behavior to societal integration, familial functioning, prevention of pathology, and development of the self. (p. 101)

The proportion of mental health professionals who acknowledge that their lives are guided by religion is lower than that of the general public, but the gap is narrowing. Bergin and Jensen (1990; cf. Bergin, 1930) found that 46% of the mental health professionals they surveyed agreed that their whole approach to life was based on their religion. It seems that interest in religion has risen recently within the field of counseling (Worthington, 1989).

Counselor and client value dissimilarity can be helpful. In their review, Beutler, Crago, and Arizmendi (1986) concluded that initial client and counselor value dissimilarity was helpful in producing more positive therapeutic outcome. Beutler et al. (1986) stated that research on therapy outcome has indicated ". . . initial patient and therapist dissimilarity of attitudes and belief systems are associated with patient [client] beliefs converging on those of their therapist" (p. 275). One response to these research findings has been to attempt to match clients and counselors in regard to their particular religious values (McMinn, 1984; Worthington, 1988). These models are intriguing and merit further investigation, but simple value congruity does not ensure that effective therapy will take place. Ridley (1985) stated that "ethnic minority membership is not a sufficient condition for treatment effectiveness, even though the therapist and client may represent the same eth-nic grouping" (p. 613).

When religious values are viewed from a cross-cultural perspective, Ridley's observations seem valid as well: Client and counselor religious value congruence does not ensure effective treatment. Referral is the ethically sound response to resolve serious value conflicts, but less serious conflicts must be resolved within the counseling process. Research has demonstrated that minimal levels of value discrepancy actually serve to promote effective thera-peutic outcome.

It is clear that counseling is a value-laden process in which the client is seeking to be influenced by the therapist to promote a more healthful exist-ence. Some members of religious groups want to seek help through coun-seling but do not seek help because they are wary of being influenced by a counselor who might change their basic values during the counseling pro-cess. They have reservations about the extent of influence to which they are willing to be subjected. Because counselors do not generally share values common to clients, some clients fear that the counselor will not be able to effectively understand their problems, or worse yet, that they will have to sacrifice their values to receive the benefit of therapy.

In support of clients' fears of counselors' negative influence, Keating and Fretz (1990) found that for clients, "Strong religious beliefs resulted in more negative anticipations about counselors" (p. 294). In support of clients' views of counselors as a positive influence, Godwin and Crouch (1989) found that Christian participants tended to view counseling more positively, and gave counselors' skills a higher rating than did non-Christian participants. More research is needed to establish what specific elements of religiosity in coun-selors and clients contribute to differences in expectations about counsel-ing. Until such research is done, counselors need to be mindful that there is potential for clients with strong religious beliefs to have negative expecta-tions about counseling, and these expectations need to be explored before effective therapy can take place.

Counselor Self-Disclosure of Religious Values

Counselors are not obligated to change their own values to work effectively with clients who have particular religious values. Counselors are in a posi-tion to promote a positive image to clients regarding religious values, if they can convey acceptance of clients' values. Beutler, Pollack, and Jobe (1978) concluded their study on therapists' attitude of acceptance toward clients' values by stating that "the therapist's attitude toward the patient's values has the greatest impact on the patient's feelings of growth" (p. 199). Beutler et al. (1986) concurred with this finding, and added "that therapists' accep-tance of patients' attitudes and values facilitates improvement and that pro-viding treatments and interventions that are consistent with the patients' beliefs enhances treatment outcome, even when therapists and patients do not adhere to the same belief system" (p. 276).

When religious value differences exist, it is the responsibility of the counselor to be educated about the values held by the clientele he or she serves, and to place the clients' value differences within a cross-cultural context (Ridley, 1985). The client's values should be openly and overtly explored as a usual part of the counseling process. For example, issues such as locus of control, acceptance of responsibility, belief in God, and guilt and shame are often explored in chemical dependency counseling. These issues and others affiliated with religious values often play a role in problems presented by clients. Carefully exploring the client's religious values allows the counselor to convey acceptance and understanding of the client's problems, thus promoting positive therapeutic outcome.

Once the client's values have been explored, the counselor should make known to the client his or her own values in a cultural context (Thesis 5). Such openness lessens the likelihood that severe values conflicts will occur, and provides the opportunity for exploration and resolution of the conflict. If serious value conflicts persist in the face of open discussion, the client should be referred to another counselor (American Psychological Association, 1990; cf. Worthington, 1988).

Guidelines for Counselors

Specific recommendations for how counselors can go about working with clients from a variety of cultural backgrounds, and clients who have a variety of religious values, are provided in this section. These guidelines represent principles that, when followed, will allow counselors to effectively deal with religious issues in the therapeutic process. These guidelines were derived from the literature reviewed in previous sections of this article and from the author's professional experience.

The implementation of these guidelines is dependent on two premises. First, if counselors are to provide professional service to clients with a variety of religious values, they need to maintain an open attitude toward religious values: Religious values need to be viewed as valid and valuable elements in the therapeutic process. Second, counselors are encouraged to consider a philosophical reorientation with regard to their understanding of the function of religious values: Religious values are part of clients' cultural make up. This reorientation represents a new prescription (Watson, 1967) for the use of the term *religious values*. As counselors come to view religious values in a cultural context, they will be more able to effect the necessary attitude change, and more freely explore clients' religious values.

Guideline 1: Help the client to feel that his or her religious values are an accepted part of the therapeutic process. Careful probing about the client's religious values and how these values relate to his or her current situation yields important information and promotes the client's feelings of being accepted by the counselor (Hill & Gormally, 1977).

The client's religious values need to be incorporated into the goal setting as part of the foundation of counseling interventions. As previously discussed in the case illustration of the wife who wished to be more self-sacrificing for her husband, the counselor and client must cooperatively determine the goals for counseling to avoid undue conflict and to help ensure the success of therapeutic interventions (cf. Purdy, Simari, & Colon, 1983). The counselor may wish to ask the client to inform him or her about areas in which the counselor's knowledge of particular religious beliefs, values, practices, or cultural context is lacking. The client is then able to appropriately educate the counselor about specific issues of culture or values that he or she holds. This approach serves to enhance the counselor's genuineness or transparency (cf. Anderson & Goolishian, 1988; Truax & Carkhuff, 1967), and promotes the establishment of rapport between the counselor and client.

Guideline 2: View religious values as part of the solution to the client's problem, not just as part of the problem. Counselors are encouraged to review the literature on the positive influence of religious values on mental health, as well as the benefits of religious communities for providing social support. Religious practices such as prayer or meditation may be effective tools for alleviating feelings of tension, sadness, or disappointment. Client religious beliefs, such as the value of human life or the purposefulness of divine providence, may be effective allies for the counselor helping a client to increase his or her self-esteem or work through the grief over the death of a spouse.

Counselors are too often inclined to challenge religious values as underlying causes of the client's presenting problems (Bergin, 1991; Cohen, 1982). It may be most appropriate for the counselor to help the client bring his or her behavior in line with religious values rather than to challenge the client's religious values as being overly rigid. In the case where an unmarried Catholic man experiences guilt and shame over ongoing sexual encounters, it may be more appropriate to help him divert sexual expression in other directions, rather than to challenge his religious value of chastity.

Guideline 3: Become more educated about cultures, religious values, beliefs, and practices; strive to understand how these issues are integrated with psychological theory and counseling practice. Specific examples of clients' religious values relevant to counseling would include: (a) the view of sin and overcoming its influence on human functioning (Watson, Morris, & Hood, 1988a; Watson et al., 1988b); (b) the significance of spiritual commitment (Albany, 1984); (c) the role of religious values in the development of mental disorders (Fitz, 1990); or (d) psychological development in the context of religious value development (Hill, 1986; Richards, 1991). Counselors are encouraged to explore these and other similar issues with clients in the early part of therapy to secure an understanding of the client's particular values.

Counselors are encouraged to seek more education about the specific religious ideologies and practices that their clients hold and observe. Furthermore, counselors need to understand the support structure or cultural context within which these beliefs and practices operate. A few illustrative resources that can aid counselors in this process are the following: Allport (1950), Ansbacher and Ansbacher (1979), Cox (1973), Farnsworth (1985), Fromm (1950), James (1982), Mathisen (1980), Meehl (1958), Van Leeuwen (1985), and Yalom (1980).

Guideline 4: Get involved with community or professional activities that promote interactions with persons from diverse cultures, who have a variety of religious values. Counselors are encouraged to gain first-hand experience with a variety of cultures and religious values through active involvement with others. The damaging effects of lack of information or misinformation about particular cultural groups can be remediated through ongoing close personal involvement with members of these groups. There are, for example, several large Amish communities throughout the midwestern and northeastern United States that offer opportunities for cross-cultural enhancement.

Guideline 5: Explore and evaluate your own personal religious values. Self-examination is essential for several reasons: (a) we all have blind spots to our biases regarding religious values (cf. Nicholi, 1990); (b) we need to be aware of our biases to work around them with clients; (c) the process of personal values clarification can help the counselor identify issues or values with which he or she can and cannot effectively or comfortably work; and (d) the counselor's struggle to get in touch with values will provide a better understanding of and appreciation for the process that clients go through. This same process is seen in cases where counselors who have experienced childhood sexual abuse undertake a self-examination process to explore their current sexual values and ability to work with clients who have had similar experiences.

Religious values self-examination should focus on how cultural factors or factors in the early family environment provided for or helped shape religious values. A series of questions serves to guide this self-examination: What were my parents' specific religious values? What religious values was I taught as a child? Were these values commonly taught to my peers, or unique to my experience? Do most other members of my ethnic or cultural group have similar values? How do I currently assimilate those values into my current beliefs and behavior? What factors have caused me to accept or reject the religious values of my family or cultural group?

A primary goal of the religious values self-examination process is to prepare the counselor to be able to effectively implement Guidelines 6 and 7.

Successful counselors will find a new understanding of their current values and how these values fit with their particular cultural experience. Counselors who find that the self-examination process is too evocative, leaving them feeling embittered or indifferent to religious values, should seriously consider referring clients with issues affiliated with religious values. Similarly, some counselors find that they are simply unable to work with victims or perpetrators of sexual abuse. Counselors in this position, who do not refer their clients to another counselor, run the risk of bringing damaging countertransference issues into the therapeutic process. Counselors who find that they are comfortable with religious values issues should make themselves available to colleagues as referral resources to provide clients with competent counseling in this area.

Guideline 6: Be aware of what counselor resistance or cautious maneuvering around religious issues may convey to clients. Counselors who do not openly discuss or integrate religious values as part of the counseling process run the risk of conveying unintended messages about the client's religious values (Beutler, Pollack, & Jobe, 1978; cf. American Psychological Association, 1990). Clients trying to establish trust in the early counseling relationship may feel distanced by such a counselor and not be sure why; clients are prone to accept responsibility for these situations, even when the tension emanates from the counselor (Basch, 1980). Similarly, a Caucasian counselor may convey uneasiness to an African American client if issues of race are not discussed in a straightforward manner early in therapy (cf. Sue, 1981). Counselors need to make an effort to avoid an approach that skirts discussion of religious values. The final guideline is provided to help counselors develop a straightforward response to clients, allowing counselors to avoid the pitfalls of miscommunications to clients about these issues.

Guideline 7: Develop a simple straightforward language with which to communicate to clients about their religious values and your religious values. Open communication about religious values should be a part of client and counselor exchanges early in the counseling process. A brief statement about the counselor's general approach to religious values in counseling can be included in the orientation statements typical in an initial interview: "From time to time we find that clients' religious values are related to the problems discussed in counseling. While I am not interested in changing your religious values, I would be interested in discussing how your values relate to your presenting problems."

When it is discovered that the client holds strong particular religious values, the simple introductory statement can be elaborated into a brief discussion of values. The counselor might say for example, "I understand that you are strongly committed to your religious beliefs and values, particularly in the area of . . . These values are an important part of your life and cultural background. Although I am not a religious person, I often work with clients with a variety of religious beliefs. As part of our counseling I will try to be sensitive to your particular beliefs and we will explore how your beliefs and values interface with your current problems as well as how they may help with the ongoing change process." The client is then encouraged to talk in more detail about his or her values and the counselor is afforded the opportunity to begin to explore the cultural origins of those values. Counselors who prefer not to work with these types of client issues or values are advised to develop a statement that reflects this preference: "I understand that religious values often play an important role in the counseling process. I am not qualified to deal directly with these sorts of issues, and I would be happy to provide you with the name of another counselor who works closely with these types of issues." This situation would be akin to an African American counselor referring an Asian American client to an Asian American counselor because of his or her limited skills in working with Asian Americans. A straightforward approach to the discussion of religious values limits the possibility for miscommunication and effectively promotes the welfare of the client.

CONCLUSION

This article represents one step in the process of developing a fully comprehensive framework for the cross-cultural nature of religious values. Further research is necessary in several areas to complete this framework: how particular religious beliefs affect psychological functioning in general (cf. Cohen, 1982; Witter, Stock, Okun, & Haring, 1985); how particular religious beliefs can enhance or limit the effectiveness of counselor interventions (Beck, 1981; Finney & Maloney, 1985; Gladding, Lewis, & Adkins, 1981); the further assessment of the specific impact of client-counselor religious value dissimilarity on counseling outcome; the impact of counselors' countertransference to client religious issues on therapeutic outcome. Researchers are encouraged to test, for example, Worthington's (1988) model of client-counselor religious values in counseling.

Even though counselors have recently become more interested in cross-cultural issues, certain aspects of culture have been minimized or virtually ignored; religious values are one such example. Counselors need to become more sensitive to the significance of clients' religious values and their implications for the therapy process. Counselors are encouraged to view religious values as an element of cross-cultural counseling that should be approached in a straightforward manner throughout the counseling process.

Counselors who follow the guidelines offered in this article will have a better understanding of the cross-cultural nature of religious values. The guidelines proposed in this article help counselors to fully explore their strengths and limitations in working with religious values in the therapy process. Counselors who clearly understand their strengths and limitations in integrating religious values in therapy can enhance their effectiveness in working with clients' religious values and avoid the pitfalls associated with values conflicts in the therapeutic process.

[Readers' Notes: The term *religious values* is used throughout this article to denote a broad range of religious issues to which a person is deeply committed; terms such as *spiritual values, religious faith,* or *religious beliefs* are analogous concepts for the purposes of this article. The reader is referred to Miller (1982) for a comprehensive review of the damaging effects of negative stereotypes; also see Fishman (1956) for a discussion of the factual inaccuracy of stereotypes.]

REFERENCES

Albany, A. P. (1984). Clinical implications of religious loyalties: A contextual view. *Counseling and Values, 28,* 128-133.

Allport, G. (1950). *The individual and his religion.* New York: Macmillan.

American Psychological Association. (1990). Ethical principles of psychologists. *American Psychologist, 45,* 390-395.

Anderson, H., & Goolishian, H. A. (1988). Human systems as linguistic systems: Preliminary and evolving ideas about the implications for clinical theory. *Family Process, 27,* 371-393.

Ansbacher, H. L., & Ansbacher, R. (Eds.). (1979). *Superiority and social interest* (3rd ed.). New York: W. W. Norton & Company.

Basch, M. F. (1980). *Doing psychotherapy.* New York: Basic Books.

Beck, J. R. (1981). Treatment of spiritual doubt among obsessing evangelicals. *Journal of Psychology and Theology, 9,* 224-231.

Bergin, A. E. (1980). Psychotherapy and religious values. *Journal of Consulting and Clinical Psychology, 48,* 95-105.

Bergin, A. E. (1991). Values and religious issues in psychotherapy and mental health. *American Psychologist, 46,* 394-403.

Bergin, A. E., & Jensen, J. P. (1990). Religiosity of psychotherapists: A national survey. *Psychotherapy, 27,* 3-7.

Beutler, L. E., & Bergan, J. (1991). Value change in counseling and psychotherapy: A search for scientific credibility. *Journal of Counseling Psychology, 38,* 16-24.

Beutler, L. E., Crago, M., & Arizmendi, T. G. (1986). Therapist variables in psychotherapy process and outcome. In S. Garfield & A. E. Bergin (Eds.), *Handbook of psychotherapy and behavior change* (3rd ed., pp. 257-310). New York: John Wiley & Sons.

Beutler, L. E., Pollack, S., & Jobe, A. (1978). "Acceptance," values, and therapeutic change. *Journal of Consulting and Clinical Psychology, 46,* 198-199.

Clinebell, H. J. (1965). *Mental health through Christian community.* Nashville, TN: Abingdon Press.

Cohen, E. J. (1982). Induced Christian neurosis: An examination of pragmatic paradoxes and the Christian faith. *Journal of Psychology and Theology, 10,* 5-12.

Cox, R. H. (Ed.). (1973). *Religious systems and psychotherapy.* Springfield, IL: Charles C Thomas.

Farnsworth, K. E. (1985). *Wholehearted integration: Harmonizing psychology and Christianity through word and deed.* Grand Rapids, MI: Baker Book House.

Finney, J. R., & Maloney, H. N. (1985). Empirical studies of Christian prayer: A review of the literature. *Journal of Psychology and Theology, 13,* 104-115.

Fishman, J. A. (1956). An examination of the process and function of social stereotyping. *Journal of Social Psychology, 43,* 27-64.

Fitz, A. (1990). Religious and familial factors in the etiology of obsessive-compulsive disorder: A review. *Journal of Psychology and Theology, 18*, 141-147.

Fromm, E. (1950). *Psychoanalysis and religion.* New Haven, CT: Yale University Press.

Gladding, S. T., Lewis, E. L., & Adkins, L. (1981). Religious beliefs and positive mental health: The GLA scale and counseling. *Counseling and Values, 25*, 206-215.

Godwin, T. C., & Crouch, J. G. (1989). Subjects' religious orientation, counselor's orientation and skill, and expectations for counseling. *Journal of Psychology and Theology, 17*, 284-292.

Hill, C. E., & Gormally, J. (1977). Effects of reflection, restatement, probe and nonverbal behaviors on client affect. *Journal of Counseling Psychology, 24*, 92-97.

Hill, C. I. (1986). A developmental perspective on adolescent "rebellion" in the church. *Journal of Psychology and Theology, 14*, 306-318.

Inouye, K. H., & Pedersen, P. B. (1985). Cultural and ethnic content of the 1977 to 1982 American Psychological Association convention programs. *The Counseling Psychologist, 13*, 639-648.

James, W. (1982). *The varieties of religious experience.* New York: Penguin Books.

Keating, A. M., & Fretz, B. R. (1990). Christians' anticipations about counselors in response to counselor descriptions. *Journal of Counseling Psychology, 37*, 293-296.

Kroeber, A. L., & Kluckhohn, C. (1952). *Culture: A critical review of concepts and definitions.* New York: Vintage Books.

Linton, R. (1945). *The cultural background of personality.* Englewood Cliffs, NJ: Prentice-Hall.

Lonner, W. J. (1985). Issues in testing and assessment in cross-cultural counseling. *The Counseling Psychologist, 13*, 599-614.

Mathisen, K. (1980). Back to the basics: A broad conceptual model for the integration of psychology and theology. *Journal of Psychology and Theology, 8*, 222-229.

McMinn, M. R. (1984). Religious values and client-therapist matching in psychotherapy. *Journal of Psychology and Theology, 22*, 24-33.

Meehl, P. (Ed.). (1958). *What, then, is man? A symposium of theology, psychology and psychiatry.* St. Louis: Concordia.

Miller, A. G. (Ed.). (1982). *In the eye of the beholder: Contemporary issues in stereotyping.* New York: Praeger Publishers.

Nicholi, A. M. (1990). The atheistic world view of Sigmund Freud and its influence on his clinical observations. *Christian Medical & Dental Society Journal, 21*(4), 4-9.

Padilla, A. M., & De Snyder, N. S. (1987). Counseling Hispanics: Strategies for effective intervention. In P. Pedersen (Ed.), *Handbook of cross-cultural counseling and therapy* (pp. 157-164). New York: Praeger.

Pedersen, P. (Ed.). (1987). *Handbook of cross-cultural counseling and therapy.* New York: Praeger.

Purdy, B. A., Simari, C. G., & Colon, G. (1983). Religiosity, ethnicity, and mental health: Interface the 80s. *Counseling and Values, 27*, 112-122.

Richards, P. S. (1991). Religious devoutness in college students: Relations with emotional adjustment and psychological separation from parents. *Journal of Counseling Psychology, 38*, 189-196.

Ridley, C. R. (1985). Imperatives for ethnic and cultural relevance in psychology training programs. *Professional Psychology: Research and Practice, 16*, 611-622.

Russo, T. J. (1984). A model for addressing spiritual issues in counseling. *Counseling and Values, 29*, 42-48.

Scarr, S. (1988). Race and gender as psychological variables: Social and ethical issues. *American Psychologist, 43*, 56-59.

Sperry, R. W. (1988). Psychology's mentalist paradigm and the religion/science tension. *American Psychologist, 43*, 607-613.

Spilka, B. (1987). Religion and science in early American psychology. *Journal of Psychology and Theology, 15*, 3-9.

Sue, D. W. (1981). *Counseling the culturally different: Theory and practice.* New York: Wiley.

Sue, S. (1988). Psychotherapeutic services for ethnic minorities: Two decades of research findings. *American Psychologist, 43,* 301–308.

Theodore, R. M. (1984). Utilization of spiritual values in counseling: An ignored dimension. *Counseling and Values, 28,* 162-168.

Triandis, H. (1987). Some major dimensions of cultural variation in client populations. In P. Pedersen (Ed.), *Handbook of cross-cultural counseling and therapy* (pp. 21-28). New York: Praeger.

Truax, C. B., & Carkhuff, R. R. (1967). *Toward effective counseling and psychotherapy: Training and practice.* Chicago: Aldine.

Van Leeuwen, M. S. (1985). *The person in psychology.* Grand Rapids, MI: William B. Eerdmans.

Vontress, C. E. (1987). Existentialism as a cross-cultural counseling modality. In P. Pedersen (Ed.), *Handbook of cross-cultural counseling and therapy* (pp. 207-212). New York: Praeger.

Watson, P. J., Morris, R. J., & Hood, R. W. (1988a). Sin and self-functioning: Part 1. Grace, guilt, and self-consciousness. *Journal of Psychology and Theology, 16,* 254-269.

Watson, P. J., Morris, R. J., & Hood, R. W. (1988b). Sin and self-functioning: Part 2. Grace, guilt, and psychological adjustment. *Journal of Psychology and Theology, 16,* 270-281.

Watson, R. I. (1967). Psychology: A prescriptive science. *American Psychologist, 22,* 435-443.

Witter, R. A., Stock, W. A., Okun, M. A., & Haring, M. J. (1985). Religion and subjective well-being in adulthood: A quantitative synthesis. *Review of Religious Research, 26,* 332-342.

Woody, R. H. (1988). *Fifty ways to avoid malpractice.* Sarasota, FL: Professional Resource Exchange.

Worthington, E. L. (1988). Understanding the values of religious clients: A model and its application to counseling. *Journal of Counseling Psychology, 35,* 166-174.

Worthington, E. L. (1989). Religious faith across the life span: Implications for counseling and research. *The Counseling Psychologist, 17,* 555-612.

Yalom, I. D. (1980). *Existential psychotherapy.* New York: Basic Books.

Preparing to Counsel Clients of Different Religious Backgrounds: A Phenomenological Approach

ROBERT T. GEORGIA

COUNSELORS IN SCHOOLS, colleges, community agencies, and other settings are confronted in the 1990s with a clientele drawn from an increasingly wide range of religious, social, and cultural backgrounds. Sue (1992) noted that "within the next 20 years, racial and ethnic minorities will become a numerical majority, while white Americans will constitute only about 48 percent of the population" (p. 9). Current immigration rates are the highest in history. Of current immigrants, 34% are Asians; many more are from African, Middle Eastern, and other non-White or non-Christian societies. In addition, the White American population is aging, with declining fertility and birth rates (1.7 children per mother, as compared with 2.4 for African Americans, 2.9 for Mexican Americans, 3.4 for Vietnamese, and 11.9 for Hmongs). The number of White students in California has already dropped below 50%. Unlike earlier immigrants, these groups are not necessarily oriented toward assimilation, often preferring instead to retain their cultural heritage (Sue, 1992).

To meet the demands of this changing environment, new approaches in conceptual framework, education and training, research opportunities, and direct service delivery are required (Pedersen, 1991). Counselors have been admonished to explore and clarify their own values, standards, and assumptions about human behavior. As a first step in understanding others, they have been advised to familiarize themselves with their clients' varying orientations in terms of religion, values, and culture (Sue, 1992). Stimulating contributions in this vein include recent cross-cultural studies of self-concept (Page & Berkow, 1991; Wood, 1991), religious values (Bishop, 1992), and counseling practices (Locke, 1992).

In dealing with clients of different religious backgrounds, counselors cannot avoid the necessity of knowing something about their clients' belief systems and practices. "An awareness of individual and group world views can help us develop the skills needed for effectiveness in cross-cultural counseling and psychotherapy" (Ibrahim, 1985, p. 626). In the study of other religions, however, we are confronted with the problem of controlling our

From "Preparing to Counsel Clients of Different Religious Backgrounds: A Phenomenological Approach," by R. T. Georgia, 1994, *Counseling and Values, 38*, 143–151.

own values, biases, stereotypes, and assumptions as we encounter others' worldviews. We cannot do justice to our clients' beliefs if we approach them wearing ideological blinders. A method or approach for studying religions that would minimize the distortion of personal prejudices and presuppositions would be of significant value to counselors. Such a method or approach should be compatible with traditional counseling values of acknowledging and respecting the client's own beliefs and values.

The study of religion can be approached from a number of perspectives, including the historical, sociological, psychological, and metaphysical. Of the various approaches to the study of religion, the author proposes that a phenomenological approach, as practiced by many scholars of comparative religion, can best satisfy counselors' needs to learn about other religions while controlling their own biases and assumptions.

This article does not offer detailed instructions or examples on how to conduct a phenomenological study of religion. The scholarly literature for this purpose is ample and extensive, from Max Weber's (1978) early 20th-century writings on the study of religions to the comparative religion of Joachim Wach (1958) to more recent works by such scholars as Mircea Eliade (1969), Niniar Smart (1973a, 1973b), and Anthony Blasi (1985). The accessibility of phenomenological method for conducting psychological research is also well documented (for example, see Giorgi, 1985; Merleau-Ponty, 1967; Packer, 1985). This article instead focuses on presenting a rationale for using the phenomenological approach in the comparative study of religion, and then draws some relevant implications for its use by counselors in their own study of religion and in their work with clients.

PHENOMENOLOGY IN THE COMPARATIVE STUDY OF RELIGION

In the comparative study of religion (CSR), a strong preference has developed for the use of the phenomenological method.

> The contemporary study of the religions of the world, in America and among scholars around the world, whether it be known under the name of *comparative religion, the history of religions, or the science of religions,* uses in large measure the method of approach to its subject that is to be identified with the phenomenological study of religions…it is today a primary scholarly discipline and tool being used to further the development of a science of religion. (Ashby, 1965, p. 29)

Employing phenomenology as a method enables comparative religionists to gather data in a philosophically unencumbering manner. In doing so, phenomenologists place their emphasis upon description, leaving the problem of value to the philosopher of religion or the theologian (Ashby, 1965).

The agenda of phenomenology in the comparative study of religion is relatively simple and straightforward. "Its aim is to view religious ideas, acts, and institutions with due consideration to their 'intention,' yet without subscribing to any one philosophical, theological, metaphysical, or psychological theory" (Wach, 1958, p. 24). As used in phenomenology, the word "intention" does not have a telic connotation, but rather denotes the meaning ascribed by the believer to religious ideas, acts, and institutions.

In CSR, pioneering work in phenomenological research was done by P. D. Chantepie de la Saussaye, Nathan Söderblom, and C. J. Bleeker, but the seminal figure in the development of this approach was the Dutch scholar Gerardus Van der Leeuw. For Van der Leeuw (1938), phenomenology has a threefold implication: "(1) Something exists. (2) This something 'appears.' (3) Precisely because it 'appears' it is a 'phenomenon'" (p. 671). Someone experiences the object, or "something."

> The "phenomenon" as such, therefore, is an object related to a subject, and a subject related to an object...its entire essence is given in its "appearance" and its appearance to "someone." If (finally) this "someone" begins to discuss what "appears," then phenomenology arises. (Van der Leeuw, 1938, p. 671)

In order to make sense of this "something" which "appears," Van der Leeuw continued, we assign names to phenomena. "In giving names we separate phenomena and also associate them; in other words, we classify" (p. 674). Classification is essential because it creates structure. "Structure," Van der Leeuw asserted, "is reality significantly organized" (p. 672). But the facts of reality must be allowed to speak to us as directly as possible. We must attain "a description which respects the data and their peculiar intentionality" (Danilou, 1959, p. 78), again understanding "intentionality" as meaningfulness to the believer.

Van der Leeuw suggests that we accomplish this end through the technique of "epoche."

> Phenomenology, therefore, is neither metaphysics, nor the comprehension of empirical reality. It observes restraint (the epoche), and its understanding of events depends on its employing "brackets." Phenomenology is concerned only with "phenomena," that is, with "appearance"; for there is nothing whatever "behind" the phenomenon. (1938, p. 675)

Epoche has been described as a "temporary suspension of all inquiry into the problem of truth" (Wach, 1958, p. 25). While observing religious phenomena, in other words, we relax for the moment our penchant for applying evaluative criteria to determine truth or falsity, content to try to absorb what the phenomena mean to the subject of the experience. Smart (1973b) defined phenomenological description as "a structure-laden account which is not theory laden" (p. 38), while Roderick Hindery (1973) noted that it is employed "in a sense of empathetic listening from a 'detached inside'" (p. 557).

The phenomenological method does not seek to tackle whether there is anything "behind" the phenomenon that corresponds to something beyond the edge of human influence (Rashke, Kirk, & Taylor, 1977). Arapura (1972) noted that "phenomenology as such, as Van de Leeuw expects, cannot permit itself to arrive at 'conclusions concerning revelation itself' even indirectly or per viam negationis" (p. 50). The purpose of Van der Leeuw's phenomenology is simply to let the phenomena appear, to assign names to the appearances, to experience them systematically while observing epoche and respecting their intentionality, to clarify what has been seen, and to testify to what has been understood (Van der Leeuw, 1938, p. 688). The intentionality of the data must shine through, and the investigator must "surrender himself" to the phenomena (Streng, 1970, p. 210).

Phenomenology in this sense has self-imposed limits. It is true, as Charles Long (1967) noted, that Van der Leeuw fails to tell us just how one must deal with the background of interpretation...a complete hermeneutic cannot avoid the interrelationship of the historical subject and object" (p. 71). However, such ability or willingness to interpret does not fall within the intended program of this use of phenomenology, since, as Arapura (1972) conceded, "evaluation is always premature in phenomenology" (p. 51). The import of the phenomenological method lies not in its hermeneutic value, but rather in the straightforward and simple way in which it advocates a presuppositionless experiencing and studying of the facts of the phenomena themselves.

The concepts of epoche, intentionality, and classification, as derived from Van der Leeuw, underlie much of the work of modern comparative religionists. Ninian Smart valued epoche as an "attempt to reach an empathetic objectivity, or if you like a neutralist subjectivity" (1973a, p.6), but he advised that, in addition to suspending judgment as to the truth of what is being investigated, the phenomenologist's "bracketing must also be a bracketing of expressions of value, feeling, etc." (p. 32). To do CSR, a person "must put aside or suspend his own value judgments as much as possible in order to let religious phenomena 'speak' for themselves" (Sullivan, 1970, p. 251). In this effort of the phenomenologist,

> ...the primary aim is to overcome the subjective element in himself as a scholar while allowing full status to the subjective element in the person or community to whom the appearance of the phenomenon is significant. (Ashby, 1965, pp. 27–28)

The ability to withhold judgment is vital for the comparative religionist. Epoche is a caution against committing one of the cardinal sins of CSR. "It is one of the basic rules of the phenomenological study of religions to avoid judgment of other religions by criteria of one's own" (Benz, 1959, p. 120). This applies, it might be added, even if "one's own" religion is atheism, agnosticism, or a sociopolitical philosophy such as dialectical materialism.

The comparative religionist is a phenomenologist "insofar as in his descriptions he respected the religious data and their peculiar intentionality" (Eliade, 1969, p. 35). The religious phenomenologist's purpose is not to interpret, criticize, or moralize, but "rather to grasp the religious intentions of these practices, no matter how bizarre or repelling they may seem to him ethically, theologically, sociologically, historically—or personally" (Sullivan, 1970, p. 251).

Phenomenology alone, even when used appropriately within its subject matter and context, cannot accomplish all that the comparative study of religion intends. In concert with the historical, sociological, psychological, and other approaches, however, it offers a useful means of attaining an empathic understanding of religions while avoiding the excesses of subjectivity. Although other approaches also contribute substantially to furthering the aims of CSR, the phenomenological method has established an abiding and central role in the discipline's pursuits.

APPLICATION OF PHENOMENOLOGICAL METHOD TO WORK WITH CLIENTS

It might be useful to construct a hypothetical example to illustrate the kinds of questions a counselor might raise in applying the phenomenological method to work with clients whose religious orientations are different from his or her own.

> Mohamed is a recent immigrant from Iraq. College-educated and employed as a computer analyst, he is torn between his adherence to Islam and a desire to "fit in" in his adapted society. He has conflicted feelings about sex, family responsibilities, career ambitions, and his sense of personal identity. He is experiencing a tremendous strain between his religion and his new social milieu. For a long time, he hesitated to see a counselor for fear of being misunderstood because of cultural differences. He is not yet convinced that he has made the right decision in doing so.

Many questions will arise in the course of the counselor's relationship with Mohamed. Some will deal specifically with religion. In utilizing a phenomenological approach, the counselor might wish to pose the following questions to himself or herself (adapted from Bishop, 1992; Farmer, 1992).

1. As a precondition, have I adequately explored and evaluated my own religious values and beliefs so that I can identify possible biases, presuppositions, limitations, doubts, and still open questions? What kinds of resistance or maneuvering might I bring to a relationship with such a client?
2. How can I familiarize myself with Islam (especially Mohamed's school or branch of Islam) so that I can appreciate the intellectual and historical context of Mohamed's thinking on religion? Which literature should I review to gain a comprehensive, open-minded, nonjudgmental understanding of the religion, particularly its influence on human functioning?
3. How can I experience Islam in practice so that I can develop a personal sense of the familial, social, and cultural dimensions and expressions of the religion? Which Islamic community and religious activities are accessible to me?
4. Which simple, straightforward language can I use to communicate openly and honestly with Mohamed about his religious values and beliefs, and mine?

5. How can I make Mohamed feel comfortable and confident enough to describe to me his religious values and beliefs, the religious experiences he has had, and how he feels his present life—its pattern, meaning, problems, and goals are influenced by those values and beliefs?
6. How can I help Mohamed to feel that his religious values and beliefs are an accepted part of the therapeutic process, and that they will play an important role in our cooperatively determining the goals of counseling?
7. How can I help Mohamed to see his religious values and beliefs as part of the solution to his problem, and not just as part of the problem, without my trying to challenge or change those values or beliefs?
8. How can I convey my therapeutic expectations and treatment approaches to Mohamed both in my accustomed counseling language and in the language of his value and belief structure?

Although this article has focused primarily on ways of responding to the second question, the other questions follow naturally and are implied by the logic of the phenomenological approach as applied to the work of counselors with clients of different religious backgrounds. Relationships with other types of clients will certainly provoke somewhat different sets of questions, but this hypothetical example may provide a flavor of the use of the phenomenological method in counseling.

IMPLICATIONS FOR COUNSELING

The phenomenological approach used in the comparative study of religion can be of significant value to counselors in their work with clients. Phenomenological method can aid counselors and researchers in directly accessing important information about their clients. For example, "in-depth phenomenological interviewing is interested in understanding the experience of other people and the meaning they make of that experience, rather than in being able to predict or control the experience" (Farmer, 1992, p. 261).

This is particularly relevant for counselors who expect to be involved with clients whose religious beliefs differ from their own. "Information about specific religious values is an important part of preparing counselors to work with these issues in counseling" (Bishop, 1992, p.180). Understanding clients' belief systems is important because "counselors who hold a world view different from that of their clients and are unaware of the basis for this difference are most likely to impute negative traits to clients" (Sue & Sue, 1990, p. 137). With its emphasis on "bracketing" one's own judgment and respecting the intentionality of the data, the phenomenological approach to the study of religion permits the counselor to view others' religious beliefs in a relatively presuppositionless and nonjudgmental manner. Such restraint is necessary for the culturally skilled counselor, who is characterized by Sue and Sue (1990) as one who "actively and constantly attempts to avoid prejudices, unwarranted labeling, and stereotyping" (p. 167) in an effort to attain a "cognitive empathy" (p. 169) with clients.

Being able to recognize, enter into, and communicate within the client's universe of discourse and belief enables the counselor to clarify and advance the methods and objectives of the intervention. As Probst (quoted in Johnson & Ridley, 1992) noted, "therapeutic expectations are most powerful when the active ingredients of psychotherapy are translated into the language and belief structures of the client" (p. 221). A phenomenological understanding of clients' belief systems can provide critical aid in developing effective intervention strategies. Beutler et al. (quoted in Bishop, 1992) have observed that "providing treatments and interventions that are consistent with the patient's beliefs enhances treatment outcomes, even when therapists and patients do not adhere to the same belief system" (p. 276).

For the counselor, controlling one's own values and assumptions in learning about other religions is a crucial factor in avoiding prejudice and stereotypes about clients, and working productively with them toward the achievement of counseling goals. Utilizing the phenomenological method, "investigators can begin to understand the subjective meaning of the acts from the perspective of the participants" (Jackson & Patton, 1992, p. 203).

CONCLUSION

Counselors preparing to do direct research or interviewing with human participants on the topic of religious belief should familiarize themselves with the phenomenological approach, and counselors engaged in a study of the various religions should pay special attention to texts with a phenomenological orientation. Through the use of the phenomenological method, counselors studying the religions of their clients can "see" the religious differences without the coloration of personal, professional, or ideological lenses. Such unbiased, empathic understanding can enable the counselor to communicate better with clients and develop sensitive and effective intervention strategies.

To assess the usefulness of the phenomenological method to the counseling profession in relation to clients' religious beliefs, several avenues of future search might be explored. Counselors might produce monographs about their use of phenomenological interviewing techniques in ascertaining clients' religious beliefs. Focusing on selected psychological variables, they might also make phenomenologically based comparisons of clients or groups of clients of different religious orientations. Where religion is an issue, studies might be conducted to determine the relative effectiveness of treatment interventions based on a phenomenological approach versus non-phenomenologicall based interventions. Finally, it might be instructive to evaluate the differences found in the nature and degree of comfort in communication between client and counselor in situations where a phenomenological approach is used as compared with situations where it is not employed.

REFERENCES

Arapura, J. G. (1972). Religion as anxiety and tranquility. In J. Waardenburg (Gen. Ed.), *Religion and reason: Method and theory in the study and interpretation of religions* (Vol. 5). The Hague, Netherlands: Mouton & Co.

Ashby, P. H. (1965). The history of religions. In P. Ramsey (Ed.), *Religion* (pp. 1-49). Englewood Cliffs, NJ: Prentice-Hall.

Benz, E. (1959). On understanding non-Christian religions. In M. Eliade & J. M. Kitagawa (Eds.), *The history of religions: Essays in methodology* (pp. 115-131). Chicago: The University of Chicago Press.

Bishop, D. R. (1992). Religious values in cross-cultural counseling. *Counseling and Values, 36,* 179-181.

Blasi, A. J. (1985). *A phenomenological transformation of the social scientific study of religion* (Vol. 10 in American University Studies: Series VII, Theology and Religion). New York: Peter Lang.

Danilou, J. (1959). Phenomenology of religions and philosophy of religion. In M. Eliade & J. M. Kitagawa (Eds.), *The history of religions: Essays in methodology* (pp. 67–85). Chicago: The University of Chicago Press.

Eliade, M. (1969). *The quest.* Chicago: The University of Chicago Press.

Farmer, L. J. (1992). Religious experience in childhood: A study of adult perspectives on early spiritual awareness. *Religious Education, 87,* 259-268.

Giorgi, A. (Ed.). (1985). *Phenomenology and psychological research.* Pittsburgh, PA: Duquesne University Press.

Hindery, R. (1973). Exploring comparative religious ethics. *Journal of Ecumenical Studies, 10,* 552-574.

Ibrahim, F. A. (1985). Effective cross-cultural counseling and psychotherapy. *Counseling Psychologist, 13,* 625-638.

Jackson, A. P., & Patton, M. J. (1992). A hermeneutic approach to the study of values in counseling. *Counseling and Values, 36,* 201-209.

Johnson, W. B., & Ridley, C. R. (1992). Brief Christian and non-Christian rational-emotive therapy with depressed Christian clients. *Counseling and Values, 36,* 220-229.

Locke, D. C. (1992). Counseling beyond U. S. borders. *American Counselor, 1*(2), 13-16.

Long, C. H. (1967). Archaism and hermeneutics. In J. C. Brauer (Gen. Ed.), *Essays in Divinity* (Vol. 1, pp. 67-87). Chicago, IL: The University of Chicago Press.

Merleau-Ponty, M. (1967). The interconnections of psychology and phenomenology. In J. J. Kockelmans (Ed.), *Phenomenology* (pp. 485-502). New York: Doubleday.

Packer, M. J. (1985). Hermeneutic inquiry in the study of human conduct. *American Psychologist, 40,* 1081-1093.

Page, R. C., & Berkow, D. N. (1991). Concepts of the self: Western and Eastern perspectives. *Journal of Multicultural Counseling and Development, 19,* 83-93.

Pedersen, P. B. (Ed.). (1991). Multiculturalism as a fourth force in counseling [Special issue]. *Journal of Counseling & Development, 70*(1).

Raschke, C. A., Kirk, J. A., & Taylor, M. C. (1977). *Religion and the human image.* Englewood Cliffs, NJ: Prentice-Hall.

Smart, N. (1973a). *The phenomenon of religion.* New York: Herder and Herder.

Smart, N. (1973b). *The science of religion and the sociology of knowledge.* Princeton, NJ: Princeton University Press.

Streng, F. J. (1970). The objective study of religion and the unique quality of religiousness. *Religious Studies, 6,* 209–219.

Sue, D. W. (1992). The challenge of multiculturalism: The road less traveled. *American Counselor, 1*(1), 6-14.

Sue, D. W., & Sue, D. (1990). *Counseling the culturally different: Theory and practice.* New York: Wiley.

Sullivan, H. P. (1970). The history of religions: Some problems and prospects. In P. Ramsey & J. F. Wilson (Eds.), *The study of religion in colleges and universities* (pp. 246-280). Princeton, NJ: Princeton University Press.

Van der Leeuw, G. (1938). *Religion in essence and manifestation* (J. E. Turner, Trans.). London, England: George Allen & Unwin.

Wach, J. (1958). *The comparative study of religion* (J. Kitagawa, Ed.). New York: Columbia University Press.

Weber, M. (1978). *Economy and society: An outline of interpretive sociology* (G. Roth & C. Wittich, Eds., 2 vols.). Berkeley, CA: University of California Press.

Wood, M. (1991). Self-concept and self-esteem: A cross-cultural perspective. *NASPA Journal, 29,* 24-30.

Spiritual and Ethical Beliefs of Humanists in the Counseling Profession

NELSON GOUD

FOR THE PAST decade political and religious fundamentalists have launched a vigorous campaign against humanism. Some charge that humanism is immoral and anti-God, and that it has taken over the government, education, and the United Nations, and is attempting to control the world (LaHaye, 1980). Lawsuits alleging that the religion of secular humanism is being practiced in schools have received wide coverage in the press (Colley, 1987; Pfeffer, 1988). Librarians and public school teachers are being accused of using books that promote godless religion and moral relativism (Dixon, 1982; Donelson, 1987; Gabler, 1982). Robinson and Wilson (1982) compare the attacks to the McCarthy era tactics of the 1950s, only now humanists instead of communists are the scapegoats. As Brodinsky describes it: "Many mighty guns—legislation, censorship, big-name leadership, high-powered propaganda—are trained on secular humanism" (Brodinsky, 1982, p. 90).

Due to the high public visibility of these criticisms, members of the humanistic community are often asked to explain the religious/ethical stance of humanism. Helping professionals, particularly front-line counselors and educators, are especially vulnerable to these inquiries. Professional humanistic associations have responded with position papers and articles describing their stances (Colley, 1987; Goud, 1982; Robinson & Wilson, 1982). Humanistic convention programs have had debates between fundamentalists and humanists, and the American Humanist Association chose "Religion, Politics, & Secular Humanism" for its 1988 annual conference theme. Some humanistic associations have debated the value of retaining the word *humanistic* in their titles because of the controversies (Arons, 1987; Goud, 1987). The American Humanist Association chose a different strategy and leveled countercharges at the fundamentalists (Edwords, 1987; Edwords & McCabe, 1987; Gibbons, 1988; McKown, 1988; Negri, 1987; Watters, 1987).

Still, many questions remain as a result of the polemic. Do humanists believe in God? Is humanism a religion? Are all humanists secular humanists? How do humanists make ethical decisions? While there have been many individual responses to these philosophical questions, there has been little, if any, systematic sampling of the beliefs of current humanists. This study is an attempt to survey selected spiritual and ethical beliefs of one group of

From "Spiritual and Ethical Beliefs of Humanists in the Counseling Profession," by N. Goud, 1990, *Journal of Counseling & Development, 68,* 571–574.

humanists, primarily identified as practicing humanistic counselors and educators. The results will be discussed from both contemporary and historical perspectives.

METHOD

Questionnaire

Table 1 contains the fifteen items used in the investigation. These items were constructed by the author based on the most commonly discussed humanism-fundamentalist issues in the literature and professional conferences. These issues clustered around four themes: humanistic identity (items 1-3), religious and spiritual beliefs (items 4-9), ethical fulfillment (items 10-12), and public school controversies (items 13-15). Participants were asked to respond to each item on a 5-point Likert scale (Stanley & Hopkins, 1972).

Participants

A random sampling of 388 members of the Association for Humanistic Education and Development (AHEAD) constituted the target population for this study. One hundred and fifty-eight members returned mailed questionnaires, for a 41% return rate. The respondents were representative of the total AHEAD membership in proportion to sex, geography, and length of membership. Their occupational affiliations were as follows: counselors/therapists (58%), college faculty (11%), administrators (9%), teachers (8%), graduate students (7%), school counselors (5%), other (2%).

Procedure

The questionnaire was mailed in January 1988, and a follow-up questionnaire was mailed in February 1988. Respondents did not sign their names to the questionnaire.

RESULTS AND DISCUSSION

Table 1 also summarizes the response frequencies and median score for each of the questionnaire items. In the following discussion, however, data are combined such that *agree* and *strongly disagree* are treated as one category and *disagree* and *strongly disagree* as another category.

TABLE 1

Questionnaire Items and Response Frequencies

Item	Response Frequencies[a]					N[b]	Median
	1	2	3	4	5		
1. I consider myself humanistic.	90	55	8	2	2	158	1.0
2. I am a secular humanist.	22	32	30	31	35	150	3.0
3. I have read *Humanist Manifestos I and/or II.*	16	16	16	23	72	143	5.0
4. I believe in the Judaic-Christian God.	55	37	29	17	17	155	2.0
5. I believe there is a universal spiritual force that can manifest itself in ways other than the Judaic-Christian God.	78	44	14	8	11	155	1.0
6. Humanism is a religion.	6	9	28	51	60	154	4.0
7. Humanists are generally anti-God and religion.	3	4	17	67	65	156	4.0
8. Humanistic and religious values have more similarities than differences.	39	9	18	6	3	157	2.0
9. If freely chosen, becoming a believer in religion is consistent with humanistic beliefs.	52	77	18	6	5	158	2.0
10. Truth and ethical fulfillment can be attained through experience alone (without religion or other supernatural beliefs).	43	47	28	25	15	158	2.0
11. One's freedom to create a life with meaning takes precedence over allegiance to any political, religious, or cultural ideology.	57	60	15	17	9	158	2.0
12. Ethical decisions concerning adult life-styles, sexual preferences, birth control, abortion, divorce, suicide are an individual's *right and responsibility* (even if they conflict with a religious doctrine).	87	48	3	13	5	156	1.0
13. Both Creationism and Evolution should be taught in public schools.	21	39	24	32	39	155	3.0
14. Prayer, in some form, should be legally permitted in schools.	18	45	25	33	37	158	3.0
15. Some form of values/ethics education is essential in public schools.	84	65	8	1	0	158	1.0

[a] 1, *Strongly agree;* 2, *agree;* 3, *undecided;* 4, *disagree;* 5, *strongly disagree.*
[b] Some respondents did not answer each item.

1. *Humanistic identity.* Almost all participants (92%) viewed themselves as "humanistic." Whatever the subjective meaning of secular humanism (the most common label fundamentalists attach to all forms of humanism), about one-third (36%) of this humanistic group classified themselves as "secular humanists." Fundamentalist critics often quote and cite *Humanist Manifestos I and II* (American Humanist Association, 1973) as being the primary source of humanistic beliefs. For this sample, only 22% had read one or both of these documents. (See Goud [1982] for a further discussion of *Humanist Manifestos I and II* as they relate to the controversy.)

2. *Religious and spiritual beliefs.* A clear majority of the participants (59%) believed in the Judaic-Christian God. Although 72% disagreed that humanism is a religion, 83% believed that there are more similarities than differences among humanist and religious values, and 83% agreed that, if freely chosen, religion is consistent with humanistic beliefs. It was also found that 79% believed in a universal spiritual force that can manifest itself in ways other than the Judaic-Christian God.

   These results suggest that a large majority of these humanists demonstrate a high compatibility with traditional religious beliefs and values. The supposed humanist aversion to religion is not supported by these findings. However, religion can take nontraditional forms for some humanists. Two-fifths of this sample were undecided about or did not believe in the Judaic-Christian God, and four-fifths believed there can be a spiritual force other than the Judaic-Christian God. So while these humanists find traditional religion a compatible choice, not all choose it. Many believe in a possible spiritual choice outside of the Judaic-Christian tradition.

3. *Ethical fulfillment.* With respect to ethical decision making, 57% of the participants believed that human experience alone was sufficient for realizing truth and ethical fulfillment. An even greater number believed that individual freedom to create a life with meaning took precedence over any ideology (74%) and that adult ethical decisions were an individual's choice even if they conflict with religious doctrine (87%). For these humanists, individual freedom and choice (in contrast to religious/political/cultural ideology) are the determining factors in making ethical decisions.

4. *Public school issues.* Participants were almost evenly divided on whether both Creationism and Evolution should be taught and whether prayer should be legally permitted (there was a slight tendency to disagree). Almost all (94%) believed that some form of values/ethics education is essential in public schools. Compared to a recent public poll (*Phi Delta Kappan*, 1987), the participants in this study were *less* inclined to allow prayer (40% compared to 68% in the general population) and substantially *more* in favor of values/ethics education (94% compared to 43% in the general population).

IMPLICATIONS

This study attempted to provide empirical evidence regarding the question: What do humanists believe concerning religion, spirituality, and ethics? The results reveal valuable information about these issues. An interpretation may aid in clarifying some of the confusion abundant in the humanism-fundamentalist controversy.

Ethical/spiritual pluralism best characterizes the positions of the humanists in this investigation. In this survey, for example, we found orthodox religious believers, nonbelievers, and those who believe in a nonorthodox spiritual force. Underlying this ethical/spiritual pluralism is the belief in individual freedom to create or choose these beliefs.

Most critics of humanism seem to think that all humanists have the same beliefs, especially in the realm of spirituality. Furthermore, a perception persists that humanism rejects any belief in a god or religion (and in some instances, that humanism is a religion itself—but one without a god). While these perceptions are valid for *some* humanists, they cannot be applied to *all* humanists. Much of the confusion and misperception is due to a lack of knowledge about the various schools of humanism. It is essential to have this knowledge if one is to accurately understand humanist's positions on religion and spirituality.

Schools of Humanism

All schools of modern humanism have their roots in Renaissance humanism. Renaissance humanists successfully reintroduced the Greek-Latin concepts of the inherent dignity of humankind, critical and free inquiry, individual expression, and the establishment of a social order based on human virtue. Their works were intended to be complementary to, and not directly opposed to, prevailing religious doctrines. (See Kriseller [1979] and Trinkaus [1983] for a fuller treatment of these ideas.)

The many variations of modern humanism generally fall under two schools: the scientific/naturalistic school and the humanistic psychology school. While maintaining similarities in the values established by the Renaissance humanists, these schools differ in their beliefs involving the transcendent nature of being human.

The *scientific/naturalistic school,* which includes selected ethical unions and "religious humanism," bases much of its approach on the scientific positivist and rationalist movements of the eighteenth century and on the earlier work of Francis Bacon. For this school the way to truth is through reason, logic, and the empirical methods of science. Advocates of this school reject belief in any form of the supernatural, because it is not accountable to the scrutiny of rational inquiry and, therefore, vulnerable to the possible arbitrary desires of religious and governmental authority. Lamont (1957) expresses this view accordingly: "The establishment of knowledge in any field requires time and trouble in the form of observation, reflection, experimentation, and testing. This fact automatically rules out religious revelation or any kind of intuition as in itself a dependable method of arriving at the truth" (p. 180). Proponents of the scientific/naturalistic school are equally skeptical about nontraditional supernatural sources of truth like astrology, mysticism, altered consciousness states, and so on. Any claim must pass the test of scientific validation.

Humanist Manifestos I and II (American Humanist Association, 1973) are documents from the scientific/naturalistic school. Both statements summarize major beliefs on religion, ethics, the individual, and civil liberties. The signers of the 1933 *Humanist Manifesto I* called themselves "religious humanists" (of the nontheistic variety). This designation did not appear in *Humanist Manifesto II*, published in 1973. Both documents assert that there is insufficient evidence for belief in the supernatural, and that humankind must look elsewhere (reason, science) for truth and fulfillment. Many of the current critics of humanism perceive *Humanist Manifestos I and II* as the prime documents of humanism. One can see then why some critics claim that humanism is a religion if they believe all humanists subscribe to *Humanist Manifesto I*. There are numerous other written documents from this school. Further and additional ideas can be found in Lamont (1957), Kurtz (1973), Beattle (1979), Edwords (1984), and in *The Humanist*, journal of the American Humanist Association.

The *humanistic psychology school* emerged in the mid-twentieth century as a more inclusive alternative to the prevailing behaviorist and Freudian models in psychology. Adherents of this school believe that behaviorists, with their insistence on empiricism, ignore the inner dimension of being human; Freudian psychologists, while willing to explore the inner life, tend to overemphasize the mentally ill aspects and neglect the "higher" human essences such as creativity, values, transcendent states like peak experiences, and undeveloped positive potentialities. Humanistic psychologists focus their work on the actualizing tendency in all humans. This drive toward actualization can incorporate transcendent qualities. Carl Rogers, a founder of this school, comments on this point accordingly:

> We are tuning in to a potent creative tendency which has formed our universe, from the smallest snowflake to the largest galaxy, from the lowly amoeba to the most sensitive and gifted persons. And perhaps we are touching the cutting edge of our ability to transcend ourselves, to create new and more spiritual directions in human evolution. (1980, p. 134)

The willingness to explore the transcendent nature of being human is one major difference between this school and the scientific/naturalistic school (it also makes the humanistic psychology school open to the criticism that it is attempting too much under the banner of science). Further explanations of the humanistic psychology school can be found in Maslow (1968, 1970b, 1971), Rogers (1961, 1977, 1983), Tageson (1982), and Goble (1970).

Given this history of humanism, issues in the current fundamentalist-humanism controversy can be seen from another perspective. We see, for example, that there are humanists who do not believe in any form of a supernatural (the adherents of the scientific/naturalistic school). We also find another school of humanists who are open to a variety of spiritual beliefs (the humanistic psychology school). The majority of the participants in this study appear to belong to the latter school.

The ethical/spiritual pluralism finding of this study is in one way in opposition to *both* the religious fundamentalists and the scientific/naturalistic humanists. Both use spiritual beliefs as a "humanist litmus test." If you are a humanist, say the fundamentalists, you do not believe in any religion or spirituality. The scientific/naturalistic humanists contend that if you believe in spiritual entities, then you are not a true humanist. This investigation refutes both of these positions.

The majority of humanists in this study seem to believe that a person should be allowed to use his or her freedom to choose or create a spiritual orientation. If this choice leads to a conventional spiritual viewpoint and is freely chosen, then this is a valid expression of human freedom. The same holds true for agnostic, atheistic, or even fundamentalist choices.

Most humanistic counselors and educators are familiar with the teachings of the humanistic psychology school. Many are not aware of the scientific/naturalistic school and the inherent antagonism it often has with selected religious groups. The findings of this study may aid in further understanding the current controversy and the varieties of humanism. The results can be useful in discussing humanistic stances on ethics and spirituality to interested inquirers (including those of a fundamentalist persuasion).

The humanist-fundamentalist controversy has been characterized by a dichotomous, "them versus us" rhetoric. It is unnecessarily divisive and combative. The ill feelings and false claims from all sides detract from working together on common values and goals. Maslow said that the pursuit of "ultimate values" is essential to both religious and scientific domains. It is "a road which all profoundly serious, ultimately concerned people of good will can travel for a very long distance" (1970a, p. 54). Attempting to enhance human rights and possibilities, shared by all, has more than enough challenge. It is time to combine resources for human betterment rather than spear throwing.

REFERENCES

American Humanist Association. (1973). *Humanist Manifestos I & II*. Amherst, NY: Author.

Arons, M. (1987, July 5). What's in a name? *AHP Perspective*.

Beattle, P. (1979). *The prospect for humanism*. Yellow Springs, OH: Fellowship of Religious Humanists.

Brodinsky, B. (1982). The new right: The movement and its impact. *Phi Delta Kappan, 64*, 87-94.

Colley, S. (1987). The secular humanism issue: An opinion. *Alabama A.C.D. Journal, 14*, 5-10.

Dixon, C. (1982). The deliberate sabotage of public education by liberal elitists. *Phi Delta Kappan, 54*, 97.

Donelson, K. (1987). Six statements/questions from the censors. *Phi Delta Kappan, 69*, 208-214.

Edwords, F. (1984). The humanist philosophy in perspective. *The Humanist, January/February*, 7-10.

Edwords, F. (1987). The religious character of American patriotism. *The Humanist, 47*, 5-10.

Edwords, F., & McCabe, S. (1987). Getting out God's vote: Pat Robertson and the evangelical's. *The Humanist, 47*, 5-10.

Gabler, M. (1982). Mind control through textbooks. *Phi Delta Kappan, 64*, 96.

Gibbons, D. (1983). Were you saved or were you hypnotized? *The Humanist, 48*, 17-18.

Goble, F. G. (1970). *The third force: The psychology of Abraham Maslow*. New York: Pocket Books.

Goud, N. (1982). Type I and Type II humanists. *Journal of Humanistic Education and Development, 21*, 9-17.

Goud, N. (1987). Point of view. *Infochange, 47*, 9.

Kristeller, P. O. (1979). *Renaissance thought and its sources*. New York: Columbia University Press.

Kurtz, P. (Ed.). *The humanistic alternative: Some definitions of humanism*. Buffalo, NY: Prometheus Books.

LaHaye, T. (1980). *The battle for the mind*. Old Tappan, NJ: Fleming H. Revell.

Lamont, C. (1957). *The philosophy of humanism*. New York: Philosophical Library.

Maslow, A. H. (1968). *Toward a psychology of being* (2nd ed.). New York: Viking.

Maslow, A. H. (1970a). *Religions, values, and peak-experiences*. New York: Viking Compass.

Maslow, A. H. (1970b). *Motivation and personality* (2nd ed.). New York: Harper & Row.

Maslow, A. H. (1971). *The farther reaches of human nature*. New York: Viking Compass.

McKown, D. (1988). Religion and the constitution. *The Humanist, 48*, 13-16.

Negri, M. (1987). Ambitions and strategies of the religious right. *The Humanist, 47*, 29-32.

Pfeffer, L. (1988). How religious is secular humanism? *The Humanist, 48*, 13-18.

Phi Delta Kappan (1987). The 19th annual gallop poll of the public's attitudes toward the public schools. *Phi Delta Kappan, 69*, 17-30.

Robinson, E. H., & Wilson, E. S. (1982). *Humanistically oriented education and counseling practices*. Position paper from the Association for Humanistic Education and Development (division of the American Association for Counseling and Development).

Rogers, C. R. (1961). *On becoming a person*. Boston: Houghton Mifflin.

Rogers, C. R. (1977). *On personal power*. New York: Dell.

Rogers, C. R. (1980). *A way of being*. Boston: Houghton Mifflin.

Rogers, C. R. (1983). *Freedom to learn for the 80's*. Columbus, OH: Merrill.

Stanley, J. C., & Hopkins, K. D. (1972). *Educational and psychological measurement and evaluation*. Englewood Cliffs, NJ: Prentice-Hall.

Tageson, C. W. (1982). *Humanistic psychology: A synthesis*. Homewood, IL: Dorsey.

Trinkaus, C. (1983). *The scope of renaissance humanism*. Ann Arbor: University of Michigan Press.

Watters, W. (1987). Christianity and mental health. *The Humanist, 47*, 5-11.

Observers' Perceptions of a Counselor's Treatment of a Religious Issue

DAVID MORROW
EVERETT L. WORTHINGTON, JR.
MICHAEL E. McCULLOUGH

IT IS GENERALLY well established that in successful counseling, clients often change their values to more closely approximate those of their counselors. The conditions under which value influence occurs are not well understood. Beutler (1981) has suggested that religious values are particularly susceptible to influence. Others have suggested that susceptibility to influence depends on the degree of commitment to those values (Goldsmith & Hansen, 1991; Worthington, 1988).

In addition, the mechanisms by which value influence occurs are not well understood. Some have suggested that value influence occurs through the counselor's position of credibility (Strong, 1968). Others have pointed to the client's sensing conditions of worth from the counselor (Rogers, 1951)—even if the counselor does not intend value influence. Truax (1966) suggested that clients might change their values because the counselor positively reinforces value change through empathy or positive regard or negatively reinforces value change through removal of directiveness. Worthington and Scott (1983) suggested that counselors influence their clients' values through selective attention to clients' goals.

One unexplored hypothesis is that counselors influence their clients' religious values by the way they handle client talk that deals directly with religious issues. When a client explicitly mentions a religious issue, the counselor has many options, three of which provide extreme prototypes. The client's religious beliefs or values may be supported, ignored, or challenged.

Previous research investigating Christians has suggested that counselors' status as a Christian or not may affect clients' expectations about counseling. For example, Keating and Fretz (1990) have shown that highly committed Christians have more positive anticipations of counseling after receiving pretherapy information that a counselor is empathic to a Christian worldview (but not explicitly Christian) or secular (without reference to Christian values). For non-highly committed Christians, however, descriptions of the explicitly Christian counselor and the empathic counselor elicited similar

From "Observer's Perceptions of a Counselor's Treatment of a Religious Issue," by D. Morrow, E. L. Worthington, Jr., and M. E. McCullough, 1993, *Journal of Counseling & Development, 71*, 452–456.

anticipations, and they were both more positive than was true for the secular counselor. Negative anticipations about counseling can prevent people from entering counseling, thus resulting in an underutilization of counseling among Christians, especially highly committed Christians (Quackenbos, Privette, & Klentz, 1985, 1986; Worthington, 1986). In another study with Christians, however, Lewis and Epperson (1991) showed that pretherapy disclosure indicating that a counselor is Christian did not influence Christian clients away from seeing an explicitly non-Christian counselor.

Moreover, even if Christians—highly or less highly committed—enter counseling, clients may respond differently to counselors who support, ignore, or challenge the clients' values. For instance, Worthington (1988) has theorized that highly committed religious individuals, especially psychologically vulnerable clients, tend to evaluate their world on religious value dimensions. Weakly committed religious people or nonreligious people are not thought to use religious values frequently. Thus, according to at least some previous research and theory, whether the counselor supports, ignores, or challenges a client's religious values would be expected to have different impacts on people with different religious values. Perceptions of the counselor could be affected by a single salient incident, which could affect the therapeutic relationship, working alliance, and success of counseling.

Like much previous research, this study involved Christians as the religious people under investigation. Christians with relatively high beliefs and those with relatively low beliefs (along conservative evangelical lines) viewed one of three videotapes of counseling in which the counselor either supported a client's concern about the impact of her Christian values on her behavior, ignored the Christian values (and focused on family influences), or challenged her Christian values. We hypothesized that main effects for neither Christian belief nor counselor's treatment of Christian values would be found, but that an interaction would be found between observers' Christian commitment and the counselor's treatment of Christian values. Observers with higher Christian beliefs were expected to rate the counselor who supported a client's Christian values higher than the ignoring or challenging counselor. Observers with lower Christian beliefs were not expected to differentiate among the three treatments of the client's Christian values.

METHOD

Participants

Participants were 102 undergraduate psychology students from a large southeastern urban university. The design was a 2 x 3 factorial—Christian Belief (high or low) x Counselor's Treatment of the Client's Religious Values (support, ignore, challenge). Of the 102 in the total sample, there were 58 in the high Christian belief group and 44 in the low Christian belief group. There were 69 women (50 White and 19 Black) and 33 men (29 White and 4 Black). The experimental design involved six cells whose ns ranged from 13 to 20. The cells were balanced by race and sex as much as possible.

Manipulated Independent Variable

Three 10-minute videotapes of counseling served as the three levels of the manipulated independent variable. The counselor in the videotape was a licensed clinical psychologist with 7 years of postdoctoral experience in full-time private practice. The client in the videotape was portrayed by a female graduate student in counseling psychology with 3 years of post-bachelor's-degree counseling experience.

The first 7 minutes of each videotape consisted of the same counseling exchange and focused on exploring presenting issues (e.g., feelings of isolation, relationship difficulties). The client expressed distress and guilt over a nonmarital sexual relationship, which she characterized as a "serious sin." She said that her Christian values were making her feel guilty. When the counselor wondered whether her distress was out of proportion to the seriousness of her behavior, she responded, "Well, it is a sin," and she cited the Bible as her authority.

The three videotapes differed only within the last 3 minutes. In each case the counselor suggested a competing belief that might help the client. The manipulation was primarily concerned with the value given the client's religious framework. The counselor responded to the client's religious values by (a) supporting, that is, suggesting that she explore these Christian values but saying that perhaps the client was focusing too much on God's judgment and should focus more on God's forgiveness; (b) ignoring, that is, suggesting that her religious values were part of other family influences, which merited more attention; or (c) challenging, that is, suggesting that the woman was old enough to question her religious upbringing and that more attention should be paid to what she wanted and how she felt about the behavior rather than what her religious upbringing prescribed. After the supportive, ignoring, or challenging intervention, an identical conclusion to the interview was viewed.

A manipulation check was performed to determine whether the videotapes conveyed a supporting, ignoring, or challenging counselor response. Students from psychology classes, who did not participate in this study ($N=59$; 19 for supportive, 18 for ignoring, and 22 for challenging), watched one of the videotapes and classified the counselor's response as most closely described by supporting, ignoring, challenging, or none of those. Of those viewing each tape, 84% identified the supporting videotape correctly, 83% identified the ignoring tape correctly, and 68% identified the challenging tape correctly.

Then the tape was rated using a 5-point Likert-type scale (from 1 = *not at all* to 5 = *perfectly*) on the degree to which each of the three adjectives accurately described the counselor's response to the client's religious values. One-way analyses of variance followed by Duncan's test identified the following differences. For the adjective "supporting," the counselor on the supporting tape was rated as more supportive (M=3.5) than on the other two tapes (ignore M=1.6; challenge M=2.3), F(2, 56)=15.69, p<.0001. For "ignoring," the counselor on the ignoring tape was rated as more ignoring (M=3.6) than on the other two tapes (support, M=1.7; challenge, M=2.4), F(2, 56)=12.94, p<.0001. For "challenging," the counselor on the challenging tape was rated as more challenging (M=3.7) than on the other two tapes (support, M=2.7; ignore, M=1.7), F(2, 56)=12.18, p<.0001. Thus, the tapes were considered to be accurate manipulations of the independent variable.

Instruments

The Shepherd Scale. Level of Christian belief was measured using the Shepherd Scale (Bassett et al., 1981). This 38-item instrument is a measure of evangelical Christian beliefs and practices. Each item is rated on a 4-point scale (1=*not true* to 4=*true*) according to the degree to which the item is true of the person. The scale is divided into a belief component that measures agreement with Christian doctrinal statements, and a Christian walk component that measures Christian life-style characteristics. A total scale score is derived by summing the subscales, and the total score was used in this article. The scale has adequate psychometric properties (Bassett et al., 1981). For example, it has 2-week test-retest reliability of r=.82, split-half reliability of .83, and alpha of .86. Its construct validity has been shown by correlating it with other validated measures of religiosity such as King and Hunt's (1975) composite religious scales (r=.65) and Glock and Stark's (1965) Dimensions of Religious Commitment (r=.41). Bassett et al. (1981) have found the Shepherd Scale to differentiate between Christians and non-Christians but not between committed Roman Catholics and Protestants. The Shepherd Scale has been used in other research to differentiate between Christian and non-Christian groups (Pecnik & Epperson, 1985).

For this study, a distance of one-half of a standard deviation was desired between the scores of the high and low Christian belief groups to ensure that the groups were truly distinct. Participants whose scores were within one quarter of a standard deviation from the midpoint score between the means of Christian and non-Christians, as reported for the Bassett et al. (1981) community sample, were not used. Thus, given the standard deviation of 8.7 cited in Bassett et al. (1981), participants whose scores ranged from 109 to 113 were not used. Because the scale was not expected to categorize participants with complete fidelity into Christian and non-Christian categories, the participants were labeled "high" or "low Christian belief." (It is easily conceivable that many of those labeled "low Christian belief" might not be Christians.)

Attraction and receptivity. The participants' attraction and receptivity to the counselor were measured by the Tape Rating Scale developed by Greenberg (1969) and used by Haugen and Edwards (1976) in their analogue study of Christian counseling. The scale consists of two subscales to measure participants' attraction to the counselor and receptivity to the counselor's influence. The attraction subscale consists of 26 items describing the positive and negative aspects of the taped counselor's interactions, which are endorsed on a 7-point scale ranging from *strongly agree* to *strongly disagree*. The receptivity subscale consists of 10 statements concerning participants' attitudes toward the counselor and indicates participants' willingness to interact with the counselor.

Persuasion. Degree to which a participant was persuaded by the counselor was measured by the Persuasibility Questionnaire (Greenberg, 1969), which was also used by Haugen and Edwards (1976). This 40-item questionnaire contains statements about the videotaped client such as "The client probably often leaves work unfinished," "The client is probably more creative than the average person," and "The client is likely to overestimate a person's abilities." Participants were informed that the counselor had also completed the questionnaire on the client and his ratings were included so the participants could compare their ratings with his. In actuality, half of the counselor's ratings were either "strongly agree" (10 items) or "strongly disagree" (10 items), assigned randomly to each extreme. These 20 extreme items were scored in terms of the participant's closeness to the counselor's ratings, with 0 being perfect agreement with the counselor. The lower a participant's score, the more that participant's opinions were assumed to be influenced by the counselor.

Expectation for change, likelihood of referral, and likelihood of client's and participant's return. Participants' ratings of expectation for client change, likelihood of referring a Christian friend to the counselor, and likelihood of referring a non-Christian friend to the counselor were assessed using three 8-point (1=*low*, 8=*high*) items used by Worthington and Gascoyne (1985) in their analogue study of preferences among Christian counselors. Another item by Worthington and Gascoyne (1985) was used as a manipulation check. Two similar items assessed participants' opinions of the likelihood that the client would return for subsequent counseling and the likelihood of their own return, had they been clients.

Social desirability. Because social influence through the observation of counseling was being studied, social desirability, as measured by the MMPI (Minnesota Multiphasic Personality Inventory; Hathaway & McKinley 1943) K scale, was used as a covariate to test for the presence of a social desirability set and to remove statistically the characterological proclivity of participants to influence. Some well-known measures of social desirability, notably the

Crowne-Marlowe Social Desirability Scale (1964), were not used because they have been found to have an anti-religious bias (Watson, Morris, Foster, & Hood, 1986). Using the MMPI K scale as a measure of social desirability is not unprecedented in religion research (see Haugen & Edwards, 1976).

Procedure

Participants were scheduled to arrive at the experimental site in groups of 5 to 20. After reading and signing a consent form, participants completed the K scale of the MMPI, then the Shepherd Scale, and another questionnaire not related to this study. Participants were divided into three groups relatively balanced for race and sex. Each group was randomly assigned to view one of the three videotapes (support, ignore, and challenge). In the final distribution, perfect balance for race and sex was not possible because participants who scored in the midrange on the Shepherd Scale were later dropped from the analyses. After completing the questionnaires, participants were then taken to a videotape viewing room and were read the following introduction: "We are interested in your reactions to the following taped portion of a counseling session. As you watch the tape, put yourself in the position of the client and imagine how you would respond to this particular counseling."

Participants watched one of the three videotapes. After viewing the videotape, participants returned to a waiting area and completed the Tape Rating Scale, Persuasibility Questionnaire, items from Worthington and Gascoyne (1985), and the two additional items.

RESULTS

Experimental Manipulation Check

Participants were assigned to conditions according to Christian commitment based on extreme scores on the Shepherd Scale. As a manipulation check, participants answered the question, "What emphasis should religion have in the personal counseling of the person you just observed?" A one-way (high versus low Christian belief) analysis of variance (ANOVA) was performed. Participants with high Christian belief thought that religion should play a larger part in counseling than did participants with low Christian belief, $F(1, 100)=7.01$, $p<.01$.

Primary Analyses

The means and standard deviations for participants' ratings of the counseling tapes appear in Table 1. A 2 x 3—Christian belief x Counselor's Treatment of the Client's Religious Values (support, ignore, challenge)—

multivariate analysis of covariance (MANCOVA) was performed, with social desirability (as measured by the MMPI K scale) as the covariate. Dependent variables were ratings of attraction to the counselor, receptivity to the counselor, persuasion by the counselor, expectation for change, referral of a Christian friend, referral of a non-Christian friend, likelihood of client return, and likelihood of participant return. Multivariate F ratios were estimated by the Hotelling-Lawley Trace.

The multivariate main effect for social desirability was not significant, multivariate $F(8, 88)=1.17$, $p<.10$. The multivariate main effect for the level of Christian belief was not significant, multivariate $F(8, 88)=1.56$, $p<.10$. The multivariate main effect for the counselor's treatment of the client's religious values was significant, multivariate $F(16, 174)=2.35$, $p=<.004$. The multivariate interaction was not significant, multivariate $F(16, 174)<1.00$, ns.

Univariate analyses of variance (ANOVAs) were performed to determine the locus of the multivariate main effect for counselor's treatment of religious values. Significant univariate Fs for the counselor's treatment of religious values were obtained for the degree to which the participant was persuaded by the counselor, $F(2, 95)=3.96$, $p=.02$; predicted change of the client, $F(2, 95)=3.96$, $p=.04$; and likelihood that the participant would have returned for the next session, $F(2, 95)=4.18$, $p=.02$ (see Table 1).

Post hoc analysis using Duncan's multiple range test was performed for the three dependent variables that showed significant univariate main effects. Participants were more persuaded by the counselor who ignored the client's religious values ($M=43.4$, $SD=15.1$) than they were by the counselor who supported the client's religious values ($M=52.0$, $SD=10.9$). The persuasion by the counselor who challenged the client's religious values ($M=48.7$, $SD=11.8$) was not different than was either of the other two conditions. (Low scores indicate greater persuasion.)

Participants predicted that the client would improve more seeing the counselor who supported her religious values ($M=5.3$, $SD=1.0$) than she would seeing the counselor who challenged her religious values ($M=4.0$, $AD=1.0$). The predicted improvement of the client seeing the counselor who ignored her religious values ($M=4.3$, $SD=1.0$) was no different than was the predicted improvement in the other two conditions.

Participants who viewed the challenging counselor rated themselves less likely to return for the next session had they been the client ($M=4.3$, $SD=2.3$) than did participants who viewed the other two counseling conditions (Supports, $M=5.5$, $SD=2.2$; Ignore, $M=5.7$, $SD=2.1$). There were no significant Christian Belief x Counselor's Treatment of the Client's Religious Values interactions.

DISCUSSION

Worthington (1988) hypothesized that highly religious individuals would respond to religious issues in counseling differently than would less reli-

TABLE 1
Means and Standard Deviations for Perceptions of a Counselor's Treatment of a Client's Religious Issue

Dependent Variable	Treatment		
	Support	Ignore	Challenge
Attraction			
M	129.4	128.8	126.5
SD	27.5	27.5	24.4
Receptivity			
M	42.7	44.0	38.1
SD	14.3	15.2	15.2
Persuasion*			
M	52.0	43.4	48.7
SD	10.9	15.1	11.8
Expectation for change*			
M	5.3	4.3	4.0
SD	1.0	1.0	1.0
Referral of Christian friend			
M	5.3	5.3	4.2
SD	2.1	2.2	2.1
Referral of non-Christian friend			
M	4.4	5.2	4.3
SD	2.3	1.9	2.0
Likelihood of client return			
M	6.1	5.6	5.7
SD	1.6	1.8	1.7
Likelihood of participant return*			
M	5.5	5.7	4.3
SD	2.2	2.1	2.3
MMPI K Scale			
M	13.6	12.7	12.8
SD	4.0	3.9	4.3

Note. MMPI = Minnesota Multiphasic Personality Inventory. Ranges of scores on items: Attraction 26–182; Receptivity 10–70; Persuasion 40–240 (high scores represent resistance to persuasion); Expectation for change 1 (low)–8 (high); Likelihood of Referral of a Christian friend 1 (low)–8(high); Likelihood of client return 1(low)–8(high); Likelihood of participant return 1 (low)–8 (high). MMPI K Scale is scored as the number of items endorsed, in which 12 items = a t score of 49 and 13 items = at score of 51. $*p < .05$.

gious or nonreligious individuals. This hypothesis was not supported in this analogue study. The participants, regardless of high or low Christian beliefs, rated the counselor differently depending on the manner in which the counselor responded to the client's religious values.

The counselor who ignored the client's religious values was more persuasive than was the counselor who supported the client's religious values. This may have been due to his responses being seen as more in line with what would be expected from a professional counselor. His responses emphasized the client's role in her family of origin as well as her relationship with her parents and thus focused on more "psychological" factors than "religious" ones. Pecnik and Epperson (1985) found that both Christian and non-Christian students expected a counselor labeled "Christian" to be less expert and effective than one whose religious views were not identified. As a result of focusing on religious material in a supportive manner, the counselor in this study may have been viewed by the participants as less expert and professional, and, consequently, less persuasive than was the counselor who focused on traditionally psychological material. Strong (1968) proposed that the perceived expertness of the counselor is an important component of social influence in the counseling relationship.

Another factor that may have been important is what Egan (1982) referred to as role competence. By belonging to a particular profession, a person is perceived as possessing the competence or expertness associated with that profession. By using overtly religious language in supporting the client's religious values, the supportive counselor may have been seen as trying to fulfill a role typically associated with the clergy rather than professional counselors. Therefore, he may have been seen as operating outside the area of his assumed expertise. On the other hand, the counselor who focused on psychological material responded in a manner consistent with the expectations of a professional psychologist and may have benefitted from the competence that the participants associated with that role.

The participants predicted that the client would improve more seeing the counselor who supported her religious values than seeing the counselor who challenged those values. They also indicated that they would be less likely to return to the challenging counselor than to either of the other two. Challenging the client's religious values was viewed less positively regardless of how similar the participants' religious values were to those expressed by the client. This suggests that the counselor's demonstration of respect for the client's religious values was more important to the participants than was their agreement with the particular content of those values. It has long been maintained that an important aspect of an effective helping relationship is the counselor's ability to understand the client's internal perspective and to communicate this understanding to the client (Rogers, 1951). The participants may have believed that the challenging counselor did not demonstrate enough understanding of the client's world as viewed through her religious values, and as a result, would not be as helpful.

The lack of Christian Belief x Counselor's Treatment of the Client's Religious Values interaction on any rating of the counselor, while contrary to the hypotheses of this study and to theorizing by Worthington (1988), is consistent with the findings of some other studies (Haugen & Edwards, 1976; Pecnik & Epperson, 1985). Haugen and Edwards (1976) found that Christian students listening to identical counseling sessions were not more attracted, receptive, persuaded, or willing to meet the counselor who was labeled "Christian" than the counselor who was labeled "non-Christian." Pecnik and Epperson (1985) found that after listening to identical counseling interactions, both Christian and non-Christian students rated the counselor labeled "Christian" as less expert. This indicates that a factor other than the counselor's similarity to the participants' identified value orientation was exerting a more powerful influence.

Worthington (1991) has suggested that a variety of other factors besides religious belief may influence religious values during counseling. Particularly strong are situational factors. Analogue studies have often not revealed differences in ratings of Christian and non-Christian counselors by Christian and non-Christian participants once the participants have been exposed to the actual counselor. This study supports previous research in this regard. Differences have routinely been found in preferences for Christian counselors by Christians—whether clients or not. This has extended to analogue studies about the effects of pretherapy information on counselor preference (Lewis & Epperson 1991) and anticipations about counseling (Keating & Fretz, 1990). Thus, it may be true that once a committed Christian person actually begins counseling, the outcome of counseling depends much more on exactly what happens in counseling than on the match of beliefs and values of counselor and client. Or, it may simply be true that this study did not assess Christian beliefs with enough precision. In addition, it may be that Christian belief is not the factor that affects observer perceptions; perhaps measures of religious values or Christian commitment would have yielded stronger effects.

Another alternative explanation exists. Goldsmith and Hansen (1991) have argued that Worthington's theorizing may apply especially to religious clients or other individuals who are experiencing psychological uncertainty rather than apply to all highly religious people. In that event, participants in this research and other analogue studies are students, not clients, and as students they may not judge religious counselors as would actual clients. Thus, future researchers should investigate judgments of counselors by people (highly committed versus less committed) who are psychologically distressed and those who are not, so that light may be shed on the validity of the numerous suggestive analogue studies that have addressed religious counseling.

Ideally, field studies of instances of counseling in which religious values are addressed are needed. Practical considerations make such studies unlikely. For example, in secular counseling and even in much religious counseling, discussion of religious topics is a low-frequency occurrence. In a field study, counselors who know that their behavior is being monitored in such low frequency events may not respond as they would had they been uninformed about the topic. If a researcher conducts a field study without informing the counselor about the topic under investigation, however, it would be necessary to listen to a prohibitive number of hours of audiotapes before an acceptable number of events (discussions of religious issues) could be collected. Researchers are encouraged to investigate religious counseling creatively, but much of what is learned will necessarily come from analogue studies.

Use of analogue methodology is obviously a limitation of the current study. Other methodological aspects of the study limit the conclusions that may be drawn. For instance, the videotape involved one male counselor and one female client, both Caucasian. Ideally, replication using other combinations of sex and race are needed to show that effects were not due simply to the particular (a) stimulus videotape and (b) race and sex combination in this study. In addition, this study considered a client with Christian values and measured only degree of commitment to Christian beliefs by the observers. Because of these limitations, findings should not be generalized to other races, sexes, religions, or even stimulus materials without circumspection.

REFERENCES

Bassett, R. L., Sadler, R. D., Kobischen, E. E., Skiff, D. M., Merrill, I. J., Atwater, B. J., & Livermore, P. W. (1981). The Shepherd Scale: Separating the sheep from the goats. *Journal of Psychology and Theology, 9*, 335-351.

Beutler, L. E. (1981). Convergence in counseling and psychotherapy: A current look. *Clinical Psychology Review, 1*, 79-101.

Crowne, D. P., & Marlowe, D. (1964). *The approval motive: Studies in evaluative dependence.* New York: Wiley.

Egan, G. (1982). *The skilled helper.* Monterey, CA: Brooks/Cole.

Glock, C. Y., & Stark, R. (1965). *Religion and society in tension.* Chicago: Rand McNally.

Goldsmith, W. M., & Hansen, B. K. (1991). Boundary areas of religious clients' values: Target for therapy. *Journal of Psychology and Christianity, 10*, 224-236.

Greenberg, R. P. (1969). Effects of pre-session information on perception of the therapist and receptivity to influence in a psychotherapy analogue. *Journal of Consulting and Clinical Psychology, 33*, 425-429.

Hathaway, S. J., & McKinley, J. C. (1943). *Minnesota Multiphasic Personality Inventory.* Minneapolis, MN: University of Minnesota Press.

Haugen, C. D., & Edwards, K. J. (1976). Religious values and their effect on the perception of a therapist in a psychotherapy analogue. *Journal of Psychology and Theology, 4*, 160-167.

Keating, A. M., & Fretz, B. R. (1990). Christians' anticipations about counselors in response to counselor descriptions. *Journal of Counseling Psychology, 37*, 293-296.

King, M. B., & Hunt, R. A. (1975). Measuring the religious variable: National replication. *Journal for the Scientific Study of Religion, 14*, 13-22.

Lewis, K. N., & Epperson, D. L. (1991). Values, pretherapy information, and informed consent in Christian counseling. *Journal of Psychology and Christianity, 10*, 113-131.

Pecnik, J. A., & Epperson, D. L. (1985). Analogue study of expectations for Christian and traditional counseling. *Journal of Counseling Psychology, 32*, 127-130.

Quackenbos, S., Privette, G., & Klentz, B. (1985). Psychotherapy: Sacred or secular? *Journal of Counseling and Development, 64*, 290-293.

Quackenbos, S., Privette, G., & Klentz, B. (1986). Psychotherapy and religion: Rapprochement or anti-thesis? *Journal of Counseling and Development, 65*, 82-85.

Rogers, C. R. (1951). *Client-centered therapy.* Boston: Houghton Mifflin.

Strong, S. R. (1968). Counseling: An interpersonal influence process. *Journal of Counseling Psychology, 15*, 215-224.

Truax, C. B. (1966). Reinforcement and non-reinforcement in Rogerian psychotherapy. *Journal of Abnormal Psychology, 71*, 1-9.

Watson, P. J., Morris, R. J., Foster, J. E., & Hood, R. W., Jr. (1986). Religiosity and social desirability. *Journal for the Scientific Study of Religion, 25*, 215-232.

Worthington, E. L., Jr. (1986). Religious counseling: A review of published empirical research. *Journal of Counseling and Development, 64*, 421-431.

Worthington, E. L., Jr. (1988). Understanding the values of religious clients: A model and its application to counseling. *Journal of Counseling Psychology, 35*, 166-174.

Worthington, E. L., Jr. (1991). Psychotherapy and religious values: An update. *Journal of Psychology and Christianity, 10*, 211-223.

Worthington, E. L., Jr., & Gascoyne, S. R. (1985). Preferences of Christians and non-Christians for five Christian counselors' treatment plans: A partial replication and extension. *Journal of Psychology and Theology, 13*, 29-41.

Worthington, E. L., Jr., & Scott, G. G. (1983). Goal selection for counseling with potentially religious clients by professional and student counselors in explicitly Christian or secular settings. *Journal of Psychology and Theology, 11*, 318-329.

The Spiritual Journey:
Explorations and Implications
for Counselors

ROBERT L. BARRET

SEVERAL TIMES IN the past few years I have felt "urged" to write about the ways in which my spiritual beliefs influence my behavior as a practicing counselor. Each time I have approached this task I have blocked myself from getting much done because it seemed so egocentric to suppose that this work would be valuable to anyone other than me. The urging persists, however, and because I have so often been touched by the way something familiar has been restated, I offer these thoughts for whatever they may be worth to you.

BACKGROUND

My family has a long-standing tradition in the church. The family Bible, printed in 1628 and filled with notations about generations of my forebears, remains in our ancestral home. One of the strongest memories of my child-hood is attending a small rural church with my grandparents. Around the sanctuary were plaques honoring various members of the Latta family, making a silent statement to me that, as a member of that family, I, too, belonged to the church. As a teenager I complied with this tradition. I was active in the youth program at my church and even attended a church-affili-ated college. Throughout those growing up years I wrestled with what I called my lack of faith and hoped that the day would come when I could participate in church services without having so many questions about whether or not I really believed all that the church said I should believe. Often I knew I had more disbelief than faith. I considered myself to be faith-ful to the church though, and I was convinced that reflection and reading would provide some of the answers that would allow me to find a place in the church.

Living in the South during the 1950s and 60s, it was hard not to question the faith that I had accepted. I remember police carting off Blacks who had come to my church one Sunday. And I recall that when Black and White

From "The Spiritual Journey: Explorations and Implications for Counselors," by R. L. Barret, 1988, *Journal of Humanistic Education and Development, 26,* 154–163.

college student leaders wanted to meet to share ideas about leadership, the only places available for meetings were the campuses of the Black colleges. The church-affiliated college I attended even admonished a student group to which I belonged for inviting an emerging Black leader to speak on campus.

Later, after marriage, I became active in another church. I liked the traditional form of worship, and I felt more "in contact" with a more active worship. Still, I never really talked about my doubts with anyone; I mostly just assumed that one of these days I would get it worked out. And so I passed through my 20s uncertain, but trying to make my faith work. Jolted at age 26 by the death of my best friend in an automobile accident, I spent weeks in intense confusion. "How can it be that Dan, who gave his life so fully to serving others, is dead, yet I, a businessman primarily involved in accumulating things, am still here?" I asked myself over and over. And at that time I decided that I could no longer put off resolving my spiritual questions. I knew that I needed to change careers, but before I made a choice I had to know my life plan.

I threw myself into church activities, and for a time, gave serious thought to going to a seminary. Looking back, I can see that a career in the church was simply an attempt to quell the doubts that worried me. As I looked into this decision, a minister friend suggested that I see a counselor who helped give me the courage to face my doubts and to understand myself more fully. So I abandoned the idea of attending seminary and became a schoolteacher instead. And, although the questions became more insistent, I continued to attend church regularly.

I sang the hymns, prayed the prayers, received the sacraments, listened to the sermons, went on retreats, and recited the creeds like my friends in church. But underneath I knew the words did not really reflect my beliefs, and I became angry with myself over what I saw as a major hypocrisy. Worship seemed as if it would be one of life's most sacred moments, an activity calling for ultimate honesty. But I knew that I had left my integrity at the door, for I did not really believe all that I repeated during the services. Unlike most of my church-going friends, I struggled constantly to understand how I could come into the presence of the God in whom I professed a belief while making statements that I knew I did not accept. The words of most of the hymns said things that I did not believe, the prayers I repeated were filled with requests for forgiveness and a salvation that has never made any sense to me.

Gradually I quit going to church, never feeling good about my decision, but knowing that I was making a mockery of the church if I simply stood there saying things I did not believe. It was hard for me to accept that I had abandoned the church; at times, I felt as if I had renounced my family. Internal criticism was pretty much constant as I wondered why I was unwilling just to let the church be what it is and not question it so much. Others seemed to be able to make this accommodation; why did I have to be so different? For a long time I considered myself not religious.

As I walked away, a part of me knew that I was giving up on something that had been an obvious source of strength and meaning to people I loved. I felt as if I had failed but knew that I had to get out, at least for a while. Almost immediately I stumbled in response to the uniquely Southern inquiry, "And what is your church?" Eventually I was able to state that I was not active in a church. Both the question and my answer left me uneasy, but I knew I was finally making honest statements about where I stood.

Even though I left the church, questions remained before me. And, if I do not go to church, where do I find the major sources of meaning in my life, and where can I celebrate and investigate my spirituality?

Of course, outwardly my life went on. I was enjoying being a teacher, having a family, and studying counseling in graduate school. Deciding to pursue a doctorate, I took a job at a church-related school. I knew this was a risk, but the chaplain there was a good friend, and I suppose on one level, I hoped that I could feel better about myself as a nonchurchgoer if I worked in a school with a religious connection. For a while that worked, but eventually, in the weekly chapel services, I found myself troubled by the suggestion that one church's love was inherently better than other forms of love. A break came when the student chapel committee asked me to speak in chapel about my religious struggle. In that talk I said, in part,

> I suspect that many of you also wonder if there is a way or a time that you will ever come to believe that God himself or herself or itself, really exists. I wonder that often: so many times I find myself upset when I go to church and see others easily reciting a creed that contains elements I do not accept.

The reaction to my talk was interesting. Many students expressed appreciation, and one faculty member thanked me. I felt that for the first time I had been honest in a worship service. I was also not too surprised when I was "given" a year's leave of absence the following spring and told that my job was being eliminated. It was clearly time for me to move on.

After finishing my degree with the completion of a clinical internship in a university counseling center, I accepted a teaching position, began a part-time private practice, and started doing volunteer counseling with cancer patients and their families. And I pretty much left the church, becoming one of a group that Bishop Jack Spong calls "the church alumni." And in some ways, leaving the church was the beginning of a new journey that is a lonely and often alienating experience. I read about the Eastern faiths while reading both the Old and New Testaments. I read contemporary theologians and talked with colleagues as often as they would put up with me. And I began to sense that my belief is in a Spirit that is available to all people, perhaps packaged in unique ways by all man-made institutions, but flowing from a universal source that touches all of us.

My readings led me to Thomas Merton (1961) who freed me with

> Our idea of God tells us more about ourselves than about God. We must learn to realize that the love of God seeks us in every situation and seeks our good. His inscrutable love seeks our awakening. True, since this awakening implies a kind of death to our exterior self, we will dread his coming in proportion as we are identified with this exterior self and attached to it. But when we understand the dialectic of life and death we will learn to take risks implied by faith, to make choices that deliver us from our routine self and open to us the door of a new being, a new reality. (p. 17)

My own sense of alienation was lessened as I read Merton's words for I knew that being true meant being outside the church, at least for now. My demand that the church speak to me suggested an attachment to the institution that blocked my growth and understanding. l had come to accept that my spiritual quest involved the asking of questions without the expectation of receiving absolute answers; yet every time I turned to the church I was given answers even before I had asked my questions.

THE PRESENT

The most difficult part of this writing is about to begin. I would like to explain where all of this searching has left me, or at least where I find myself at this particular point in time. Each of us is on a journey, and sometimes we meet each other along the way and share some time together. But ultimately I must go my own way aware that one of life's ironies is that my God is already with me and that my search is not for the answer but instead to find out how I can best be spiritual in all that I do. What being spiritual means for me in any given moment may be different from what that would mean to others. And being spiritual does not mean doing simply what "feels" good or worshipping at the shrine of the "Me generation." Being spiritual means letting go of attachments and living an intentional life where I try to give witness continually to the "that" which is within me. Being spiritual also means trying to live a life that is focused on acting spiritual.

> Every theology arises out of a certain praxis [practice], and it is also true that every praxis articulates, consciously or unconsciously, a certain theological view cr reality. This fact has largely been overlooked, especially in the religious life of the West. One reason it has been overlooked is that in many instances theology has been divorced from the idea of ministry; theology has become an abstract discipline, whereas ministry has been reduced to uniformed practice.... If no theology can be separated from the praxis that gives rise to it, then no praxis can be separated from the theological understanding that supports it. (Evans, 1986, p. 19)

A belief such as that expressed above calls for a faith that is action oriented in such a way that people live their lives at a more satisfactory level, and, at the same time, at a more intentional level.

My God surrounds the world filling rocks and trees and fish and grass and turtles and humans with spirit. My God is not "up there" but here with us, and life is lived with the simultaneous experience of both divinity and sin. As I live, one task is to have reverence for that divine spirit that is in all things. Life can become a constant experience of worship, once attachments can be given up. My more difficult attachments include the ego that I massage by using my God's power to glorify myself as a teacher, or counselor, or parent, or man who drives a new car and lives in a big house. Being spiritual means letting go of ego and "simply being."

So I "let go" and began to trust in myself more and to realize that God, or Spirit, or Whatever surely is within me, and that all I have to do is simply *be* so the spirit can flow out into the world through me. My quest then turned into a search for awareness of the sacred elements in my daily life. If I can shut off my ego and its demands for gratification and denial of pain, I often find myself in very profound places. Sometimes these are moments alone, and sometimes they are shared with others. Sacred moments exist all around me and offer opportunities to experience the spirit as I create my life. "Living in the spirit" or living an intentional life does not guarantee happiness, just a fuller awareness of being. Life demands that I encounter my own pain along with my joy and that I not allow my ego to demand a constantly "joyful" life. Often when I am true to the spirit in me I make choices that are the most difficult. The spirit calls me to risk in ways that frequently seem quite threatening and are, in fact, painful.

To summarize, as a spiritual person I affirm the divine that is in all things, and I attempt to live a life that continually reflects the divine in me, knowing that divinity and ego are mutually exclusive and that I must guard against getting confused and seeing them as one and the same. My life can become a constant worship experience when I succeed in shutting Me off and letting the spirit flow through me. In those moments, all is prayer and sacred. One of the hardest aspects of this belief is that I do often feel very alone and alien as I see people around me finding abundant meaning and company in their church lives. And sometimes I get quite frustrated as I attempt to justify my spiritual life to them, for, true to their belief, they attempt to justify their spiritual life to me.

I do not worry much about salvation or the hereafter. Instead, I try to concentrate on being as true to the spirit as I can in this life; the next life, if it exists, will then take care of itself. I believe Jesus would be embarrassed by what churches have done to him, just as I think Buddha would not rejoice at seeing temples erected in his memory. Creating religious institutions is a natural human activity, but is often a flawed endeavor because institutions, once established, have a way of subverting their original purpose to protect themselves. The dogma that permeates and protects the institution often wanders far from the theology and practice espoused by prophets.

My belief does suggest a life of service. And the service goes two ways. First, there is the service of the spirit in which I shut down my ego and my own selfish needs and examine the ways that my activities illuminate the spiritual parts of my being. And second, probably everything (although I constantly fall short of this ideal) that I do is best done in the service of others. I must put myself in situations that allow the spirit in me to flow out to lessen the pain that others may feel. This act can be something as simple as a greeting or as complex as a counseling session.

COUNSELING AND THE SPIRITUAL LIFE

My work as a counselor is one of the places in my life that is most sacred. I have come to understand that the process is most helpful when I can leave my ego with its demands that the client change or acknowledge my power and simply let myself be with this other human and his or her pain. When I can "not try" but simply "be," both of us enter a highly reverent moment that can be filled simultaneously with pain and joy and lead to much insight and new behavior. Sometimes, however, puffed up with my own importance and power, I work very hard at getting the client to the place I believe is most desirable and expend much energy pushing and pulling with a variety of techniques, my "bag of tricks," to force movement. What I need to remember is that movement will come when the person is ready, and that when I simply accompany my clients along the way, shining my light on significant events, and going with them into their pain, experiencing that pain with them, and then watching their transformation as the pain takes on new shapes, the most growth occurs. As I see their transformation take place I am filled with an awareness of the sacredness of that moment, and I, too, am transformed. I try to help them formulate their questions and then to be present as they struggle to find their answers. And it may be that in the time of transformation, my sense of reality may differ from theirs, but we are joined in a moment that we both perceive as profound and sacred. We are united in a spiritual experience that changes both of us.

Counseling is an art, and communicating its message depends on the gifts of the aspirant who must reinvent the art within himself or herself. I believe that, as a counselor, I am practicing from two sources: a vast spiritual experience that I share with all humans, and a set of theoretical and technical beliefs that may help me understand the person before me. Once the relationship is established, if the spiritual in me touches the spiritual in the other, both of us are transformed. It is not necessary that my illusions about reality be affirmed, nor that I accept the other's reality. Despite our poverty and fragmentation, what is powerful is that always-present depth of being that simply is. It is this depth that both unites and isolates us, but that allows us to relate so that the other is changed. The separation and fusion that we both experience in the moment of transformation flow not only from the extremes of experience, but also from a source outside both of us, yet permeating everything around us. The union of consciousness that we experience together has no boundaries; it both is and is not. And this deep spirit allows us to be both created and destroyed as we contact it. Pain in our lives is simply one way of calling us back to it so that we can be transformed anew, freed from the oppressions that have captured and bound our spirit (Smith, 1980).

I am suddenly aware that many might accuse me of making psychology into a religion, or that I am suggesting that the spiritual process is simply that which is called secular humanism by more conservative groups—the idolization of the individual who functions at the highest level when doing "what feels right for me." Psychology is not a religion. And not all counseling is a spiritual experience. But, the process of counseling enables many to tap into an inner source that, previously denied or lost to awareness, imbues life with abundant meaning and purpose. In this sense, counseling may be a deeply spiritual event, not because it enables the client simply to "feel good" but because it does refresh a soul that has been impoverished, and it does reduce feelings of alienation and loneliness by freeing the client to enter more fully, more completely, and more wholly into relationship with others. As this happens the counselor becomes a spiritual guide for the client (Jones, 1982).

Perhaps you are wondering how anyone can tolerate the intensity of such a process when seeing five or six clients every day? For me, every counseling session does not carry the wallop of such emotional intensity; it definitely involves bits and pieces of it. But over time, I believe that we will enter that sacred spot where defenses are dropped and things begin to shift so that the client is changed. I am not altogether sure how to maximize that moment, or how to encourage its coming sooner. Often I leave my office at the end of the day absolutely deflated, feeling that I have given and given, and nothing much has happened. But when the spirit strikes and I have been with a client in one of those special moments, I am refreshed and absolutely certain that both of us have been changed.

So what, then, is the connection with my spiritual life and the work I do with clients? For some, those who are in the deepest despair, I am the watchman in the night, the person who is willing to accompany the client on a fearsome inward journey that has an indistinct destination, at best. And as I travel along with these persons, I am helpful when I follow their lead and shine a light on specific content so that it may be further illuminated for them. I liken the experience of being a counselor to that of going into a dark cave with a person who is afraid of what may be found. As we walk along, my client in front of me, the client describes what we pass. My job is to shine the light on particular places and say something like, "Look at that more closely. Tell me more about that." As this previously clouded and perhaps forbidding content becomes more familiar, the client is less afraid and more able to make sense of current behavior. Sometimes this "illumination" takes place slowly and without a tremendous amount of emotion; but other times the client experiences the "Aha" and a shift occurs that touches both of us, and heals both of us in unknown ways.

This account may sound a bit like confession, absolution, and redemption. And in some ways those terms do fit parts of this process. As clients talk about material that has been very frightening, often the sense of disappointment and shame is abated as their deeds are accepted by another. Using words like *confession* is probably not helpful to clients mainly because those words are so often laden with meanings that can lead the process away from the critical issue at hand. I do not want to "lay my experience" on the client; I am hopeful that I can provide the freedom for the client to find personal meanings without being influenced more than necessary by my beliefs. It is not my place to offer forgiveness; the client must find a personal forgiveness, if that is what is required.

I have learned that it is not so important to find answers to the questions that nag at me. I will probably never make peace with the church. But I will go on asking my questions, aware that in the asking, a vital part of me is being expressed. And now at mid-life, I am beginning to understand that the questions change a bit over the years. The answers I sought when I was 16 do not seem nearly as important as those I seek today. And sometimes I am aware that a bit of an answer has been found, that I am at peace with my search, perhaps more comfortable going it alone rather than insisting that the church or some other group reach out to me and say "yes, you are right." This awareness does not mean that my spiritual authority rests within. It does mean that I must use my own experience, the thoughts of others, and much meditative thought to come to conclusions that work for me.

Peck (1972) has noted a simple, but profound truth, "Life is difficult" (p. 15). This teaching, borrowed from the Four Noble Truths given by Buddha, is explained by Buddhists as Life is suffering or Life is out of joint. This suffering can be seen in the trauma of birth, the pathology of sickness, the fear of old age, the fear of death, the anguish of being tied to what one hates, being separated from what one loves, and the painful input that comes from the five senses. The cause of such suffering is the desire to pull apart from life and seek fulfillment through self. Acknowledging that life is difficult and is filled with pain can free people to focus their attention on the corresponding meaning that life also provides. And just as certainly, with intent, humans can rise above this angst, not forsaking all of the pain, but living with the pain in such a way that the meaning of life is experienced more fully.

I suppose the crux of this article is that counseling, just as religion does, seeks to ameliorate the pain of living and to focus the individual on the more positive aspects of life. Psychological growth begins when one accepts himself or herself as he or she is in that moment. Spiritual growth begins when one experiences acceptance just as one is. And for me, at times, these two "growths" come together as I am privileged to be with another person who is attempting to bring clarity and meaning from a life that seems painful and hopeless. The healing awareness of both the source and meaning of this pain often comes as a surprise to both of us. It is a gift that comes from "something" beyond both of us, something I believe is spiritual and profoundly sacred. In that moment both of us are renewed and strengthened. I hope for more of those moments in my experiences both as a counselor and as a human.

REFERENCES

Evans, J. H. (1986). Faith and praxis in theology. *Counseling and Values, 31,* 17-28.

Jones, A. (1982). *Exploring spiritual direction: An essay on Christian friendship.* Minneapolis: Winston Press.

Merton, T. (1961). *New seeds of contemplation.* New York: New Directions.

Peck, M. S. (1978). *The road less traveled: A new psychology of love, traditional values and spiritual growth.* New York: Simon & Schuster.

Smith, A. H. (1980). Reflections at the grave of a mystic. *Voices, 16*(1), 58-63.

Soul Healing:
A Model of
Feminist Therapy

PATRICIA M. BERLINER

DOROTHY RIDDLE DECLARES, "Our revolution is about how we relate to our love and our power, and about finally realizing that they are the same" (1975, p. 16).

The convergence of love and power is lived out in my life as a sister of St. Joseph, a psychologist and practicing psychotherapist, and a member of the multidisciplinary team of Women for a New World. The ideas of the other two members, Donna Flynn and Sister Judith Shea, helped shape our psychospiritual perspective. I wish that you could all take part in one of our retreat-workshops, but because this is not possible, I will try to communicate to you the spirit and power of our work and explore its implications as a model of therapy as soul healing.

Although it may be difficult for some psychotherapists to acknowledge the spiritual dimension in a person's life, I believe that any therapist who calls a client to change through deeper self-knowledge is in the gray area of connectedness between psychology and spirituality (Allport, 1950; Batson & Ventis, 1982; Conn, 1978, 1981; Frank, 1977; Jung, 1933; Maslow, 1964; May, 1969; Sellner, 1990). Both psychological growth and spiritual conversion draw the person out of old ways of being, through the deaths such letting go requires, and into liberating forms of life consistent with one's true self. Whether or not they consider their work to be *spiritual*, therapists who are able to do this are effecting the original meaning of the work *therapeia*, of which one meaning was *soul healing*.

The work of Women for a New World and of therapy as soul healing, is to help women and men discover the nurturing god, the spark of the divine feminine, in themselves and to love what they discover. Author-playwright Ntozage Shange celebrates "I found god in myself and I loved her, loved her fiercely" (1980, p. 67). This discovery of the divine in ourselves begins in the dark, scary places of our own personal and social histories, the places where powerlessness and fear, potential and hope converge. In this convergence, often experienced as conflict and sometimes as crisis, transformation becomes possible.

From "Soul Healing: A Model of Feminist Therapy," by P. M. Berliner, 1992, *Counseling and Values, 37,* 2–14.

The psychospiritual workshops developed by the team of Women for a New World are intended to provide an environment where that transformation can take place. Combining the feminist principles of consciousness raising and networking with practice in introspective and expressive techniques (cf. Harris, 1989; Iglehart, 1983; West, 1987), we endeavor to model and foster egalitarian, growth enhancing relationships (Greenspan, 1983; Rosewater & Walker, 1985; Sturdivant, 1980; Tschirhart-Sanford & Donovan, 1984; Young-Eiserdrath, 1987). We work to create an alliance in which both participants and facilitators feel safe enough to move inward, where the process of soul healing begins.

HISTORY OF WOMEN FOR A NEW WORLD

The history of Women for a New World is a long one that is, in many ways, itself a chronicle of convergence and transformation. The seed of change took root in my own life in the early 1970s. I came to adulthood when Pope John XXIII was opening the windows and doors of the Roman Catholic church, and Betty Friedan started the women's movement by asking "Is that all there is?" But in 1966, the year that I graduated from a Catholic women's college and entered the sisters of St. Joseph, I was much more conscious of the freedom a women's environment provided than of our subordination within the institutions that had shaped us.

My awareness began to change one day in 1974 when a friend commented on the sexist language in church hymns. I told her it didn't much matter since no one heard the words anyway. Soon after, I heard the words!

In 1975, I accepted an invitation to write the religion chapter for a textbook on women as strangers. My research put me in contact with women from several religious traditions—orthodox Jewish women to Salvation Army workers, Lutheran deaconnesses to cloistered nuns. None of us thought of ourselves as being radical, but all of our stories reflected deep pain and awareness that something was very wrong within each of our denominational structures.

One of the women I interviewed, a Roman Catholic theologian, invited me to join a group of women she was forming. I did not know the term *consciousness raising* then, but I did know that it was unusual and refreshing for married women, single women, and nuns to be meeting together. At first we discussed books; soon we began talking about ourselves, our problems, lives, and visions.

Gradually we moved outward. Four of us named ourselves Women for a New World and sponsored a series of lectures by women experts in their fields. Unaware of the fame of some of our speakers, we invited such women as Robin Morgan, and they came, without fee, to our borrowed storefront. After this series, Women for a New World was absorbed by a women's center, but one of the women, Donna Flynn, and I had become friends and began dreaming about what Women for a New World could be. Donna has always believed that the simple yesses we said then—yes to a women's discussion group, yes to a lecture series, yes to a friendship—shaped the vision that has transformed our lives.

At that time, unknown to myself, I was gaining a reputation for my interest in women's issues and, in 1980, I was invited to give a three-evening course for religious educators on Women in Today's World.

Because we were all living examples of women in today's world and church, I decided to draw on our own life experiences. Rather than lecturing, I created a reflective environment, structuring sessions around three themes: lifethread (Who am I when I am most true to myself?), demons (What keeps me from being that self?), and angels (What helps me to be that self?). I located each theme within a psychological and spiritual context, and introduced questions for reflection and time for discussion.

The presentation-reflection-discussion format proved to be effective within a framework that had both strengths and limitations. Participants had time for reflection between sessions, but because they were involved in their normal routines, quality time and space were not easy to find. Also, feedback indicated that three 2-hour sessions just weren't enough.

The response of participants challenged me to develop this workshop further. The opportunity to do so came from Sister Dorothy Mennis, who invited me to offer a weekend at the retreat house where she was a spiritual director. I thought that another person's expertise and perspective could broaden, augment, and balance my own, so I invited Dorothy to work with me on the program. The first *for women only* weekend was based around the three themes I had introduced in the earlier workshop.

I learned a lot about myself and about women's needs on this weekend. First, because I was working with a person whom I identified as the *spiritual* part of the team, I focused on the *psychological*. I was so careful not to mention the word *God* that I contributed to the very separation of psychology and spirituality I was trying to bridge. Then, because I thought the women needed time for reflection, I determined that the weekend would be a mostly quiet time. I was angry and appalled when the women used their free time to talk among themselves. Only later did I realize that they were meeting their own needs to bond, to share their stories, and to create the environment that would be most beneficial for them. When I recognized that given the opportunity, women would choose what they needed, I was able to loosen my hold on the process. I learned the hard way that women did not want to be told what to do or have words put into their mouths.

The third change was made because most of the women who attended the weekend were not members of religious congregations and both team members were. I thought that this might cast doubt on the credibility and relevance of our experiences. Before we offered the weekend a second time, I invited Donna Flynn, who had attended the first weekend, to become part of the team.

We thought that Donna would represent primarily the experience of a married Catholic woman and jokingly introduced ourselves as *the psycho, the spiritual,* and *the dash in between.* But Donna's honest sharing of her life, her *housewife hiding behind the apron* stories, proved to be the piece that changed the tenor of the weekend from the giving of information to the telling of stories. Donna's professional expertise as a nurse and religious educator as well as her introduction of relaxation techniques, creative expression, and guided imagery encouraged further emphasis on the concrete and experiential and completed the body-mind-spirit dialectic.

As we reviewed what happened on our weekends, we realized that we were most comfortable and effective when we entered the process as participant-facilitators, as catalysts rather than experts. This choice allowed all of us, participants and facilitators, the freedom to enter into an evolutionary process. Letting go of our expectations of ourselves and others, we could create a safe space, coming together to reflect on our experiences, tell our stories, give creative expression to our struggles and discoveries, and celebrate our feminine qualities in ritual forms.

Encouraged by the success of our weekends, Donna and I continued to work together. For a long time, we created programs only at the invitation of interested church-related groups (primarily because we did not have the finances to risk sponsoring our own programs). Then in May 1989, we resurrected our identity and sponsored our first program as Women for a New World. For this weekend, entitled *Touching the Sacred: Play as Sacrament,* we invited Judith, an artist, art educator, and longtime friend, to join the team. Her gift of being able to create a prayerful, aesthetic environment from the simplest of materials and to bring out the artist in all of us has become an invaluable addition.

As a result of this weekend, we began to develop programs for women who had expressed an interest in our work. For example, one year we offered a five-part series on *Celebrating the Season.* Remaining faithful to our Roman Catholic tradition, these days provide an opportunity for community building and creative celebration of feminine ritual that is not available in the institutional church. We think of ourselves as offering *feminist* programs for *nonfeminist* women. Through our orientation, we help the women to recognize that *good women* have a centuries' old tradition of resistance to and overcoming of oppression within the structures of church and society (Harris, 1989; Kohlbenschlag, 1986; Osiek, 1986; Reuther, 1985, 1988; Solle, 1984). Discovering role models whose lives they can identify with enables the women to define their own spirituality within a "feminist heritage and history they can feel good about" (Rader, 1980, cassette tape) and be a part of.

Interestingly, although the primary focus of our work is still Roman Catholic women, we have accepted an increasing number of invitations from mixed groups, including the Christophers, divorced and separated Catholics, advocates for the homeless, and people affected by AIDS (including family and friends of those with AIDS).

Whenever we are invited to create a program, we first try to understand the issues and needs of the people who will be coming. We ask ourselves what we would want from this experience if we were participants, and then we struggle together to shape our unique perspectives, gifts, and visions into a common vision of what we hope to communicate. When the process works, we touch the divine in ourselves and one another and are empowered to be channels of that creative power for others.

Judith believes that Brigit, a Celtic goddess, is an apt patroness for Women for a New World. Although Brigit is a unified being, she presents herself in three aspects, a feminine trinity. As the muse, Brigit reflects the spirit of truth; as warrior, keeper of the forge and fire, she provides tools for meeting life's struggles courageously; as the lady of the land, she is guardian of the healing elements of nature, opening us to our own healing powers.

HOW WOMEN FOR A NEW WORLD WORKS

What Does Judith's Metaphor for Who We Are and What We Do Look Like in Practice?

One of the programs we were invited to give was a winter day for people affected by AIDS. The group sponsoring the day had no idea of who or how many people would come. All we had to work with was a title, *Flowers in the Snow.* The three of us immediately related to the title, then panicked as we questioned our qualifications to speak to this group. We finally decided that we knew about flowers, about snow, and about people, and proceeded from there.

In the several times we met to plan and to pray for the people who would attend, we reflected on the title and offered ideas about how it might be expressed. We argued for our own perspectives and struggled to listen to one another's. After we came up with a tentative overview and some content, each of us chose the piece of the presentation-reflection-experiential format we wanted to work on and went to work. It takes a great deal of trust to leave with things unfinished and believe that it will turn out well.

When we arrived on the day of the program, we found an ugly church basement transformed into a welcoming setting of flowers in the snow. Greeted by Robert, the man who had created the title of the day, we invited him to join us in our prayer for the success of the day. Then we were ready to start.

As theme setter, I began by telling the group how drawn we had been by the title and asked what it had meant to them. The responses had a power shaped by their own experiences of pain, love, and presence to healing in the face of tragedy. Framing my presentation around their responses, I reflected on the image of flowers in the snow as mirroring the process of growth from resistance to receptivity to responsiveness. I closed with the song *The*

Rose (1979). Donna built a guided imagery from my introduction, drawing people into their own places of flowers in the snow. Judith then invited us to make our own and ritualize the experiences through the work of our hands. After showing us how to transform circles of white tissue paper and pipe cleaners, she sent us off to reflect and to make our flowers a prayer. I sat next to a man who was writing name after name of people on his circles. All I could do was say "so many names" and begin to cry. A woman across from me took my hand, saying "but they're here with us." Later, as she drew the face of a child who had died of AIDS, I could take her hand. When we reconvened, people talked about their flowers and about the day. One man was grateful that we had not talked at (lectured) him. A tough looking teenager spoke of how hard it is to be HIV positive and thanked the group for making him feel welcome and safe. A petite woman told how struck she had been by the dainty, delicate flowers being made by "the biggest man here." An 80-year-old nun talked about the patients she visited, and the woman who had taken my hand grieved for the 3-year-old who had died. As we ended with a prayer of thanksgiving for the passing of winter, we gathered our flowers and prayers into one large basket.

What we did was so simple. We brought people together. We created an environment where they felt safe enough to share pain, struggles, successes, and hopes. We offered time for reflection and left them free to accept or reject an invitation to move more deeply into their own inner places. We affirmed the wisdom of their lives. We provided a variety of techniques that heightened the body-mind-spirit connection. Mostly, we trusted our humanity, reflected the struggle to live our own truth, and offered hope and support for the journey.

IMPLICATIONS FOR THE PRACTICE OF THERAPY

What Does This Have To Do With Soul Healing?

Women for a New World has taught me about the political as well as the personal dimension of my work as a psychotherapist. After the first few *for women only* weekends, I began to realize that we were not providing just a socially acceptable weekend away. When I started to ask participants what had attracted them and what they got from the weekend, I discovered a consistency in their responses. Most said that they felt as if there were a crack in their world, whose pieces no longer fit together. These women, raised in the patriarchal ideal of the *good woman* (Belenky et al., 1986; Bepko & Krestan, 1990), were taught to believe that, if they took care of everyone else's needs, theirs, too, would be met. When the women's movement touched their lives, they began to suspect that this ideal was neither true nor healthy. The women's movement challenged *good women* to accept that they had both the right to have their needs met and the obligation to find ways to fulfill those needs.

I discovered that the attempt to reconcile their traditional ideals with their new insights constituted a major conflict for the women in our population. These women were struggling to define for themselves what it means to be *good*. They were looking for ways to liberate themselves from the oppressive elements of the ideal of the good woman without having to sacrifice their traditional values and lifestyles. They also were seeking ways to continue to be caring persons, finally able to include themselves in that caring. I believe they were trying to *revalue the feminine* (Berliner, 1990). In my understanding, this involves women's learning to value themselves as unique individuals and as women and to reclaim the power of the feminine in their lives.

To better understand the process of change, I decided to develop a schema. This schema included feedback from workshop participants about their lives and the process of the weekends. It helped us to conceptualize their conflicts and the process of resolution that was taking place. Representing growth as a continuum of change from self-hatred to self-esteem, I identified four marker points, or phases, of the good woman in transition: the *self-less* woman, who has no sense of herself as a person of value, the *self-ish* woman, whose validity depends on her adherence to rules and roles, the *self-centered* woman, who has moved toward establishing a personal identity, and the *centered self*, whose contemplative stance contributes to her acceptance of herself as a unique and valuable individual, at home in both her inner and outer worlds (see Figures 1-4). (Sister Karen Cavanagh [personal communication, February, 1991], adapting this schema for a seminar on the psychology of women, framed the phases as: Am I? What am I? Who am I? And I am who I am.)

Each of the points on the continuum is characterized by pulls to oppression and liberation, which constitute the conflict of that stage, and by psychological and spiritual developmental issues, whose resolution moves the good woman into the next phase of growth. One of the contributions of the retreat-workshops is their ability to provide an environment and tools with which good women can resolve their conflicts in ways that lift the pulls to oppression and strengthen the pulls to liberation. Further research needs to be done to assess the applicability of this model to the lives of *good men*, but it would seem that whatever is liberating for women may also be liberating for men.

My life experiences as a good woman and my professional experience in working with this population have led me to conclude that using my love and power as a therapist consists in helping people resolve the conflict manifested in pulls to oppression and pulls to liberation.

Although our retreat-workshops do not represent formal therapy, they do provide a therapeutic environment. I have found that people who come for therapy, like those who attend our programs, are hurting and are looking

FIGURE 1
"Self-less": No Self

Characteristic of the Stage	Contribution of the Workshop
Oppression	*Lifts Oppression*
Devaluation of women	Presents a model of women as valid
Abuse	and valuable, inherent goodness
Women as weak, secondary, inferior	Points out the oppressive elements of
Female role models perpetuate the	the ideology and ways in which
ideology	women contribute to, or can refuse to
	contribute to, their own oppression
Liberation	*Liberation*
Experiences of self as valid	Experiences affirmation as a person
Experiences of the validity and strength	through telling and hearing of
of women and of caretaking qualities	personal stories, unfolding and
Realizing that a woman does not need	sharing of personal creativity
to see herself as a victim or as	
responsible for the problems of a	
nonnurturing ideology	
Conflict	*Creates New Conflict*
Are women really valid?	Do I have a right to change?
If I don't blame myself, whom can I	What will happen when I stop hating
blame?	myself?
Am I responsible for others?	What will my world look like? Who will
How can I be a caretaker without being	be in it?
responsible?	
Do I want to be a caretaker? Can I care	
for me?	
Developmental Issues	*Resolution of Developmental Issues*
Misplaced anger—turned inward and	Directing anger outward
not directed against the real sources	Refusing to be a victim
of devaluation	
Fear of one's own power—being able to	
take care of oneself	
Fear of abandonment	
Spirituality	*Converted Spirituality*
God as patriarch: creator of the	God who cares about us and accepts
ideology	us as we are
Vengeful God: rewards and punishes	We do not have to prove ourselves to
God of Fear	God
Uncaring God	We are created in God's love, not "No-
Why did God make me to begin with?	selves"
Church perpetuates fear	God accepts our anger—even at God—
Unloved by parenting figures: cannot	there is justifiable anger
experience being loved by God	"I have loved you with an everlasting
	love"
	"God looked upon creation and saw
	that it was good"

FIGURE 2
"Self-ish": Rules and Roles

Characteristic of the Stage	Contribution of the Workshop
Oppression Male-defined femininity Rules protect women and give them identity Women defined as weak Ideology conveys idea of reachable perfection of womanhood: perfect = inferior, weak	*Lifts Oppression* Gives women options; nothing on weekend is mandatory Permits and invites naming and choosing what she needs Offers a searching environment, supportive of her questioning and in company with other searchers
Liberation Realize that perfection is impossible See the strengths in caretaking, but the oppressive nature of the ideology See other models of caring persons who reflect possibility of including self without depriving others	*Liberation* Affirmation of gifts and strengths Validation of need and obligation to take care of self Self-caring as freeing of self and others Offers women opportunity to learn techniques of self-care and relaxation and explore personal forms of creativity
Conflict Good is bad condundrum—caring is limited, if I do what is good for me, I will deprive others; if I take care of others, to the exclusion of myself, I will not have my needs met. How can I balance the two?	*Creates New Conflict* What will happen to her world and relationships if she begins to include herself in her caring? What will happen if she begins to see herself as strong instead of weak and dependent?
Developmental Issues Not enough sense of self to build from Guilt Dependency issues	*Resolution of Developmental Issues* Make choices in spite of guilt about choosing for self Begin to identify the negative impact on others of supposed caring behaviors Letting go of ideological definition of perfection
Spirituality God as Authority/Lawgiver God of Justice No room for error or deviation from rules; rules provide security, but also structure Rituals ensure relationship and rightness with God External relationship with God and faith	*Converted Spirituality* Meeting the God who supports her well-being and personal integrity Begin to see church as human institution Begin to see that we are all part of what makes church Question childlike relationship to God "I set before you life and death: Choose life" Parable of the talents

FIGURE 3
"Self-Centered": Personal Identity

Characteristic of the Stage	Contribution of the Workshop
Oppression Lack of support for emerging identity Autonomy versus dependence	*Lifts Oppression* Support from others who are also struggling with conflict between autonomy and dependence or who have moved beyond this struggle and provide role models Affirmation of strengths and successes
Liberation Experience of personal strength Making choices for one's own needs and experiencing success and affirmation Sense of self-esteem begins to emerge when taking responsibility for choices	*Liberation* Opportunities for self-expression and creativity Introduction to process of discernment: What is moving me and what feels congruent and right; inferiority of decision making God's spirit moves within me Now has a self to measure against
Conflict Where do I belong? Accepting the consequences of taking responsibility for personal choices, especially when not affirmed or supported by significant others Struggle to go on in face of opposition	*Creates New Conflict* Coming to grips with recognition that she has choices and that her choices make a difference Needing to set up means for support systems to enable follow-through on choices, especially stresses related to becoming autonomous woman
Developmental Issues Need to protect self Move forward or retreat Accept personal power	*Resolution of Developmental Issues* Gaining personal autonomy and independence without losing connectedness with other persons Discovering identity and meaning outside of traditional roles; finding different meaning within traditional roles Integrating past; not rejecting it
Spirituality God as beyond the limits of the institution God is inside me as well as beyond Church institution may be rejected for a time to allow for discovery and deepening of relation with personal God Church rules lose power	*Converted Spirituality* God of integrity, history, community I-Thou relationship with God The gift you have received, give as gift Parable of the vine and the branches Movement to interior awareness of relationship with God I am the Church Co-creation with God

FIGURE 4
"Centered Self": Contemplative Womanhood

Characteristic of the Stage	Contribution of the Workshop
Oppression Danger of navel gazing Overwhelmed by realities of world's needs	*Lifts Oppression* Encourage women to see themselves as containing inner resources and unity of community of women Inherent unity and wholeness of all creation
Liberation Enabled to be freer caretakers of self, others Recognition of relation to, but not domination over, all of creation— being part of a larger picture Experience of meaningful, loving relationship	*Liberation* Frees women to see the power in the feminine qualities Caring = caring about Develops feminine images of God
Conflict Freedom creates responsibility Role of the good woman contributes to perpetuating oppression Recognition of gifts and limitations Acceptance of mortality	*Creates New Conflict* Shows that women have the power to effect change, however limited, and encourages them to take and use that power (ripple effect) Encourages rejection of victim stance and victim behavior
Developmental Issues Freedom and responsibility: being feminine and adult Forgiveness of self and reconciliation with life for oppressive or death-dealing elements	*Resolution of Developmental Issues* Recognition of power of caretaking qualities as different from power over Recognition of mortality and limitation Rejection of victim stance in favor of active participation in life
Spirituality God as mystery, adventurer Finding God in the inner depths, at the central core of being Church as faulted, limited, human but a place created by people who come together to find and bring God	*Converted Spirituality* God of love, person as co-creator Active, responsible stance toward life Contemplative dimension nourished, generating response to all of creation: one with the source We are the church "You are the salt of the earth; you are the light of the world" "Love God and love your neighbor as you love yourself"

for ways to stop their pain They are not likely to recognize that in the pain and conflict lies the opportunity for growth.

In my practice of individual psychotherapy I have adapted the participant-facilitator role to that of companion-guide (Berliner, 1983). As companion-guide, I accompany my clients into the yet to be discovered hurting and healing places in themselves. I try to create a safe place in the midst of their upturned worlds and offer them weapons for the struggle and tools for the reconstruction of their world. If I am teaching my clients to trust the process, I, too, must trust the process, letting go of answers so that I have room to listen to the questions. I try to reflect to each person the voice that I hear and the wisdom that it speaks. And I try to open myself to their struggle, because I, too, am on a journey and need to learn from them. If it works, then all of us, having walked together for a while, can say "I found god in myself and I loved her, loved her fiercely" (Shange, 1980, p. 67).

REFERENCES

Allport, G. (1950). *The individual and his religion: A psychological interpretation*. New York: Macmillan.

Batson, C. D., & Ventis, W. L. (1982). *The religious experience*. New York: Oxford Press.

Belenky, M. F., Clinchy, N. G., & Tarule, J. (1986). *Women's ways of knowing: The development of self, voice and mind*. New York: Basic Books.

Bepko, C., & Krestan, J. (1990). *Too good for her own good: Free from the burden of female responsibility*. Grand Rapids: Harper and Row.

Berliner, P. (1983). Journey into being: The counselor as companion-guide. *Counseling and Values, 27*, 105-111.

Berliner, P. (1990). *Revaluing the feminine: The process of psychospiritual change in contemporary Roman Catholic women*. (University Microfilms, No. 9102606).

Conn, W. (Ed.). (1978). *Conversion: Perspectives in personal social transformation*. New York: Alba House.

Conn, W. (Ed.). (1981). *Conscience development and self-transcendence*. Birmingham, AL: Religious Education Press.

Frank, J. (1977). Nature and the functions of belief systems: Humanism and transcendental religion. *American Psychologist, 32*, 555-559.

Greenspan, M. (1983). *A new approach to women and therapy*. New York: McGraw Hill.

Harris, M. (1989). *Dance of the spirit: The seven steps of women's spirituality*. New York: Bantam.

Iglehart, H. (1983). *Woman spirit: A guide to women's wisdom*. San Francisco: Harper and Row.

Jung, C. (1983). *Modern man in search of a soul*. New York: Harcourt Brace.

Kohlbenschlag, M. (1986, October). *Feminist spirituality: Beginnings*. Presented at the Women in Church Conference, Washington, DC.

Maslow, A. (1964). *Religion, values and peak practices*. New York: Viking Press.

May, R. (1969). *Existential psychology*. New York: Random House.

Osiek, C. (1986). *Beyond anger: On being a feminist in the church*. New York: Paulist.

Rader, R. (1980). *The myths and realities of the history of religious women*. (Cassette tape). Collegeville, MN: Liturgical Press.

Reuther, R. (1985). *Woman church: The theology and practice of feminist liturgical communities*. San Francisco: Harper and Row.

Reuther, R. (1988). Christian quest for redemptive community. *Cross Currents, 28*, 3-16.

Riddle, D. (1975). New visions of spiritual power. *Quest, 1*(4), 7-16.

The Rose. (1979). New York: Atlantic Recording Company.

Rosewater, L. B., & Walker, L. (Eds.). (1985). *Handbook of feminist therapy: Women's issues in psychotherapy.* New York: Springer Publishing Company.

Sellner, E. (1990). *Mentoring: The ministry of spiritual kinship.* Notre Dame, IN: Ave Maria Press.

Shange, N. (1980). *For colored girls who have considered suicide where the rainbow is enuf.* New York: Bantam.

Solle, D. (1984). *The strength of the weak: Toward a Christian feminist identity.* Philadelphia: Westminster Press.

Sturdivant, S. (1980). *Therapy with women: A feminist philosophy of treatment.* New York: Springer Publishing Company.

Tschirhart-Sanford, L., & Donovan, M. E. (1984). *Women and self-esteem.* Garden City: Anchor Press/Doubleday.

West, M. (Ed.). (1987). *The psychology of meditation.* Oxford: Claredon Press.

Young-Eisendrath, P., & Wiedemann, F. (1987). *Female authority: Empowering women through psychotherapy.* New York: Guilford Press.

Moving Through Loss:
The Spiritual Journey of Gay Men
and Lesbian Women

KATHLEEN Y. RITTER
CRAIG W. O'NEILL

FROM BIRTH, ALL human beings embark on a journey that entails a series of losses at every stage of life. Just as there are losses associated with being heterosexual, there are also losses that are frequently a part of the lesbian and gay experience in our society. As they move through their lives, gay men and lesbian women often turn for renewal in the same directions as heterosexuals, namely, to traditional religion and to mental health professionals. In the course of looking to these groups for enabling and understanding, they can sometimes find their pain intensified.

Representatives and followers of traditional religion have often hurt lesbians and gay men by weaving a moral and historical tapestry of guilt, shame, and repression rather than by providing validation and inspiration for their inherent goodness. Additionally, some mental health professionals, by being ignorant of the pain and unique searchings of the gay or lesbian soul, may miss the opportunity to provide support and healing as well as possibly short-circuit the journey toward identity synthesis and self-actualization.

The purpose of this article is to help counselors better understand the deep losses of lesbian and gay clients relative to both their sexuality and their religious faith and to provide guidance in helping clients work toward spiritual integration. Although some gay or lesbian people feel a profound alienation with regard to organized religion, others who have never bonded with a faith tradition experience an inner void that can only be called spiritual. We hope this article can provide counselors with the perspectives not only to appreciate the spiritual losses of many gay and lesbian individuals but also to take clients developmentally beyond mere acceptance of the loss to an internalization of the concept that inherent in their experience is the basis for a truly transformed and transforming spirituality.

Crucial to an understanding of this article is the current research by Money (1987, 1988), who pointed to the notion that sexual orientation is strongly influenced by prenatal brain *hormonalization* as well as postnatal socialization. As is true for all learning, this early learning (often within the first months of life) involves changes in both brain chemistry and structure. As Money stated: "When nature and nurture interact at crucial developmental periods, the residual products may persist immutably" (1987, p. 398). Despite this evidence that sexual orientation is biologically intrinsic in each human being, however, many individuals, churches, and much of society in general persist in believing otherwise. Even well-meaning individuals can fall into this trap and, despite good intentions, inadvertently violate the inherent sacredness of gay or lesbian people, perhaps even terminating their journeys toward wholeness.

TRADITIONAL RELIGION

Because most of the core norms, values, and structures of American society have evolved from the Judeo-Christian heritage, it is important to initiate the discussion of the losses of persons of same-gender orientation from the perspective of traditional organized religion. Commonly accepted scriptural interpretation, custom, doctrinal pronouncements, and historical tradition (Boswell, 1980) have heaped accusations of shame, contamination, and sinfulness upon the heads of lesbian and gay people that, in turn, have established the framework of society's attitude toward them. It is no wonder then that many gay men and lesbian women have found their experience in traditional religion to be something less than viable. Some contend that for a religious experience to be viable it must be philosophically reasonable, morally helpful, spiritually illuminating (James, 1928), and communally supportive (Callahan, 1985). The discussion of traditional organized religion that follows will examine the experience of gay men and lesbian women from each of these perspectives.

Philosophically Reasonable

Two of the major tenets of the Judeo-Christian tradition are the unconditional goodness of the human being and the unfailing love of the Creator for each person. These two fundamental principles do not always seem to apply to gay and lesbian people. One major religion has recently described same-gender orientation as "objectively disordered" and "inclined toward evil" (Ratzinger, 1986), which can leave the impression in the minds of lesbian women and gay men that there *are* conditions on their goodness. Furthermore, to attain that evidence of God's unfailing love, which much of traditional religion defines as salvation, individuals of same-gender orientation often try to do what they believe is necessary to be lovable to the Creator (i.e., to be either heterosexual or repent or repress their homosexual nature). Either of these actions can thrust religiously bonded people into a powerful double bind: on the one hand, the pain of living with denial, frustration, or continual attempts to change their immutable nature or, on the other hand, the anguish of remaining forever in a state of perceived sinfulness or unlovableness.

Thus, traditional organized religion, rather than assisting with integration and wholeness, often fragments individuals by seeming to demand that individuals change or be forgiven for their *very* nature. If, as it is now becoming apparent, sexual orientation is as biologically inherent as one's gender (Money, 1987, 1988), much of organized religion is demonstrating to gay men and lesbians its philosophical unreasonableness by demanding the impossible. To many people, being asked to repent of their orientation is like asking a man to be forgiven for his maleness or a woman to be forgiven for her femaleness.

Morally Helpful

In addition to being perceived as philosophically unreasonable, much of Judeo-Christian moral teaching has not proven helpful to many gay men and lesbian women. The preponderance of "official" moral guidance as it relates specifically to lesbian and gay people is posited in the negative and focuses directly on the prohibition of intimate and sexual relationships between same-gender couples. By casting their inclinations in pejorative language (i.e., "unnatural" and "abominable"), traditional organized religion usually leaves gay men or lesbian women with few morally credible ways to express themselves either sexually or in relationships unless their biologically intrinsic sexual orientation were to change. In this regard and in spite of scientific evidence to the contrary (McNeill, 1985, 1988; Money, 1987, 1988), some Christian groups have activated programs expressly designed to support conversion to heterosexuality and/or to encourage repression of homosexual inclinations.

The three moral choices gay men and lesbians perceive as offered to them by traditional Judeo-Christian religions (i.e., conversion/repentance, celibacy, or an often spurious heterosexual marriage) are frequently perceived as deeply offensive and contrary to their desire for wholeness. Thus, many churches are viewed by lesbian women and gay men as neither trustworthy nor particularly creditable and, as such, forfeit their role as exemplars of moral wisdom and teachers of truth. In this regard, they are perceived as undeserving of loyalty and affiliation.

Several Catholic theologians and writers (Curran, 1983; Maguire, 1984; McNaught, 1988; McNeill, 1985, 1988; Woods, 1988) have attempted to offer gay men and lesbians a more positive and life-affirming theology than that promulgated by the Official Church. Although these attempts have often been met by censure, criticism, and, in the case of McNeill, the loss of his priestly community, they are providing a voice of hope, a vision of authentic gay spirituality, and the impetus for lesbian women and gay men to re-examine the path to the Creator from different moral perspectives.

Literature of an encouraging nature has also been issued by Protestants and by the gay/lesbian-affirming Universal Fellowship of Metropolitan

Community Churches (Clark, 1987; Edwards, 1984; Fortunato, 1982; Nelson, 1982, 1983; Perry, 1987; Scanzoni & Mollenkott, 1978; Uhrig, 1986), but the effect has sometimes been diminished by proclamations and rhetoric of condemnation and dehumanizing bigotry from the religious Right. Some of these Christian denominations cite seven scriptural passages as the basis for their moral positions, but many contemporary writers and theologians (Curran, 1983; Edwards, 1984; Fortunato, 1982; Maguire, 1984; Mollenkott, 1985; Nelson, 1982, 1983; Perry, 1987; Scanzoni & Mollenkott, 1978, 1980) believe that "questions of inspiration, critical interpretation, textual criticism, historical criticism, source criticism, and form criticism" have been neglected (Uhrig, 1986, p. 17).

Spiritually Illuminating

For many gay men and lesbian women, traditional organized religion has simply not inspired them to want to assimilate into the broader community of faith. In their minds, most mainline churches have not provided models of sacred gay lives and same-gender relationships nor identified the gay or lesbian person's central role in a variety of sacred traditions nor presented a mythology broad enough to encompass the life questions of lesbian and gay individuals, and thus have not offered them a pathway to holiness.

Only in the last decade has writing emerged that pointed to the very real possibility of gay and lesbian saints (Boswell, 1980) or of gay and lesbian clergy and theologians (Clark, 1987; McNeill, 1985, 1989; Perry, 1987). Until recently, those who would be able to act as mentors have been reluctant to disclose their orientation for fear of retaliation or the loss of their ministries. Thus, with few models of individuals who could reconcile their orientation with a life of spiritual commitment, lesbians and gay men have had difficulty believing this synthesis was possible. In light of the scarcity of these identifiable models, spiritually committed lesbian and gay people have often been forced either to adopt a spirituality that did not address them on the deepest levels or to become pioneers in discovering a religious, ritual experience suitable to their nature. Some of these alternatives will be discussed later in this article.

To the lesbian or gay person, traditional religion's stories of saints and biblical heroes accentuate either heterosexual values or the values of virginity or sexual repression. Models of same-sex love and friendship such as Jesus and John (John 13:23-25, 21:7), Ruth and Naomi (Ruth 1:16-17), or David and Jonathan (I Samuel 18:1-3, 20:41; II Samuel 1:26) are few and rarely highlighted. Never is a sexually intimate relationship between two people of the same sex used as an example of perfect or divine love. Thus, without a spirituality that is authentic to the gay or lesbian experience, there often seems little with which to identify or toward which to aspire.

Lives are formed by "master" or shaping stories (Fowler, 1981). Everyone has a plan or overall idea of his or her future and how this future will unfold. Judeo-Christian tradition provides people with only two types of life plans, heterosexual marriage/family: or celibacy/virginity. As a result, not only is there an absence of mythos that gives support to loving lesbian or gay relationships, characterized by constancy and fidelity, but most stories of traditional religion also distort the picture of the gay man as depraved, debased, sinful, and shamed. (In fact, the pejorative term *sodomite* has emerged from a biblical misinterpretation that was passed down as fact [McNeill, 1985; Nelson, 1982].) In the absence of positive-forming stories, many gay men and lesbian women have simply not found illumination or inspiration for their faith journeys from traditional religion.

Communally Supportive

Openly gay men and lesbians rarely find much communal support from traditional organized religion Not only is support for the development of a healthy Judeo-Christian ethic for their relationships generally lacking but also churches often actively attempt to dissolve same-gender couples, effecting the heterosexual equivalent of fostering divorce (Mollenkott, 1985). Lack of support is also demonstrated by the refusal of most traditional religions to ordain openly lesbian or gay people, thus leaving the impression that they are not wanted or trusted in leadership or ministerial roles. Furthermore, most mainline churches deny marriage to same-sex couples and offer not a single ritual to celebrate any gay or lesbian life event (such as the passage involved in "coming out"). In fact, almost all church-sponsored events, social and otherwise, seem to assume that everyone is heterosexual.

The ultimate irony for many gay or lesbian individuals is to hear about traditional Christianity's concern for the poor, the oppressed, and the "marginalized." The stories of these denominations often have Christ himself reaching out in a manner of genuine concern to the outcast. The Catholic bishops of the United States elaborated on this theme when they wrote the following in their pastoral on the U.S. economy (1986):

> The ultimate injustice is for a person or group to be actively treated or passively abandoned as if they were nonmembers of the human race. To treat people this way is effectively to say that they simply do not count as human beings. This can take many forms, all of which can be described as varieties of marginalization or exclusion from social life. (No. 77)

It is hardly paradoxical then that many lesbian women and gay men feel "abandoned as if they were nonmembers of the human race" by the very organization that attempts to speak so prophetically for the marginalized and oppressed. It seems that what they want from their churches is to be respected as human beings, included in the broader faith community, and recognized for the contribution that is theirs to make, rather than be cast as sinful, sick, or unfortunate.

The best case scenario for a gay or lesbian person in most Judeo-Christian denominations is to be treated as invisible, with one's orientation merely whispered about but never openly mentioned, and the worst case scenario is to be excommunicated or ostracised. These sacred communities that purport to instil and inspire faith for gay men and lesbians often contribute to the shattering of their faith, the further fragmentation of self, and the derailing of their journey toward self-actualization.

THE MENTAL HEALTH PROFESSION

The mental health profession, much like organized religion, has within its power both the ability to heal or to harm. Unfortunately in the eyes of many gay men and lesbians, psychologists, psychiatrists, and counselors have too often poured salt on their wounds. A healthier development, however, is that "Mental health practice with gay and lesbian populations has undergone enormous change in the past 20 years" (Gonsiorek, 1982, p. 5). Although more and more clinicians are practicing gay-affirming psychotherapy, there are still a number who believe that homosexuality is a condition requiring a cure (see Coleman, 1982; DeCrescenzo, 1985). This notion relates to the belief that heterosexuality is the mature condition and that homosexuality is indicative of an arrested Oedipal stage. Although there is a preponderance of evidence contradicting this position (Gonsiorek, 1982; Tripp, 1975), well-intentioned clients still come for a "conversion" that is not possible and depart empty-handed, feeling more hopeless than when they began.

Although sex-object choice is formed at an early stage in life (Coleman, 1982), the initial reaction of most lesbian and gay people to their same-gender attractions is to vehemently deny that something so reprehensible to society is a part of them. To deal with the horror of being so different, many will naturally seek the services of a mental health professional. Faced with their clients' ostensible request to achieve "normality," many counselors will, in good faith, attempt to help orient them toward heterosexuality. By not knowing that confusion and panic about sexual identity is a common and normal early stage in the establishment of a positive gay or lesbian identity (Cass, 1979; Coleman, 1982), counselors can inadvertently assist in premature foreclosure of the developmental trajectory.

Often, in the name of God or in the cause of faith, counselors can hold out a hope for "alteration" or "modification" of one's homosexual sense (Augsburger, 1984). Employing techniques to strengthen willpower, encourage prayer, devalue homosexuality, and positively portray heterosexuality, such counselors may, sadly, leave clients "with such a degree of self-hatred" that not only will the clients' developmental journeys be terminated but so also may be their lives (Cass, 1979, p. 229).

Aside from strategies of cure and conversion, there are other far more subtle ways that counselors can use to short-circuit the full developmental path of gay men and lesbians. Although accepting the same-gender orientation of their clients, some therapists perceive their role only in terms of helping people navigate through the shoals of prejudice and discrimination that society afflicts upon those labeled as *homosexual*. Other mental health professionals, also accepting of their clients' orientation, tend to view them the same as they do heterosexuals except for what they do in bed. Rarely, in the counseling process, is the reality of the clients' "gayness" acknowledged—almost as if they were talking to a Black individual without mentioning "Blackness." By failing to acknowledge the unique character of the gay or lesbian experience and orientation, the counselor may presume a life path parallel to that of the heterosexual and thus separate clients from their souls.

COUNSELORS AND THE SPIRITUAL JOURNEY

The discussion thus far has examined directions toward which lesbian women and gay men typically look for spiritual and personal wholeness. By understanding that deep losses may have resulted from their clients' associations with traditional organized religion and mental health professionals, counselors can help in a number of ways. They can further the spiritual journeys of the clients by positively recasting images of gay and lesbian people, by working to reframe their losses into opportunities for growth and transcendence, and by acquainting themselves and their clients with a variety of paths, both ancient and new, by which the spiritual questing of lesbian women and gay men might be facilitated.

Recasting Images

A sense of the mystical, the transcendent, the generative, the creative, and the symbolic are all characteristics of people possessing an evolved or developed faith (Fowler, 1981; O'Neill & Ritter, 1987). These are hardly characteristics that one would identify with the historical imagery of depravity and debasement associated with gay men and lesbian women since at least the latter half of the twelfth century (Boswell, 1980). Recent evidence, however, suggests that these elements have been present in many gay men and lesbians since the origin of the human species. For example, E. O. Wilson, in his Pulitzer Prize-winning book, *On Human Nature* (1982), suggests that "homosexuality . . . is a distinctive beneficent behavior that evolved as an important element of human social organization. Homosexuals may be the genetic carriers of some of mankind's rare altruistic impulses" (p. 149). Although not all would subscribe to the sweeping nature of Wilson's statement, Jung (1959) apparently had a sense of an evolved spirituality among some [male] homosexuals when he wrote that "he is endowed with a wealth of religious feelings . . . and a spiritual receptivity which makes him responsive to revelation" (p. 86). Few gay men and lesbian women, however, know that their ancestors have been the spiritual leaders and shamans throughout the history of civilization. These healers were highly esteemed and have been found in at least 88 Native-American tribes, in numerous African and South American civilizations, as well as in Polynesia, India, China, Japan, Tibet, and Malaysia, in addition to ancient Celtic, Greek, and Roman cultures (Clark, 1987; Evans, 1978; Grahn, 1984). According to Grahn:

> In tribal culture we often formed a pool of potential initiates some of whom became the shamans and medicine people who can enter the spirit world, the wind, the mountains and rivers and the bottom of the sea; the worlds of the dead, or spirits, or other people's minds, of the gods and their forces; we it is who bring back the strange and old messages, interpreting them for the benefit of our tribe. (p. 273)

Another reason to perhaps recast the image of gay men and lesbian women is the findings of three recent dissertations, two (Bordisso, 1988; Wilson, 1984) of which demonstrated that gay and lesbian populations were significantly more advanced in Kohlberg's moral developmental level than were their heterosexual counterparts, and a third one (Mitchell, 1983) that found that 120 gay and nongay individuals were not significantly different in their level of moral development as measured by Rest's Defining Issues Test (DIT) (1979). In C.V. Wilson's (1984) study, which controlled for age, sexual orientation, and sex, the DIT was administered to 192 subjects. Wilson saw the higher level of gay and lesbian moral development as a result of the disequilibrium inherent in living with an orientation that is in conflict with society's prevailing norms and rules. Bordisso (1988), also employing the DIT, controlled for age and education when studying 30 gay and 30 heterosexual Catholic priests and explained his similar findings as follows: "For homosexually oriented priests, it appears that the issue of their sexuality, introspection, conflict, anguish, fear of rejection, and alienation, provoked them to seek a more adequate stage of moral reasoning regardless of age or education" (pp. 106-107).

Although undoubtedly not applying to all persons of same-gender orientation, the findings of Wilson, Bordisso, and Mitchell, as well as the writings on shamanistic spirituality, do seem to contradict the prevailing imagery of gay men and lesbian women as being morally inferior and lacking in spiritual lineage. Counselors can assist clients in achieving spiritual wholeness by holding up to them these more inspirational and hope-renewing images. If, rather than accepting the tendency to see themselves as creatures of a dark or spiritually bankrupt life-style, gay and lesbian people could be encouraged to experience themselves as potentially rich with spiritual receptivity and as inheritors of a sacred tradition of leadership, their self-image as a people of faith could be recast. Thus, by redirecting clients toward more evolved mystical and symbolic possibilities inherent within themselves, gay men and lesbian women may be helped to reconcile the losses of their past and assimilate the gifts that are uniquely theirs to give.

Reframing Loss

Developmental literature and theory, as well as the themes and motifs of most of the world's major religions, stress the interrelatedness of loss and gain, crisis and opportunity, and death and resurrection. For gay men and lesbian women then to proceed toward individuation and spiritual wholeness, their path will be through their grief and loss (Fortunato, 1982, 1987; Fowler, 1981; Topper, 1986; Whitehead & Whitehead, 1986). It will be through the reality of their orientation, rather than in spite of it, that they will reach a sense of the mystical and transcendent. In other words, their losses become a spring-board for spiritual transformation.

"The pain and suffering that a homosexual in a homophobic culture undergoes can be either redemptive or alienating" (Fox, 1984, p. 190). Fox goes on to say that when suffering is redemptive, it leads to a sensitivity, a compassion for other oppressed people such as "the Jew, the Black person, the Native American, [and] women in a patriarchal society" (p. 190), the outsider of any description. Not only can this increased compassion prompt gay men and lesbians to a higher sense of personal and spiritual generativity (or a "giving back" to the culture) but it also models a sensitivity of response to the alienated of society.

Building upon the civil rights and women's movements of the 1960s and particularly the Stonewall Rebellion of 1969 (which is considered by many to be the starting event of the gay liberation movement), the AIDS crisis seems to be further empowering some gay men and lesbian women to assume the role of models. Confronting issues as disturbing as death, loss, and injustice has compelled many to tap deeply into themselves and to emerge with personal and spiritual resources to share with the entire community (Clark, 1987; Fortunato, 1987).

The losses of gay and lesbian people are many and they are profound—their feelings of not belonging to church, family, society, or the workplace; the loss of friends and loved ones to AIDS; the psychic destruction caused by heterosexual society's often projecting upon them its greatest fears and secrets; and the general loss of respectability, knowing that their very beings are unhesitatingly and unquestioningly despised by many. In the process of grieving through their losses, gay men and lesbian women are frequently faced with personal and spiritual developmental choice points. At any juncture they can get so mired in grief and pain that they may fail to realize the paths that lead to wholeness and, instead, take those that lead to further mistrust, shame, guilt, inferiority, confusion, isolation, stagnation, and ultimately despair (Fowler, 1981).

By highlighting and engendering the more life-affirming responses at each of these developmental junctures, counselors can assist lesbians and gay men in gaining a spirit of generativity and integrity and, hence, the individuation necessary to achieve a Conjunctive or Universalizing Faith (Fowler, 1981). As the alcoholic or child of an alcoholic begins to recover by talking, trusting, and feeling, so must many people of same-gender orientation. By aiding these clients to consciously and repeatedly identify, come to terms with, and release anger and pain in the face of their losses, a truer sense of autonomy, initiative, industry, identity, generativity, and integrity can be gained. Counselors, then, can assist gay men and lesbian women in freeing their souls of the negativity and death-dealing emotions that may be preventing them from proceeding along their spiritual journeys.

Facilitating a Spiritual Path

In the process of recasting self-images and reframing their losses, some gay men and lesbian women are meeting their communal religious needs by retaining full affiliation in traditional religions, or becoming members in a gay or lesbian subgroup of these organized denominations, or joining alternative churches. Still others are finding their way into ancient, or non-Judeo-Christian spiritual expressions.

It is the purpose of this section to acquaint counselors with these various options so that they might better facilitate whatever healthy and viable paths along which their clients may be called. The discussion will most likely not prove relevant for those with little concern for religion or spirituality. To assist those clients who might have such an interest, however, some of the references at the end of this article might prove helpful. Those starred with a single asterisk indicate literature dealing with traditional Judeo-Christianity; those marked with a double asterisk relate to ancient or non-Judeo-Christian expressions.

Traditional religion. Some gay and lesbian clients have been able to find a home within traditional organized religion. For those who remain there sometimes exists a blindness to the discrimination that surrounds them. For others, the struggle to stay is painful and is by no means resolved. A third group may find itself welcomed by denominations (e.g., Quakers, Unitarians) or by individual congregations within denominations (e.g., Episcopalian, United Methodist Reconciling Congregations [Cook, 1988]), some of which are actively trying to reverse previous ill-treatment by Judeo-Christianity. For yet another population, mainline religion is perceived as exclusionary and unresponsive to their needs, and affiliation is transferred to a gay and lesbian subgroup within that religious body. In this regard, most major cities in the United States have lesbian and gay synagogues that are branches of the Reformed Movement of Judaism and are members of the American Hebrew Congregation. The partial list available at the end of this article contains reference to the umbrella Jewish organization as well as other denominational affiliates. Likewise, many of the books in the reference list contain information concerning the beliefs of such groups.

The best example of an alternative church that serves the needs of gay men and lesbian women is the Universal Fellowship of Metropolitan Community Churches (MCC), which has more than 40,000 members in 12 countries. It has been in existence more than 20 years and is the largest organization in the world designed to serve lesbian and gay individuals. Perry (1987), the founder of MCC, indicates that this denomination invites gay and lesbian individuals to worship God freely and to stand before God's altar, as a people unashamed and proudly gay. In this regard, MCC is thus seen as philosophically reasonable, morally helpful, spiritually illuminating, and communally supportive.

Non-Judeo-Christian spiritualities. Some lesbian women and gay men have begun a quest to reconceptualize spiritual imagery and to connect themselves with ancient, more gay-affirming traditions by re-examining non-Judeo-Christian religions (Christ & Plaskow, 1979; Thompson, 1987a). Particular themes in these spiritualities seem to relate to the search for a more integrating, less dualistic approach to faith, a return to prepatriarchal mysteries and traditions, and the creation of rituals and symbols to reconnect gay men and lesbian women at the deepest level of their dreams.

There seems to be a trend toward viewing creation on a continuum (Rich, 1976), to seeing the unity and relatedness of all realities—inner and outer, God and humanity, the masculine and feminine as divine images, self and community, earth and "mankind," body and spirit—and to believing in the integrating power of dreams (Goldenberg, 1979; Rich, 1976; Starhawk, 1979, 1982).

Another direction being taken by some lesbian women and gay men is toward prepatriarchal religious expressions (Daly, 1973; Evans, 1978). These are exemplified by Native-American Spirituality with its emphasis on the sacred nature of the earth and humanity's oneness with it, by Old Religion based on the principle of the Goddess as imminent in the world (Starhawk, 1979), and by Eastern and ancient mystery religions with their emphasis on the oneness of all beings and experience with a divine Source (Doore, 1988; Downing, 1981; Grahn, 1984).

A third theme weaving itself through the previous two is that of lesbian and gay people reimagining and retelling their lives and creating a spirituality unique to their experience. By means of ritual and symbol, lesbian women and gay men are giving expression to the cycle of death and rebirth intuitively understood by many of them as they have progressed through the stages of coming out and moving through the accompanying losses (Clark, 1987; Evans, 1978; Grahn, 1984; Thompson, 1987a).

These three themes are perhaps indicative of the spiritual rebirth occurring with the gay and lesbian community. By moving through the losses of life and encountering the accompanying darkness, a new spiritual vitality and vision is taking place. It is through this transformed vision that creativity emerges. "The darkness of letting go and letting be are precursor to the energy of birth and rebirth. Living marginal existences is conducive to creativity, while comfort seldom is…" (Fox, 1984, p. 199).

Personally and spiritually evolved gay men and lesbian women are beginning to express this creativity in transformative ways. Some perceive themselves as vital links in a chain from shamans to modern day priests, celebrating and reverencing their own and the earth's innate beauty and magic. Others become healers, tapping deeply into their own compassion and birthing the dying into death—or life. Coming out of injustice often builds justice makers who themselves join the struggle to help others as marginalized as they. Some are seen as mentors, guiding by wisdom and shared experience those who are beginning to walk the path toward wholeness. Still others, out of a more developed sense of identity synthesis (Cass, 1979), are able to bridge between the sexes as well as between the inner world of creative inspiration and the outer world of society.

By appreciating the sacredness of gay and lesbian people, the richness of their spiritual questing, and the opportunities for transformation as they move with their clients through loss and grief, counselors can facilitate spiritual wholeness. The reality of being lesbian or gay can be reframed as "a 'gift' allowed to a certain percentage of humanity, offering a different set of biological, social and spiritual receptors through which the world can be perceived and interpreted" (Thompson, 1987b, p. 184). By such recasting, counselors can hold up an illuminating vision of gay men and lesbian women as healers, justice makers, mentors, and bridge builders.

REFERENCES

Augsburger, S. W. (1984). The church as a change agent for the male homosexual: Etiology, intervention, and change. *Dissertation Abstracts International, 45*, 19056B.

Bordisso, L. A. (1988). *The relationship between level of moral development and sexual orientation of Roman Catholic priests.* Unpublished doctoral dissertation, The University of San Francisco.

*Boswell, J. (1980). *Christianity social tolerance and homosexuality: Gay people in Western Europe from the beginning of the Christian era to the fourteenth century.* Chicago: University of Chicago Press.

Callahan, S. (1985). The laity and alienated Catholics. In M. Glazier (Ed.), *Where we are: American Catholics in the 1980s* (pp. 51-63). Wilmington, DE: Michael Glazier.

Cass, V. C. (1979). Homosexual identity formation: A theoretical model. *Journal of Homosexuality, 4*, 219-235.

**Christ, C., & Plaskow, J. (Eds.). (1979). *Womanspirit rising: A feminist leader in religion.* San Francisco: Harper & Row.

**Clark, J. M. (1987). *Gay being, divine presence: Essays in gay spirituality.* Las Colinas, TX: Tangelwuld.

Coleman, E. (1982). Developmental stages of the coming out process. In J. C. Gonsiorek (Ed.), *Homosexuality and psychotherapy* (pp. 31-43). New York: Haworth.

*Cook, A. T. (1988). *And God loves each one.* Nashville, TN: Reconciling Congregation Program. (Available from Reconciling Congregation Program, P.0. Box 24213, Nashville, TN 37202)

*Curran, C. (1983). Moral theology and homosexuality. In S. Gramick (Ed.), *Homosexuality and the Catholic church* (pp. 138-168). Chicago: The Thomas More Press.

**Daly, M. (1973). *Beyond God and the Father: Toward a philosophy of women's liberation.* Boston: Beacon Press.

DeCrescenzo, T. A. (1985). Homophobia: A study of the attitudes of mental health profession-als toward homosexuality. In R. Schoenberg, R. S. Goldberg, & D. A Shore (Eds.), *With compassion toward some: Homosexuality and social work in America* (pp. 115-136). New York: Harrington Park Press.

**Doore, G. (Ed.). (1988). *Shaman's path.* Boston: Shambhala.

**Downing, C. (1981). *The goddess: Mythological representations of the feminine.* New York: Cross-road.

*Edwards, G. (1984). *Gay/lesbian liberation: A biblical perspective.* New York: The Pilgrim Press.

**Evans, A. (1978). *Witchcraft and the gay counterculture.* Boston: Fag Rag Books.

*Fortunato, J. E. (1982). *Embracing the exile: Healing journeys of gay Christians.* New York: Harper & Row.

*Fortunato, J. E. (1987). *AIDS, the spiritual dilemma.* San Francisco: Harper & Row.

Fowler, J. W. (1981). *Stages of faith: The psychology of human development and the quest for meaning.* San Francisco: Harper & Row.

*Fox, M. (1984). The spiritual journey of the homosexual...and just about everybody else. In R. Nugent (Ed.), *A challenge to love: Gay and lesbian Catholics in the church* (pp. 189 204). New York: Crossroad.

**Goldenberg, N. (1979). *Changing of the gods. Feminism and the end of traditional religions.* Boston: Beacon Press.

Gonsiorek, J. C. (1982). Introduction: Present and future directions in gay/lesbian mental health. In J. C. Gonsiorek (Ed.), *Homosexuality and psychotherapy* (pp. 5-7). New York: Haworth.

**Grahn, I. (1984). *Another mother tongue.* Boston: Beacon Press.

James, W. (1928). *The varieties of religious experience: A study in human nature.* New York: Longmans, Green.

Jung, C. G. (1959). *The collected works* (Vol. 9, part 1). New York: Pantheon.

*Maguire, D. C. (1984). The morality of homosexual marriage. In R. Nugent (Ed.), *A challenge to love: Gay & lesbian Catholics in the church* (pp. 118-134). New York: Crossroad.

*McNaught, B. (1988). *On being gay: Thoughts on family faith and love.* New York: St. Martin's Press.

*McNeill, J. J. (1985). The church and the homosexual (3rd ed). Boston: Beacon Press.

*McNeill, J. J. (1988). *Taking a chance on God.* Boston: Beacon Press.

Mitchell, H. R. (1983). Moral development and sexual orientation. *Dissertation Abstracts International, 44,* 4412A.

*Mollenkott, V. R. (1985). *Breaking the silence, overcoming the fear: Homophobia education.* (Available from The Program Agency, United Presbyterian Church [U.S.A.], 475 Riverside Drive, Room 1101, New York, NY 10115)

Money, I. (1987). Sin, sickness, or status? Homosexual gender identity and psychoneuroendocrinology. *American Psychologist, 42,* 384-399.

Money, I. (1988). *Gay, straight, and in-between.* New York: Oxford University Press.

National Conference of Catholic Bishops. (1986). *Economic justice for all.* Washington, DC: United States Catholic Conference.

*Nelson, J. B. (1982). Religious and moral issues in working with homosexual clients. In J. C. Gonsiorek (Ed.), *Homosexuality and psychotherapy* (pp. 163-175). New York: Haworth.

*Nelson, J. B. (1983). *Between two gardens: Reflections on sexuality and religious experience.* New York: The Pilgrim Press.

O'Neill, C. W., & Ritter, K. Y. (1987). Who leaves and rejoins the church? *Human Development, 8,* 28-36.

*Perry, T. D. (1987). *The Lord is my shepherd and He knows I'm gay.* Austin, TX: Liberty Press.

Ratzinger, J. (1986). Letter to the bishops of the Catholic church on the pastoral care of homosexual persons. Rome, Italy: Vatican Congregation for the Doctrine of the Faith.

Rest, J. (1979). *Revised manual for the Defining Issues Test: An objective test of moral judgment development.* Minneapolis, MN: Moral Research Project.

**Rich, A. (1976). *Of woman born.* New York: W. W. Norton.

*Scanzoni, L., & Mollenkott, V. R. (1978). *Is the homosexual my neighbor?* San Francisco: Harper & Row.

**Starhawk. (1979). *The spiral dance: A rebirth of the ancient religion of the great Goddess.* San Francisco: Harper & Row.

**Starhawk. (1982). *Dreaming the dark: Magic, sex, and politics.* Boston: Beacon Press.

**Thompson, M. (Ed.). (1987a). *Gay spirit: Myth and meaning.* New York: St. Martin's Press.

**Thompson, M. (1987b). Harry Hay: A voice from the past, a vision for the future. In M. Thompson (Ed.), *Gay spirit: Myth and meaning* (pp. 182-199). New York: St. Martin's Press.

*Topper, C. J. (1986). Spirituality as a component in counseling lesbians-gays. *Journal of Pastoral Psychology, 21,* 55-59.

Tripp, C. A. (1975). *The homosexual matrix.* New York: McGraw-Hill.

*Uhrig, L. J. (1986). *Sex positive: A contribution to sexual and spiritual union.* Boston: Alyson.

*Whitehead, E. E., & Whitehead, J. D. (1986). *Seasons of strength: New visions of adult maturing.* New York: Doubleday Image.

Wilson, C. V. (1984). The relationship of sexual orientation and gender to adult moral development. *Dissertation Abstracts International, 45,* 7002B-7012B.

Wilson, E. O. (1982). *On human nature.* New York: Bantam.

*Woods, R. (1988). *Another kind of love: Homosexuality and spirituality* (3rd ed.). Ft. Wayne, IN: Knoll.

Single asterisk denotes traditional Judeo-Christian sources; double asterisks denote non-Judeo-Christian spiritual expressions.

RELIGIOUS ORGANIZATIONS

Affirmation (Gay and Lesbian Mormons)
Box 26302
San Francisco, CA 94126
(415) 641-4554

Affirmation (United Methodists for Gay and
  Lesbian Concerns)
Box 1021
Evanston, IL 60204
(312) 475-0499

Dignity, Inc. (Catholic)
1500 Massachusetts Avenue, NW
Suite 11
Washington, DC 20005
(202) 861-0017

Evangelicals Concerned
c/o Dr. Ralph Blair
311 East 72nd
New York, NY 10021
(212) 517-3171

Friends for Lesbian and Gay Concerns
(Quakers)
Box 222
Sumneytown, PA 18084
(215) 234-8424

Seventh Day Adventist Kinship International, Inc.
Box 3840
Los Angeles, CA 90078-3840
(213) 876-2076

Unitarian Universalists for Lesbian/Gay
Concerns
25 Beacon Street
Boston, MA 02108
(617) 742-2100

Universal Fellowship of Metropolitan Community Churches (MCC)
5300 Santa Monica Boulevard
#304
Los Angeles, CA 90029
(213) 464-5100

World Congress of Gay and Lesbian Jewish
Organizations
Barrett Brick, Executive Director
P.O. Box 18961
Washington, D.C. 20036
(202) 483-4801

Interreligious Encounter Group: A Psychospiritual Experience for Faith Development

VICKY GENIA

MOST TRADITIONAL PSYCHOTHERAPEUTIC approaches do not address the needs of the religiously committed client. This failure stems from a long tradition among psychologists and psychiatrists, rooted in Freud's (1927) antireligious position, of viewing religion as antithetical to psychological and emotional health. When clients present dominant religious themes and concerns in therapy, these issues are often ignored, challenged as inadequate and irrational, or analyzed as symbolic representations of neurotic fears, wishes, impulses, or conflicts.

Even when therapists are sympathetic toward religion they seldom work directly with the client's religious material. Instead, such therapists may refer spiritually troubled clients to clergypersons for spiritual guidance as adjuncts to therapy, without assessing whether such a referral is appropriate or necessary. These clinicians automatically assume, without critical examination of the specific dynamics involved, that religionists can best deal with the client's spiritual dimension, thereby leaving the psychotherapist free to work with the more tangible and palatable therapeutic material. This discontinuity of treatment may leave some clients confused and angry or torn between contradictory worldviews (see Wick, 1985).

Techniques to help healthy religious development, however, can be incorporated into traditional psychological practices. Although still in the embryonic stage, a new trend is slowly emerging. Framed by an evolving psychology of religious development, the assimilation and integration of spiritual interventions into secular therapeutic approaches is giving birth to a psychospiritual psychotherapy.

It is the thesis of this article that religious development may be helped within a religiously divergent, interactive group context having both a psychological and spiritual focus. The interreligious encounter group concept was developed from both psychological and religious influences including religious psychology, developmental psychology, pastoral counseling, moral

From "Interreligious Encounter Group: A Psychospiritual Experience for Faith Development," by V. Genia, 1990, *Counseling and Values, 35,* 39–51.

education, and traditional group psychotherapy. In this article I present the theoretical foundation for the group experience and examine the dynamics of the group process.

PSYCHOLOGY OF RELIGIOUS DEVELOPMENT: A BRIEF HISTORICAL OVERVIEW

The psychological study of religious development is rooted in efforts to distinguish psychologically healthy from unhealthy forms of religious expression. William James (1902) in his classic work *The Varieties of Religious Experience* distinguished between "healthy minded religion" and the pessimistic religious outlook of the "sick soul."

James's formulation became a prototype, which stimulated a tradition of dichotomizing religiousness into two opposing types, one representing a mature form of religious functioning and the other a psychologically unhealthy religious outlook (Broen, 1957; Evans, 1952; Fromm, 1950; Lenski, 1961). This tradition culminated in Allport's (1963) intrinsic and extrinsic religious orientation dimensions. Intrinsic and extrinsic religiousness were defined in terms of specific psychological motivations for being religious. When extrinsic religious motivation is present, religion is used defensively by an individual to provide a powerful, in-group justification of one's formula for living, or a defense against reality. Allport considered this instrumental, utilitarian approach to religion to be less healthy than an intrinsic motivation in which one's religious faith is lived as an end in itself, functioning as a foundation for one's choices and giving meaning to life's experiences.

Other multidimensional theoretical frameworks have also been proposed (Allen & Spilka, 1967; Batson, 1976; Brown, 1964; Glock, 1962; King & Hunt, 1972). These frameworks, however, neither illuminate the relationships among the religious dimensions (Meadow & Kahoe, 1984) nor explain the dynamic processes underlying individual differences on the various dimensions. These failures have led recent investigators to shift away from the multidimensional approach toward a developmental theory of religiousness.

This shift was initiated when investigators began to analyze the religious functioning of persons at different age levels in light of theoretical models of psychosocial, ego, cognitive, and moral development (e.g., Aden, 1976; Fowler, 1981; Kao, 1981; Meadow & Kahoe, 1984). This creative synthesis of religious and developmental psychology suggested that the less mature, extrinsic form of religiousness observed in some adults represents functioning in the earlier phases of a normal religious developmental pathway beginning in early childhood and continuing throughout life's journey (Fowler, 1981; Kao, 1981; Meadow & Kahoe, 1984). Adults functioning at a more mature intrinsic level were seen as having progressed to higher levels of religious development.

These ideas germinated into several proposed stage models of religious and faith development (Fowler, 1981; Kao, 1981; Meadow & Kahoe, 1984). Each of these models describes a general, normative process of faith development independent of specific theological content. The models attempt to elucidate the general structural changes in religious thinking, feeling, and experiencing that occur as the individual grows and matures. This process begins with a highly egocentric religiosity of childhood and, if conditions are favorable, culminates in a well-integrated and autonomous religiousness of middle adulthood.

CAUSES OF RELIGIOUS UNDERDEVELOPMENT

Stage theories of religious development appear intuitively valid and empirically promising. The stage concept has not, however, explicitly related practical applications of the theory to clinical practice. Although stages provide useful guidelines for roughly determining a client's level of religious development, the task remains of prescribing specific psychological interventions for the adult client whose religious functioning has remained in earlier stages of development. Because recommendations for intervention must be based on assumptions of underlying causes, it is first necessary to examine the causes of delayed religious development. These causes fall into two major categories: (a) lack of opportunity for growth and (b) psychological, emotional, or spiritual conflicts that impede higher levels of religious development.

Lack of Opportunity for Religious Growth

Individual development has two prerequisites: innate potential and growth-enhancing experience. A child will not develop cognitively beyond a minimal level if not given an education. Psychosocial development will not unfold in a child who is isolated from interaction with family, teachers, friends, and peers. Similarly, religious development will not proceed beyond an early stage if the person is not exposed to growth-enhancing religious experiences. If one remains committed to a religious institution that emphasizes unquestioned acceptance of religious authority or doctrine, one is not likely to mature religiously. In other cases an individual may be exposed to religious ideas and images in childhood and then become religiously inactive in adolescence when he or she is no longer required to attend worship services or religious education classes. Lying dormant and unintegrated into other areas of the adult's life, this religious residue remains immature.

Psychological, Emotional, or Spiritual Conflicts

Religious development does not unfold in isolation, detached from other facets of personal functioning (Fowler, 1981; Kao, 1981; Meadow & Kahoe, 1984). Instead, it is intertwined with the cognitive, social, emotional, and psychological components of the personality. Therefore, deficits in one or more of these areas are likely to be reflected in the individual's religious functioning.

For example, consider the individual who functions interpersonally on a need gratification level. This person is likely to perceive God as a narcissistic extension of self, to use prayer egocentrically to petition personal favors, and to view moral responsibility in terms of punishment avoidance. This type of individual lacks the ego structuralization necessary to develop a mature religious outlook. As another example, consider the religious experience of the emotionally constricted individual with an overdeveloped superego. This person's oppressive conscience is externalized and projected onto a punitive God representation, thereby transforming fear of one's own unacceptable impulses into fear of God's punishment. In both of these cases, as in many others, it is unlikely that the individual can develop a healthy religious outlook without therapeutic work to reshape psychological functioning.

NEED FOR PSYCHOSPIRITUAL INTERVENTION

Specific techniques and interventions are needed that help religious developmental progression by changing the underlying causes of underdevelopment. This area has been given little attention in the psychological literature. Although interest in the psychological study of religion has been accelerating at a rapid pace, efforts have primarily concentrated on theory building or empirical testing of theoretical models, with little energy directed toward explicating practical applications of these conceptualizations for the psychotherapist or counselor working with religious clients. In rare instances authors do suggest implications of their theory or investigation for the practitioner (e.g., Bergin, Masters, & Richards, 1987). These recommendations, however, are usually formulated as vague therapeutic objectives, such as helping the client to obtain a more intrinsic religious commitment, while offering little guidance on how to actually go about effecting such a change. The few sources that offer specific interventions for incorporating religious content into therapeutic work are predicated on a Judeo-Christian theological orientation (cf. Lovinger, 1984), which is not relevant for clients whose religious identifications are not within this tradition.

By incorporating psychological theory and techniques into spiritual care and guidance, pastoral counseling possesses the tools to address conflicts that are undermining religious growth. Again, because the foundation of pastoral counseling is built on a Judeo-Christian theology, the model is inapplicable to individuals outside of this tradition. Also, many individuals have spiritual and religious outlooks but are not affiliated with any formal religious tradition or institution (Vernon, 1968). Such individuals are not likely to seek help from pastoral counselors. In fact, one study has shown that even though a large percentage of persons feel that religious values are an important topic to be explored in therapy, many are reluctant to seek pastoral counseling (Quackenbos, Privette, & Klentz, 1985).

Certainly, pastoral counseling is an important and visible source of spiritual growth and guidance for many individuals. There are, however, many other spiritually troubled persons for whom these methods are not therapeutically applicable. For these individuals I propose an alternative experience, which I have labeled the *interreligious encounter group.* This experience addresses the two major causes of religious underdevelopment and is relevant to a broad range of spiritually committed clients.

FORMULATION OF THE INTERRELIGIOUS ENCOUNTER CONCEPT

The major contribution and therapeutic value of this approach to religious development lies in its *pluralistic* emphasis and *psychological* focus. Issues are not formulated in accordance with any particular theological system and may be expressed in spiritual or existential language. Although the concerns of theology and spirituality overlap (i.e., death, guilt, freedom and responsibility, isolation, and meaninglessness), the distinction is more than semantic. The interreligious encounter emphasizes the importance of each individual's unique solution to ontological and spiritual concerns based on open, personal exploration and free thinking. Thus, avenues of exploration are much wider in the interreligious encounter than in most religious settings. For example, reincarnation is not accepted within Christian denominations but may be explored within the interreligious encounter group.

Although spiritual in focus, the experience is based on principles and techniques of group psychotherapy. Because the group does not depend on any source of religious authority, it is likely to be relevant for persons of divergent faiths. A religiously diverse participation enhances the group process by exposing members to a wide range of religious ideas.

Forerunners

The interreligious encounter is based on three major influences: (a) spiritual growth groups within pastoral counseling, (b) Kohlberg's moral discussion groups, and (c) traditional psychotherapy and encounter groups. It is the purpose of the interreligious encounter group to synthesize the strengths of these three methods into an effective psychospiritual intervention to help religious development.

Spiritual Growth Groups

The possibilities of using various kinds of small groups for providing support, learning experiences, and opportunities for growth in spiritual and religious settings have recently been examined (Clinebell, 1972, 1984; Zimpfer, 1986). The potential for such group experiences seems promising. Spiritual growth groups, however, are based on a Biblical interpretation of religious truth emphasizing concepts such as sin and salvation (Clinebell, 1972, 1984). Acceptance of the authority of Biblical scripture by the group participant is assumed and provides the foundation and reference point for the group experience. Furthermore, the primary focus of the group is placed on the spiritual dimension. Instead of being viewed as a complementary goal, salubrious psychological effects that occur from the experience are considered only as incidental to the spiritual uplift.

Although these groups have tremendous value for some people, they may fail to provide the spiritual breadth or psychological depth needed for individuals experiencing more intense psychological, emotional, or spiritual conflicts.

Kohlberg's Moral Discussion Groups

A second major underlying theoretical rationale for the interreligious encounter group emerges from educational applications of Kohlberg's theory of moral development. For example, Blatt and Kohlberg (cited in Kohlberg, 1970) have empirically demonstrated a positive effect of moral discussion groups in helping moral development in children. Their studies yielded strong evidence that "a child at an earlier stage of development tends to move forward when confronted by the views of a child one stage further along (Kohlberg, 1970, p. 155). Movement through the stages is attributed to the creation of cognitive dissonance in the child. Discussion of moral dilemmas serves as a catalyst for moral growth by inspiring cognitive conflict, thereby opening avenues of thinking previously dormant (Kohlberg, 1970; Kohlberg & Wasserman, 1980).

Traditional Psychotherapy and Encounter Groups

Discussion of spiritual issues is an important element of the interreligious experience. An overemphasis on the cognitive component may, however, reduce the encounter to an intellectual theological debate among group members, thereby diminishing its therapeutic effectiveness. Religious discussion that excludes the emotional dimension may undermine the encounter's growth potential on a deeper psychological and spiritual level. To enhance the encounter's therapeutic potential, the cognitive aspect must be integrated with feelings and emotions.

By incorporating principles and techniques of psychotherapy and encounter groups, the interreligious encounter group becomes a therapeutic environment in which participants can explore memories and emotions related to spiritual conflicts and personal problems of a religious nature. It is a goal of the experience to provide a supportive environment in which members can share feelings such as sexual guilt, pervasive sense of meaninglessness, disturbing fears of death and punishment, and apprehension over religious doubts and uncertainty. Although psychotherapy and encounter groups were developed to be a medium for sharing deep personal concerns, such groups have traditionally lacked a spiritual focus (Meadow & Kahoe, 1984). To my knowledge, none exists for the specific intent of exploring religious issues and spiritual concerns within a psychological context.

In summary, the interreligious encounter group concept helps religious development by integrating ideas and techniques from spiritual growth groups, moral discussion classes, and group psychotherapy. By synthesizing elements from all three, a therapeutically valuable, psychoreligious growth-enhancing tool is created.

THEORETICAL RATIONALE

In spite of efforts toward rapprochement, religion and psychology exist primarily as separate and distinct disciplines with different functions. A fundamental goal of pastoral and spiritual counseling is to inspire deep commitment to Judeo-Christian ideals. Techniques to accomplish this goal include preaching, pastoral counseling, spiritual growth groups, and religious education (Clinebell, 1984).

Psychology, on the other hand, attempts to increase one's general level of mental and emotional health. The individual's religious functioning, if not viewed as a negative influence to be eliminated, is either ignored as unimportant or assumed to develop naturally after development in other areas. To focus exclusively on spiritual development or general psychological and emotional functioning, however, is to ignore the dynamic interaction between these two important dimensions in the religiously committed individual. Clinebell (1984) expressed this point well.

> If, for whatever reasons, counselors are tuned mainly to the wavelength of psychosocial aspects of human problems, they tend not to hear the profound spiritual longings often present.... On the other hand, lopsided attention to the religious dimension may

149

diminish awareness of complex psycho-social factors that are always interwoven with spiritual issues. (p. 105)

Others have expressed similar viewpoints. Meadow and Kahoe (1984) stated that "religious development is not independent of physical and psychological maturity" (p. 39), and Fowler (1981) emphasized that "structural [faith] change is in part a function of...psychosocial, cognitive, and moral development" (p. 276).

For the religious individual, religion is woven into the fabric of the personality, and religious beliefs and ideas often express and symbolize the individual's deepest concerns and inner experiences. Therefore, we cannot refer to spiritual maturity as an entity separate and apart from the person's total development. The lines of development within the individual are interrelated and influence one another, so that failures of development along one line are likely to impede growth in other areas. Thus, we oversimplify matters if we seek to stimulate religious maturity without taking into consideration other areas of development and the functioning of the personality as a whole.

On the other hand, although religious development is influenced by the individual's general level of psychological and emotional health, the reverse is also true. That is, religiousness affects psychological and emotional functioning. Therefore, changing the client's religious outlook is likely to provide therapeutic leverage in other areas of functioning. Spilka, Hood, and Gorsuch (1985) have theorized that psychological functioning may be enhanced by changing religious attributions. For example, inducing changes in one's perception of God from an oppressive, punitive figure to a divine source of forgiveness and unconditional love may help increase self-esteem. Also, empirical studies indicate that extrinsic religiousness is associated with external locus of control, and an intrinsic faith relates to internal locus of control (Strickland & Shaffer, 1971; Sturgeon & Hamley, 1979). Therefore, it is not unreasonable to expect that inspiring a more intrinsic religious commitment may lead to a decrease in feelings of powerlessness and an increase in acceptance of personal responsibility for behavior. Furthermore, psychological problems may be expressed in religious symbolism. (It should not automatically be assumed, however, that religious interest symbolizes neurotic needs. Religious motivation must be carefully and individually assessed.) By discounting or ignoring religious issues in therapy, important therapeutic material may be lost.

The dual focus of the interreligious encounter group on both the psychological and spiritual aspects of the person can create a powerful therapeutic process. By employing techniques derived from psychotherapy and encounter groups, psychosocial development is set into motion as group members constructively challenge one another, gain insights, work through unfinished business from the past, identify goals, and test new behaviors. Psychosocial growth then provides therapeutic fuel and energy for faith development as religious issues and spiritual conflicts are explored and confronted. As the spiritual dimension develops and matures, the interpersonal, cognitive, and psychosocial dimensions continue to expand as new religious meanings and deeper spiritual commitment enrich the person's life.

Although research has not demonstrated that small group therapeutic approaches integrating religious content are superior to their secular counterpart (Zimpfer, 1986), studies reported were of religiously based psychosocial treatment predicated on Judeo-Christian ideology. Future research is necessary to establish the effectiveness of the interreligious experience compared with other religious and purely secular group approaches.

A Note on Terminology

The term *interreligious encounter group* was chosen for this conceptualization for several reasons. Interreligious was selected to highlight diversity. The goal of the interreligious encounter experience is to create a spiritually diverse context that welcomes persons of all religious traditions (Unitarians, Moslems, Jews, Christians, Bahaists, Buddhists, Hindus, and so forth) as well as individuals who are unaffiliated with any particular faith tradition but who wish to explore the spiritual side of their nature.

The term interreligious was also chosen to avoid misunderstanding the purpose of this encounter as "ecumenical." Although the religiously diverse members unite in a common goal of progressing toward greater psychospiritual maturity, the group is not ecumenical in focus in that it makes no attempt to unify individual religious differences. Instead, such differences are theorized as enhancing the growth process. The greater the diversity of group membership, the greater the potential for growth as each participant encounters within the group the heritage, ideas, and wisdom of the great spiritual traditions of our time.

Encounter was chosen to underscore the confrontive, challenging nature of the exploration while also emphasizing the importance of support and sensitivity associated with traditional encounter groups. Zimpfer (1986) suggested that a confrontive group in which members challenge and question one another, as well as offer care and support, may be more growth producing than a group that merely offers nurturing and communal cohesiveness. Similarly, Yalom (1980) advocated creation of an existential crisis in therapy to stimulate action toward constructive change.

In the psychology of religion literature, Clark (1958) stated that "mature religion...[is] heightened through conflict" (p. 242). This point is also underscored by Kao's (1981) assertion that "a mature encounter with...other ideologies...enriches the believer's faith" (pp. 221, 222). Also, Fowler (1981) hypothesized that movement to higher stages of faith in the developmental process is helped when persons...*encounter* [italics added] and respond to situations or contexts that lead to critical reflection on their tacit value systems.... Stories, symbols, myths and paradoxes from one's own or *other traditions* [italics added] may insist on breaking in upon the neatness of the previous faith...[and] press one toward a more dialectical and multileveled approach to life truth.... Significant *encounters with other traditions* [italics added] ...may complement or correct [one's] own. (pp. 162, 183, 186)

Additionally, the interreligious interaction is intended to help participants experience the "existential...*encounter,* that special, intimate, and verbally undefinable personal relationship that is felt rather than understood" (Crumbaugh, 1979, p. 190).

Finally, a *group* format was chosen because it has been consistently held by experts of religious psychology that faith development emerges in a community (e.g., Clark, 1958; Feinsilver, 1960; Fowler, 1981; Meadow & Kahoe, 1984; Miller, 1965). Additionally, some secular psychotherapists believe that the most effective medium for constructive change is the group. For example, Yalom (1975) identified group cohesiveness and interpersonal learning as potent curative factors in effecting positive personality change. In particular he cites cohesiveness as being critical for influencing group members. Thus group influence fostered by cohesiveness, coupled with caring and confrontation (Clinebell, 1972), may catalyze cognitive and emotional restructuring in members, thereby effecting both psychosocial and spiritual growth.

Working Through Unfinished Business From the Past

Although I have used the terms psychotherapy and encounter groups interchangeably, the two are not synonymous and contain important distinctions. One primary difference relevant to this context is time focus. Encounter groups emphasize feelings and experiencing in the here and now, whereas one important facet of the psychotherapy group is relating current conflicts to past traumatic events (Corey, 1985).

According to Yalom (1980), behavior is influenced by the push of the past, forces in the present, and the pull of the future. Thus, to be maximally effective the interreligious encounter experience must balance a here-and-now focus with the need of some members to rework unhealthy religious motivations resulting from destructive early influences. This suggestion is consistent with Fowler's (1981) recommendations for faith transformation. According to Fowler, faith development is dependent on current personality patterns, psychological integration, and methods of coping with the environment. These in turn are molded in large part by earlier familial and cultural experiences. Reviewing in depth the religious experiences of a 28-year-old woman named Mary, Fowler recounted how Mary's childhood and adolescent experiences negatively influenced her choice of faith, which then set into motion a self-defeating interplay between an immature religious motivation and a maladaptive psychosocial style.

To enable Mary (and others) to acquire a more mature religious outlook, Fowler suggested that "recapitulation in the service of faith development" (p. 289) must be undertaken. By this Fowler means that shifts in religious faith toward higher levels of development can sometimes only occur by reworking past experiences that contributed to the development of an unhealthy religious orientation. For Mary, Fowler recommended

> a combination of consistent experiences of community worship and education supplemented by individual or *small-group work in spiritual direction and psychotherapy* [italics added].... Mary needs a context for and help in a process that will enable her to recapitulate earlier stages of development through a skillful *combination of therapy...and spiritual direction* [italics added].... When the recapitulative process has done its work, the person has a new foundation of inner integration from which to move decisively toward the next stage. (pp. 287, 288, 291)

THE INTERRELIGIOUS ENCOUNTERING PROCESS

As theoretically formulated, the process of movement toward religious maturity within the interreligious encounter group is helped by the following experiences.

1. Exploring religious concerns in light of past familial, cultural, and religious experiences. Exploration focusing on parental, cultural, and institutional religious indoctrination as well as other childhood events may help the group member "recapitulate" spiritual and emotional conflicts. Resolution of internal conflicts and greater acceptance of self and others will then begin to loosen the defensive functions of religious doctrine, thereby helping the member become receptive to a more creative, integrative, and healthier religious outlook.

2. Sharing, confronting, and clarifying current religious and spiritual beliefs, feelings, and experiences to gain awareness of how these influence one's values and life-styles. Permission to express religious doubts is especially crucial. Institutional religion sometimes discourages open expression of doubt by equating uncertainty with lack of faith. Sharing such doubts within the group context normalizes the fear of religious uncertainty. Knowledge that one is not alone in one's uncertainty and that doubt need not imply lack of faith creates a universalizing experience (Yalom, 1975) for members that is therapeutic. Other spiritual and existential concerns, including death, freedom and responsibility, and isolation and meaninglessness (Yalom, 1980), may be explored from the viewpoints of a variety of faith traditions and spiritual ideological systems. Supporting each individual's quest to discover his or her own spiritual truth and meaning in life is paramount to the encountering experience.

3. Developing goals for the future in light of one's emerging psychospiritual growth. Fostering integration of new spiritual insights into one's self-system, consolidating one's developing religious and spiritual identity, and learning to apply spiritual resources to daily living are important components of the group process. Group members may contribute practical suggestions on how to direct one's spiritual energy in ways that maximize mental health and emotional well-being.

SUMMARY AND CONCLUSION

The interreligious encounter experience begins with a group of religiously divergent individuals who come together in a challenging but caring environment. This context, if skillfully helped, should stimulate a cyclical and upwardly spiraling process of psychospiritual growth.

By combining Fowler's insights on faith transformation with ideals from pastoral counseling, moral education, and traditional group psychotherapy, I hypothesize that religious development for many individuals can be helped within an interpersonal, interactive context having both a psychological and spiritual focus. The interreligious encounter group is conceptualized as such a socioreligious context in which psychological and spiritual conflict may be confronted, explored, and reworked, thereby effecting a therapeutic and growth-producing psychospiritual experience.

REFERENCES

Aden, L. (1976). Faith and the development cycle. *Pastoral Psychology, 24*, 215-230.

Allen, R. O., & Spilka, B. (1967). Committed and consensual religion: A specification of religion-prejudice relationships. *Journal for the Scientific Study of Religion, 6*, 191-206.

Allport, G. W. (1963). Behavioral science, religion, and mental health. *Journal of Religion and Health, 2*, 187-197.

Batson, C. D. (1976). Religion as prosocial: Agent or double agent? *Journal for the Scientific Study of Religion, 15*, 29-45.

Bergin, A. E., Masters, K. S., & Richards, P. S. (1987). Religiousness and mental health reconsidered: A study of an intrinsically religious sample. *Journal of Counseling Psychology, 34*, 197-204.

Broen, W. E. (1957). A factor-analytic study of religious attitudes. *Journal of Abnormal and Social Psychology, 54*, 176-179.

Brown, L. B. (1964). Classifications of religious orientations. *Journal for the Scientific Study of Religion, 4*, 91-99.

Clark, W. H. (1958). *The psychology of religion.* New York: Macmillan.

Clinebell, H. (1972). *Growth groups.* Nashville: Abington Press.

Clinebell, H. (1984). *Basic types of pastoral care and counseling.* Nashville: Abington Press.

Corey, G. (1985). *Theory and practice of group counseling.* Monterey, CA: Brooks/Cole.

Crumbaugh, J. C. (1979). Logotherapy as a bridge between religion and psychotherapy. *Journal of Religion and Health, 18*, 188-191.

Evans, R. J. (1952). Personal values of factors in anti-semitism. *Journal of Abnormal and Social Psychology, 47*, 749-758.

Feinsilver, A. (1960). *In search of religious maturity*. Yellow Springs, OH: Antioch.

Fowler, J. W. (1981). *Stages of faith: The psychology of human development and the quest for meaning*. San Francisco: Harper & Row.

Freud, S. (1927). *The future of an illusion*. New York: Doubleday.

Fromm, E. (1950). *Psychoanalysis and religion*. New Haven, CT: Yale University Press.

Glock, C. Y. (1962). On the study of religious commitment. *Religious Education, 42*(Res. Suppl.), 98-110.

James, W. (1902). *The varieties of religious experience*. New York: Modern Library.

Kao, C. L. (1981). *Psychological and religious development: Maturity and maturation*. Lanham, MD: University Press of America.

King, M. B., & Hunt, R. A. (1972). Measuring the religious variable: Replication. *Journal for the Scientific Study of Religion, 11*, 240-251.

Kohlberg, L. (1970). Moral development and the education of adolescents. In R. F. Purnell (Ed.), *Adolescents and the American high school* (pp. 144-162). New York: Holt, Rinehart and Winston.

Kohlberg, L., & Wasserman, E. R. (1980). The cognitive-developmental approach and the practicing counselor: An opportunity for counselors to rethink their roles. *The Personnel and Guidance Journal, 58*, 559-567.

Lenski, G. (1961). *The religious factor*. New York: Doubleday.

Lovinger, R. J. (1984). *Working with religious issues in therapy*. New York: Jason Aronson.

Meadow, M. J., & Kahoe, R. D. (1984). *Psychology of religion: Religion in individual lives*. New York: Harper & Row.

Miller, S. H. (1965). Religion: Healthy and unhealthy. *Journal of Religion and Health, 4*, 295-301.

Quackenbos, S., Privette, G., & Klentz, B. (1985). Psychotherapy: Sacred or secular? *Journal of Counseling and Development, 63*, 290-293.

Spilka, B., Hood, R. W., & Gorsuch, R. L. (1985). *The psychology of religion: An empirical approach*. Englewood Cliffs, NJ: Prentice-Hall.

Strickland, B. R., & Shaffer, S. (1971). I-E, I-E, & F. *Journal for the Scientific Study of Religion, 10*, 366-369.

Sturgeon, R. S., & Hamley, R. W. (1979). Religiosity and anxiety. *Journal of Social Psychology, 108*, 137-138.

Vernon, G. M. (1968). The religious "nones": A neglected category. *Journal for the Scientific Study of Religion, 7*, 219-229.

Wick, E. (1985). Lost in the no-man's-land between psyche and soul. In E. Stern (Ed.), *Psychotherapy and the religiously committed patient* (pp. 13-24). New York: Haworth.

Yalom, I. D. (1975). *The theory and practice of group psychotherapy*. New York: Basic Books.

Yalom, I. D. (1980). *Existential psychotherapy*. New York: Basic Books.

Zimpfer, D. G. (1986). The use of groups in religiously based helping relationships. *Counseling and Values, 30*, 155-168.

Beliefs of Professional Counselors and Clergy About Depressive Religious Ideation

JANICE MINER HOLDEN
RICHARD E. WATTS
WILLIAM BROOKSHIRE

IN A RECENT counseling session, a client, experiencing major depression with suicidal tendencies, stated that she sometimes wondered whether her depression was evidence that God wanted her to suffer. The client, an adherent to a Judeo-Christian religion, further expressed that if God did not prevent her attempts at suicide, God must at least condone her suicide and might even want her to die. That almost identical words were dejectedly exclaimed by the main character in an educational movie depicting a typical depression (Lazarus, 1973), seems to substantiate our observation that such religious ideation occurs commonly in depression.

Despite this possibility, the phenomenon of depressive religious ideation is not mentioned in the *DSM-III-R* discussion of affective disorders (American Psychiatric Association, 1987). It is at best only touched on in the cognitive therapy literature, wherein attitudes toward religious ideation of any kind range from nonexistent (Burns, 1980; Emery, 1988; Williams, 1984), to very negative (Ard, 1971; Ellis, 1962, 1971, 1973, 1984; Ellis & Harper, 1975; Maultsby, 1975; Walen, DiGiuseppe, & Wessler, 1980), to rather more tolerant (Beck, 1976; Beck, Rush, Shaw, & Emery, 1979; Weinrach, 1988), to strongly affirmative (Hart, 1987). Of all these cognitive therapists, only Hart briefly stated that erroneous ideation about God can be a factor in a client's depression. None of these positions were substantiated by references to actual research.

Some theological as well as noncognitive secular literature on depression has touched on the potentially positive effect of religious convictions in the prevention of depression-related suicide. Peschke (1977), a Roman Catholic theologian, referred to the lower incidence of suicide among Catholics than among adherents to other Judeo-Christian faiths, presumably because of the specific prohibition against suicide in Roman Catholic theology. Similarly, the secular author Wetzel (1984) suggested that "if [suicide] violates the client's religious beliefs, you may be able to use these beliefs as a thera-

From "Beliefs of Professional Counselors and Clergy About Depressive Religious Ideation," by J. M. Holden, R. E. Watts, and W. Brookshire, 1991, *Counseling and Values*, 35, 93–103.

peutic tool" (p. 304). Neither the presence of possibly *erroneous* religious ideation in depression, however, nor its potential to *exacerbate* depression and suicide was addressed in either of these sources. A thorough review of the journal literature for the last 10 years yielded no journal articles addressing these phenomena (Loftus, 1983). Thus counselors seeking further information on these phenomena face an apparent paucity in the literature.

This paucity may be the result of a belief that religious issues are outside the domain of the secular counselor. Indeed, a recent general counseling textbook admonished counselors not to use "religious values to solve clients' problems" (Meier, 1989, p. 35). Such general statements may reinforce secular counselors' impressions that a client's religious ideation is therapeutically "off limits," even when such ideation conflicts with the theology of the church to which the client purportedly belongs and seems to be an exacerbating factor in the depression.

Thus, it seems that secular counselors are without guidance regarding whether or how to deal with depressive religious ideation. To begin to bridge this apparent chasm in the literature, we undertook to assess and compare professional counselors' and clergy's beliefs about depressive religious ideation.

METHOD

Development of the Instrument

A questionnaire was designed to assess issues related to religious ideation in depression. It began with a brief case study of the client described at the beginning of this article. It then addressed to what extent respondents (a) perceived such religious ideation to be a *misinterpretation* of Judeo-Christian thinking, (b) believed that addressing such ideation during counseling would *benefit* the client, (c) believed they had the *right* to address it, (d) felt *able* to effectively address it, and (e) expected *resistance* from the client if they were to address such religious ideation. To further analyze these issues, the questionnaire also assessed various respondent characteristics: occupation; sex; age; years of formal religious training, formal counselor training, professional clergy experience, and professional counselor experience; extent to which a cognitive approach is used in counseling; religious denomination; rating of beliefs of religious denominations and personal religious beliefs from conservative to liberal; and willingness to consult about such a client with a professional from the other field (i.e., clergy with professional counselor or vice versa).

The pilot instrument consisted of six Likert-type items for each of the five issues, about half worded "positively" and the remainder "negatively." These were randomly ordered and followed by 12 items assessing the respondent's characteristics. After piloting and revision, the final instrument consisted of 31 criterion and 12 predictor items.

Participants

The sample consisted of 150 National Certified Counselors, selected at random from the *1988 National Directory of Certified Counselors,* and 150 clergy. To sample clergy from churches ranging from relatively conservative to relatively liberal, 50 were selected at random each from the *Annual of Southern Baptist Convention* (Executive Committee, 1988), the *Episcopal Clerical Directory, 1987* (1987), and the Presbyterian's *Minutes of 199th General Assembly, Part 2—Statistics* (1987).

Procedures

Three hundred cover letters, questionnaires, and business-reply envelopes were mailed, requesting anonymous response. Shortly before the requested return date, reminder postcards were mailed.

TABLE 1
Descriptive Patterns for Predictor Variables

Variable	Range	Median	*M*	*SD*
Age				
(1 = 20 to 29)	2-6	3.0	3.33	1.05
Years of religious training	0-4 or more	4.0	2.57	1.74
Years of clergy experience	0-58	7.0	12.07	13.85
Years of counselor training	0-4 or more	3.0	2.55	1.46
Years of counselor experience	0-35	8.0	9.70	9.69
Use of cognitive approach				
(1 = almost never)	2-5	3.0	3.56	.77
Religious denomination[a]				
(1= conservative)	1-4	2.0	1.94	.86
Denomination beliefs[b]				
(1 = very conservative)	1-5	3.0	3.08	1.17
Personal beliefs[c]				
(1 = very conservative)	1-5	3.0	3.24	1.19
Willingness to consult				
(1 = very unwilling)	1-5	5.0	4.05	1.27

Note. Occupation: clergy, n=31; counselor, n=40; both, n=24. Sex: women, n=30; men, n=65.
[a] n = 89; does not include 4 respondents categorized as "other or non-Judeo Christian" and 2 missing cases.
[b] n = 92; does not include 3 respondents categorized as "other."
[c] n = 94; does not include 1 respondent categorized as "other."

RESULTS

Return Rate

Thirty questionnaires were returned undelivered. Of the 270 questionnaires presumed to have been delivered, 95 usable questionnaires were returned, yielding a 35% return rate. By occupation, usable questionnaires were returned by 33% of the counselors and by 37% of the clergy (29% of the Baptists, 47% of the Presbyterians, and 36% of the Episcopalians).

Scoring

The first 31 items were reorganized into appropriate subscales (misinterpret, benefit, and so forth). Scoring was adjusted for positive or negative syntax. Thus, a response of *strongly agree* to the item, "It would be helpful for this client to take a close look at the source of her religious ideas," was scored 5; a response of *strongly disagree* to the item, "Nothing would be gained by this client examining the foundation of her religious ideation," was also scored 5.

Reliability

For this study, a Cronbach alpha of .80 or higher was considered acceptable; .60-.79, marginal; and .59 or below, unacceptable for further statistical analysis. The reliability for each subtest was misinterpretation (after elimination of one item) alpha=.76, benefit alpha=.83, right alpha=.85, able alpha=.88, and resistance alpha=.86.

Descriptive Patterns

Descriptive patterns for responses to the 12 predictor variables are reviewed in Table 1.

A preliminary task of this study was to describe patterns for each occupational group regarding issues related to depressive religious ideation. Because 25% of respondents described themselves as *both* professional counselors and clergy (35% of "clergy" and 14% of "counselors"), a third occupational category was formed: "both." Descriptive patterns for responses on each of the five criteria are reviewed in Table 2.

Three of the five subtests were strongly skewed, with overall medians at or above 4.5, in the direction of agreement on the misinterpretation, benefit, and right variables. Skewing also occurred, but not so strongly, in the direction of agreement on the able variable. Responses were more normally distributed around a slight tendency to expect resistance.

TABLE 2
Descriptive Patterns for Issues Related to Religious Ideation in Depression

Issue	Median	M	SD
Misinterpretation[a]	**5.00**	**4.76**	**.46**
Clergy	5.00	4.84	.34
Both	5.00	4.85	.41
Counselors	5.00	4.65	.54
Benefit	**4.67**	**4.38**	**.68**
Clergy	4.68	4.38	.65
Both	4.75	4.38	.83
Counselors	4.42	4.38	.61
Right	**4.50**	**4.27**	**.77**
Clergy	4.25	4.31	.66
Both	4.83	4.49	.86
Counselors	4.25	4.12	.79
Able	**4.17**	**4.02**	**.87**
Clergy	4.33	4.16	.73
Both	4.75	4.49	.61
Counselors	3.75	3.62	.93
Resistance	**3.43**	**3.45**	**.79**
Clergy	3.43	3.45	.65
Both	3.50	3.58	.81
Counselors	3.43	3.38	.86

Note. Bold typeface indicates overall scores: $n = 95$. Occupational subgroups: counselors, $n = 40$; both $n = 24$; clergy, $n = 31$.
[a]Marginally reliable.

Regarding the misinterpretation variable, loading was very similar and most extreme among the clergy and "both" groups, and only slightly less extreme among the counselor group. Regarding the variables benefit, right, and able, loading was most extreme among the "both" group, followed by the clergy, with the relative least loading in that direction among the counselor group. This was particularly the case for the able variable; the central tendency of counselors' scores dropped, relatively speaking, to the range of *uncertain* to *agree,* (a) as compared with their central tendency scores in the *agree* to *strongly agree* range on misinterpretation, right, and benefit and (b) considering that the other two occupational groups' central tendency scores were in the *agree* to *strongly agree* range for all four of these skewed variables. Regarding the resistance variable, loading was slightly greater among the "both" group as compared with the clergy and counselor groups.

TABLE 3
Regression Coefficient Values

Predictor variables	Criterion variables: Issues related to religious ideation in depression				
	Misinterpretation*	Benefit**	Right**	Able**	Resistance**
Occupation 1 (clergy)	.050	.232	.262	.252	- .054
Occupation 2 (both)	.067	- .073	.391	.061	.064
Sex	n.s.	.322	n.s.	n.s.	n.s.
Age	n.s.	n.s.	n.s.	-.274	.172
Religious training	n.s.	n.s.	.195	.192	n.s.
Clergy experience	n.s.	n.s.	n.s.	n.s.	n.s.
Clergy	n.s.	-.021	-.021	n.s.	n.s.
Both	n.s.	-.084	-.064	n.s.	n.s.
Counselor training	n.s.	n.s.	n.s.	n.s.	n.s.
Counselor experience	n.s.	n.s.	.050	.027	n.s.
Both	n.s.	.087	n.s.	n.s.	n.s.
Counselors	n.s.	-.010	n.s.	n.s.	n.s.
Cognitive approach	n.s.	.261	.246	.293	n.s.
Religious denomination	n.s.	n.s.	n.s.	n.s.	n.s.
Denomination beliefs	n.s.	n.s.	n.s.	n.s.	n.s.
Personal beliefs	n.s.	n.s.	n.s.	n.s.	n.s.
Willingness to consult	n.s.	n.s.	n.s.	n.s.	n.s.
Constant		4.75	4.43	4.96	2.91

*Marginally reliable subtest; $p \leq .05$.
**$p \leq .10$.

Analyses

A second task of this study was to determine what predictive factors might be contributing to differences among occupational groups. Multiple regression was used to analyze the data. Occupation was effect coded, while all other variables were either dichotomous or continuous. For each of the five criterion variables, occupation was forced into the equation and all other predictor variables were subjected to backward elimination. Regression coefficients for significant predictors are reviewed in Table 3.

Misinterpretation. The reduced model for the misinterpretation variable included only occupation but was not significant ($R^2=.039$; $F=1.74$; $df=2,87$; $p \leq .18$).

Benefit. Preliminary analyses regarding the benefit variable indicated interaction between occupation and counseling experience and occupation and religious experience. Therefore, the product terms between the effect codes for occupation and counseling experience, and for occupation and religious experience, were included in this model, along with sex and the extent of use of the cognitive approach in counseling. The reduced model R^2 was .419

(F=7.31; df=8,81; p≤.0001). The R^2 change due to the interaction terms was .281 (F=9.80; df=4,81; p≤.0001).

The regression coefficient on sex indicated that men were more likely to score higher on the benefit variable than were women, as were respondents who were more likely to use the cognitive approach in counseling. For clergy, as the years of religious experience decreased, benefit variable's score increased. For respondents who were reportedly both clergy and professional counselors, counseling and religious experience tended to balance each other out if these two experience factors were about equal. The regression weights indicated that in the "both" group as counseling experience increased and religious experience decreased, benefit variable's scores tended to increase. For the counselor group, less counseling experience tended to be associated with slightly higher benefit variable scores.

Right. Preliminary analyses regarding the variable right indicated an interaction between occupation and clergy experience. Therefore, the product terms between the effect codes for occupation and clergy experience were included in this model along with religious training, use of the cognitive approach in counseling, and counseling experience. The R^2 for the reduced model was .341 (F=6.07; df=7,82; p≤.0001). Religious training, counseling experience, and use of the cognitive approach were directly related to the right variable scores.

The R^2 for analysis of the interaction was .162 (F=10.08; df=2,82; p≤.0001). The regression weights indicated that among the clergy less experience was associated with slightly higher right variable scores. For the "both" group, less clergy experience was associated with considerably higher right variable scores unless moderated by counseling experience, in which case only slightly higher scores for the right variable resulted. Regarding counseling experience, interaction was not a factor.

Able. The reduced model for the able variable included occupation, age, cognitive approach, counselor experience, and religious training, yielding an R^2 of .362 (F=7.85; df=6,83; p≤.0001). Occupation did not make a significant unique contribution to the model. Age was inversely related to the able variable's score. Counselor experience, religious training, and use of the cognitive approach were all directly related to the able variable's score. Regarding counseling experience, interaction was not a factor.

Resistance. The reduced model for the resistance variable included occupation and age, yielding a nonsignificant R^2 of .062 (F=1.91; df=3,86; p≤.13). Age was left in the model because it did make a significant unique contribution to the model with a change in R^2 of .055 (F=5.04; df=1,86; p≤.027). Higher age was associated with higher resistance variable scores.

DISCUSSION

The limited response rate and consequent self-selected nature of the sample used in this study greatly limit the external validity of these results. Although it cannot be assumed that the attitudinal tendencies found in this research are representative of all professional counselors and clergy, the results suggest some possible trends.

It is noteworthy that some factors seemed in this study to be unrelated to any differences in beliefs about depressive religious ideation. Among these were respondents' religious denominations as categorized from *very conservative* to *very liberal* by either ourselves or the respondents themselves and personal beliefs as categorized by respondents. Some respondents complained that such categories were difficult to apply, highly subjective, and potentially unreliable. A follow-up correlation between our categorizations and those of respondents' regarding Christian respondents' religious denominations yielded a significant direct correlation ($r=.73$, $p \leq .001$), suggesting some reliability. This increased our confidence in the finding that among these responders, religious affiliation and personal beliefs were unrelated to beliefs about depressive religious ideation.

Also seemingly unrelated were willingness to consult with a member of the other profession and years of professional counselor training. Although the occupational groups varied on the former factor, and correlation between occupational group and willingness to consult yielded significantly less willingness on the part of the counselors ($r=-.298$, $p \leq .01$), this difference apparently did not contribute to the variance in scores on any of the five issues. Similarly, although the occupational groups varied a great deal on professional counselor training, the clergy having loaded at 0 and 1 years and the counselor and "both" groups having loaded at "4 or more years," this difference apparently did not contribute to variance in scores on any of the five issues.

Possible patterns did emerge regarding some of the remaining predictors, but not on the issue of misinterpretation. Respondents were apparently in strong accordance that the depressed client's religious ideation was a misinterpretation of Judeo-Christian principles. It cannot be concluded from this study that all professionals, both clergy and secular, find such ideation to be erroneous; these data merely suggest this possibility. If further research were to substantiate this finding, that knowledge could help secular counselors who are uncertain on this issue to feel more justified in targeting such ideation.

Respondents of all occupational groups also tended to agree or strongly agree that the client would benefit from examining her religious ideation and that they had the right to challenge such ideation. Clergy and "both" groups tended to agree or strongly agree that they felt able to effectively challenge such ideation, whereas secular counselors tended to drop to the *uncertain* to *agree* range.

Respondents who reportedly used the cognitive approach more frequently in their counseling tended to believe it relatively more beneficial to the client to examine his or her seemingly erroneous religious ideation, to believe it more their right to challenge such ideation, and to feel more able to do so effectively. The fundamental tenet of the cognitive approach is that alleviation of client depression results from the client having learned how to identify irrational or dysfunctional thoughts and replace them with more rational and functional ones. Addressing erroneous *religious* ideation would simply be a special case of that general principle. It is easier for us to imagine that skill with the cognitive approach fosters belief in benefit, right, and especially ability, rather than the opposite; in particular, if one already feels able to challenge effectively such beliefs, why seek training in cognitive counseling skills? It is possible, however, that some predisposing factor, such as a forceful personality or a tendency to operate on intellect more than affect, leads to both belief in ability and use of the cognitive approach.

Also regarding the benefit, right, and ability to challenge seemingly erroneous religious ideation, at least two of the three beliefs tended to increase with more religious training, less clergy experience, and more counselor experience. The tendency to feel less able to challenge erroneous religious ideation seems consonant with the expectation of more client resistance if attempting to do so; why older respondents expressed these tendencies to a relatively greater degree is not so clear.

Of particular interest to us was the relative drop in secular counselors' beliefs in their ability to effectively challenge seemingly erroneous religious ideation. Of the factors shown to contribute to belief in ability among these respondents, the only one that is the exclusive domain of the clergy and "both" groups is more years of formal religious training. It seems most likely to us that relatively more formal religious training enhances the professional's ability to effectively challenge erroneous religious ideation. It cannot, however, be concluded that simply *providing* secular counselors with some compensatory formal religious training will increase their ability; the reported absence of formal religious training among some secular counselors may not be just a case of benign omission, but rather one of active avoidance. If the latter is the case, opportunities for compensatory formal religious training might be bypassed or resisted. This raises an interesting area for potential research.

These findings, tentative as they are, might be used in at least three possible future studies. Does challenging seemingly erroneous religious ideation *actually* contribute to the alleviation of depression? Recent research demonstrating the efficacy of cognitive therapy in the treatment of depression (Grinspoon, 1988) would lend support to the pursuit of a study targeting erroneous religious cognitions. Assuming that the researcher would want to use clinicians with the most positive attitudes toward such clinical intervention, he or she might send potential cooperating clinicians a questionnaire such as the one used in this study. At least from among those who respond, the researcher might select those who identify themselves as secular counselors with at least some formal religious training or as counselor-clergy (the "both" group in this study), both of whom are relatively experienced as counselors, who describe themselves as frequently using a cognitive approach to counseling, and who are relatively younger.

If such intervention were shown to be even somewhat clinically effective, variations in clinicians' effectiveness might be assessed at least on the basis of beliefs studied herein. For example, are clinicians who *believe* themselves more able to effectively challenge erroneous religious ideation *actually* more effective? And what relationship exists between the predictors found to be significant in this study and clinicians' actual effectiveness?

The results of both of these studies could be applied to develop ways to train clinicians best in this type of intervention. Further research could examine the value of various training strategies, such as the teaching of cognitive counseling skills and compensatory formal religious training for secular counselors reportedly having had little or no such training. Regarding the latter, of particular interest might be whether such training is sought after and accepted by that group, and if so whether it enhances their belief in their ability and their actual ability to effectively challenge seemingly erroneous religious ideation.

REFERENCES

American Psychiatric Association. (1987). *Diagnostic and statistical manual of mental disorders* (3rd ed., rev.). Washington, DC: American Psychiatric Association.

Ard, B. N. (1971). The case of the black and silver masochist. In A. E. Ellis (Ed.), *Growth through reason* (pp. 15-45). N. Hollywood, CA: Wilshire.

Beck, A. T. (1976). *Cognitive therapy and the emotional disorders*. New York: International Universities Press.

Beck, A. T., Rush, A. J., Shaw, B. F., & Emery, G. (1979). *Cognitive therapy of depression*. New York: Guilford.

Burns, D. S. (1980). *Feeling good: The new mood therapy*. New York: Morrow.

Ellis, A. E. (1962). *Reason and emotion in psychotherapy*. New York: Lyle Stuart.

Ellis, A. E. (1971). *Growth through reason*. N. Hollywood, CA: Wilshire.

Ellis, A. E. (1973). *Humanistic psychotherapy*. New York: McGraw-Hill.

Ellis, A. E. (1984). Rational-emotive therapy. In R. J. Corsini (Ed.), *Current psychotherapies* (3rd ed., pp. 196-238). Englewood Cliffs, NJ: Prentice-Hall.

Ellis, A. E., & Harper, R. A. (1975). *A new guide to rational living*. Englewood Cliffs, NJ: Prentice-Hall.

Emery, G. D. (1988). *Getting undepressed*. New York: Touchstone.

Episcopal clerical directory, 1987. (1987). Welton, CT: Morehouse-Barlow.

Executive Committee. (1988). *Annual of Southern Baptist Convention*. (Available from Harold C. Bennett, Pres. and Treas., 901 Commerce St., Nashville, TN 37203)

Grinspoon, L. (Ed.). (1988). Treatment of mood disorders: Part III. *Harvard Medical School Mental Health Letter, 5*(5), pp. 1-4.

Hart, A. D. (1987). *Counseling the depressed*. Waco, TX: Word.

Lazarus, T. (Producer & Director). (1973). *Depression: A study in abnormal behavior* [Film]. New York: McGraw-Hill Films.

Maultsby, M. C. (1975). *Help yourself to happiness*. Boston: Marlborough/Herman.

Meier, S. T. (1989). *The elements of counseling*. Pacific Grove, CA: Brooks/Cole.

Minutes of 199th General Assembly Part 2—Statistics. (January-December, 1987). Louisville, KY: Office of General Assembly, Presbyterian Church.

Peschke, C. H. (1977). *Christian ethics: A presentation of special moral theology in the Light of Vatican II* (Vol. 2). Westminster, MD: Christian Classics.

Walen, S. R., DiGiuseppe, R., & Wessler, R. L. (1980). *A practitioner's guide to rational-emotive therapy*. New York: Oxford.

Weinrach, S. G. (1988). Cognitive therapist: A dialogue with Aaron Beck. *Journal of Counseling and Development, 67*(3), 159-164.

Wetzel, J. W. (1984). *Clinical handbook of depression*. New York: Gardner.

Williams, J. M. G. (1984). *The psychological treatment of depression: A guide to the theory and practice of cognitive-behavior therapy*. New York: Free Press.

Religious Beliefs and Practice: An Integral Aspect of Multicultural Awareness

ROBERT H. PATE, JR.
AMY MILLER BONDI

THE *ETHICAL STANDARDS* of the American Counseling Association (ACA, formerly the American Association for Counseling and Development [AACD]) (AACD, 1988) and the Council for Accreditation of Counseling and Related Educational Programs (CACREP) standards for accredited programs (CACREP, 1988) recognize the importance of cultural diversity in the training and work of counselors. If counselors are to guard "the individual rights and personal dignity of the client" (AACD, 1988; *Ethical Standards* Section A, 10), they must learn during their professional education to respect the importance of spirituality and religion in the lives of clients and how to incorporate that respect in their practice.

Spirituality, which is usually defined as a view of one's place in the universe, is a more inclusive concept than religion. Religious faith, practice, and values may result from one's spirituality, but we use the term *religious* because the research we have reviewed uses the term *religious* to refer to specific religious faith and practice. When we are referring to a broader view than specific religious faith and practice, the more inclusive term *spiritual* is added.

We believe religious values and their importance to clients should be presented as an essential element of all counselor education programs. One reason is to respond to the CACREP (1988) Social and Cultural Foundations Standard (Section II, J, 2). The basic standard states that entry-level programs should include "studies that provide an understanding of societal changes and trends; human roles; social subgroups; social mores and interaction patterns; and differing lifestyles" (p. 25). A substandard specifically lists religious preference as one topic to be included in the curriculum.

A proposed draft of revisions to the CACREP standards (1991) changes the Social and Cultural Foundations Standard (Section II, J, 2) to "studies that provide an understanding of issues and trends in a multicultural and diverse society." A subsection of the proposed standard includes religious preference in a list of factors on which attitudes and behavior can be based.

From "Religious Beliefs and Practice: An Integral Aspect of Multicultural Awareness," 1992, *Counselor Education and Supervision, 32,* 108–115.

To meet the spirit of the CACREP standards, counselor educators must recognize the importance of religious beliefs and values as a component of client culture and make counselor education students aware of that importance.

We have three purposes for this consideration of the role of religious factors in counseling. Our first purpose is to present a rationale for the position that the religious beliefs of clients must be considered if cultural and value diversity among clients is to be truly respected. Second, we demonstrate that religious beliefs and values have a legitimate place in the multicultural component of the counselor education curriculum. Third, we offer suggestions for counselor education programs, which, if implemented, will ensure that religious beliefs are not ignored in the preparation of counselors.

THE IMPORTANCE OF RELIGIOUS BELIEFS IN COUNSELING

The 1990 *Statistical Abstract of the United States* reports that 142 million citizens are members of religious bodies with memberships of 50,000 or more. There are numerous independent religious organizations that have fewer than 50,000 members. Based on their review of literature on religious beliefs, Kroll and Sheehan (1989) concluded that more than 90% of the general public profess a belief in God, compared with 40%-70% of psychiatrists and 43% of psychologists. Likewise, Bergin and Jensen (1990) cited a 1985 Gallup survey of more than 29,000 persons, two thirds of whom responded that religion was the most important or a very important dimension of their lives.

The need for religious factors to be included in the training and practice of mental health professionals is well documented. For example, Bergin and Jensen (1990) surveyed 425 therapists representing 59% of a national sample of clinical psychologists, psychiatrists, clinical social workers, and marriage and family therapists. Of this national sample, 77% agreed with the statement, "I try hard to live by my religious beliefs," and 46% agreed with the statement, "My whole approach to life is based on religion." Yet, only 29% of them expressed a belief that religious matters were important in the treatment of all or many of their clients. As part of a discussion about the discrepancy between the personal investment of therapists in religion and their consideration of religion in therapy, Bergin (1991) concluded, "This discrepancy probably reflects the fact that such matters have not been incorporated into clinical training as have other modern issues such as gender, ethnicity, and race" (p. 396).

The topic of the role of religious values in counseling is not absent from the counseling literature. An article in *The Counseling Psychologist* by Worthington (1989) and the previously cited *American Psychologist* article by Bergin (1991) are the most comprehensive current sources. Worthington identified five compelling reasons to give attention to the implications of religious faith in understanding both normal development and remediation. His reasons were that (a) a high percentage of the population in the United States identifies itself as religious; (b) many people who are undergoing emotional crises consider religion as they manage their dilemmas, even if they have not recently been active in formal religion; (c) many clients are reluctant to bring up their religious considerations as part of secular therapy; (d) in general, therapists are not as religiously oriented as their clients; and (e) as a result of being less religiously oriented than their clientele, many helpers might not be as informed about religion as would be maximally helpful for many of their clients.

The AACD *Ethical Standards* (1988) certainly implies in the preamble that ethical counselors should be able to recognize and accept the religious values of clients as they would other important attributes that contribute to client uniqueness. Religion is specifically recognized in Section B: Counseling Relationship (19) of the AACD standards and in Section A: General (11) of the National Board for Certified Counselors *Code of Ethics* (1987). Of far more importance than the explicit mention of religion are the implicit requirements of the cited ethical codes, and others that govern counselors, which require respect for the unique values of clients. For counselor educators the question should not be whether religious beliefs will be presented and discussed as a critical component of client diversity, but how to include religious faith in the curriculum.

RELIGIOUS BELIEFS AS AN ASPECT OF CULTURE AND MULTICULTURAL CURRICULUM

Counselor educators recognize and accept the necessity for multicultural training, but what does "culture" include? Our review of dictionary definitions of *culture* indicates that religion is typically part of the definition of culture. Counselor educators may give examples of how ethnic traditions, race, and sex can affect a client's response to a counselor, but how many of our examples include the effect religious beliefs and values have on clients and the counseling process? Yet, Pedersen (1990) stated that the multicultural perspective is a forceful influence in mental health counseling and takes a broad view of culture. That broad view includes the following:

> Ethnographic variables such as ethnicity, nationality, religion, and language, as well as demographic variables such as age, gender, and place of residence, [and] status variables such as social, economic, and educational factors, and affiliations. (p. 93)

Likewise, Coughlin (1992) reported that social scientists are showing increased interest in cultural diversity and ethnicity, and "religion is understood to be intimately tied to ethnic identity" (p. 6).

A recent special issue of the *Journal of Counseling & Development* (Pedersen, 1991), which had a multicultural focus, contained 33 articles, 11 of which specifically included religion in the discussion of multicultural components of counseling. The importance of religion and spiritual values in counseling is likewise described by Lee (1991) in his discussion of the role of cultural dynamics in multicultural counseling. The significance of religious beliefs is made more explicit in Richardson's (1991) chapter in the same book. Richardson specifically addressed the influence of the African American church in the lives of African American clients and the implications of the church for those providing mental health services to this group. Although the prominence of the church for many African American clients makes the tie to multicultural awareness explicit, the influence of religion in the lives of other groups is no less important. For example, the role of guilt and psychological disturbance as a result of "sins" has been discussed by Ellis (1981), among many others. Beyond those who appreciate the doctrine of certain fundamental Christian groups, the consequence of guilt produced by the belief that "if I were a good Christian, I would not have problems that cause me to need counseling" is not well understood.

Two additional examples illustrate the tie between religion and culture. A U.S. Supreme Court decision (*Employment Division, Department of Human Resources of Oregon v. Smith*, 1990), which involved substance abuse counselors, addressed the issue of the use of an illegal substance, peyote, as part of the worship practices of the Native American church. A *Washington Post* feature article (Snead, 1991) described the use of snakes in the religious practice of some people in the Appalachian mountain region, an area recognized in the *Journal of Counseling & Development* special issue on multicultural counseling as a distinct cultural setting (Wesner, Patel, & Allen, 1991).

We endorse the concern raised by Locke (1990) that to view multicultural counseling simply as counseling that recognizes individual differences is to deny that clients are both individuals and members of groups. We suggest, however, that both ethnic minority group members and majority group members bring meaningful differences in their religious beliefs and values to counseling. Those differences are in some instances related to group membership and in others are related to individual experiences. The United States is such a religiously diverse society that any group characterization is impossible. What is possible, is for counselors to learn that part of the cultural development of many of their clients has involved religion; thus, to omit this aspect of their clients' lives from counseling is to omit a significant part of the identity of those they are attempting to serve. Coughlin (1992) stated that more social scientists and mental health professionals must consider the role a person's religious or spiritual values play in personality or mental health, because personality, attitudes, and behavior are shaped by these cultural values.

We found one initial client assessment procedure that included religion, and it was based on a multicultural model. In the previously cited special multicultural counseling issue in the *Journal of Counseling & Development*, Ibrahim (1991) suggested that the counselor first assess the worldview of the client using the Scale to Assess Worldviews. The "religion subscribed to" is specifically identified as an element of cultural identity in Ibrahim's worldview assessment.

SUGGESTIONS FOR COUNSELOR EDUCATION PROGRAMS

Counselor education students need to be taught the importance of religious beliefs in the lives of many of their clients. The CACREP standard that requires the recognition of client diversity should be addressed by the inclusion of religious and spiritual values in the multicultural component of the counselor education curriculum. We recognize the necessity to stress other influential cultural elements and social issues in this aspect of the curriculum, but examples and material that demonstrate the relevance of religion in the counseling process should also be included.

One benefit of including religious values and practice in the multicultural sensitivity component of the curriculum is to reinforce the point that cultural awareness and sensitivity are imperative in all counseling. Just because clients may give an initial impression of being "just like us," they may differ in fundamental ways that are important for the counseling relationship. We offer the following actions as means to implement our suggestions.

Course Content

Counselor education courses should include spiritual and religious values as important differences among clients. Religious beliefs should be included, among other vital client differences, in the elements of the curriculum that ensure that counselor education students understand cultural diversity. Like other important elements of cultural diversity, recognizing client differences in religious experience requires more than simply recognizing individual differences. Specific examples of how religious beliefs affect clients (for example, the feeling of being different) should be used in the curriculum. Training in intake, client assessment, and diagnosis should include religious beliefs and values as an area for counselor sensitivity and, if appropriate, inquiry.

Student Experiences

Patterson (1992) recognized that counselor values, including religious values, are implicit in the counseling process, style, and goals. The experiences in counselor education curricula that allow students to become aware of their attitudes, feelings, and beliefs and that provide for personal awareness and growth should include spiritual issues. Counselors must be comfortable with their own spirituality before they can allow clients' religion to have a place in the counseling process. Counselors should become aware that there may be times when they cannot be effective because of their own strong religious beliefs or because unresolved spiritual issues in their lives limit their ability to truly focus on the client. Exercises and disclosure activities should encourage students to discuss their religious values and questions as well as how those beliefs affect their counseling.

Case Studies

Training examples, role-plays, and seminars at which case discussions occur should include instances in which the religious values and experiences of clients are critical in the helping process. Similarly, the influence of the counselor's religious beliefs and values should be illustrated. Counselor educators should not limit such examples to the teaching of the Roman Catholic church regarding abortion. Examples should be found that students know are relevant for the clients they will serve in their geographic region. For instance, the beliefs of many born-again Christians as sources of guilt and strength should not be ignored.

Collaboration With Religious Helpers

Counselors should be taught to use religious counselors as allies at appropriate times, yet should also know the ethical and professional limits of working with religious counselors. The range of professional approaches and training of religious-pastoral counselors should be included in the section of the curriculum in which other professions are presented. Counselor education students need to know that whereas some religious counselors will use concepts and techniques identical to those taught in their program, others will simply quote scripture in response to client problems.

CONCLUSION

Bergin (1991) stated, "Psychologists' understanding and support of cultural diversity has been exemplary with respect to race, gender, and ethnicity but the profession's tolerance and empathy has not adequately reached the religious client" (p. 399). We are encouraging counselor educators to be equally exemplary and to be leaders in taking religion "out of the closet" (McWhirter, 1989). Religious beliefs are an aspect of culture that we, as counselors, must consider if we are to serve diverse populations. Counselors can and should learn from those who say that all good multicultural counseling is based on respect for and appreciation of the uniqueness of each individual. As counselor educators, we must also learn to incorporate in our curricula the concepts of multicultural counseling that are so important if we are to serve culturally, ethnically, racially, and *religiously* diverse populations.

REFERENCES

American Association for Counseling and Development. (1988). *Ethical standards*. Alexandria, VA: Author.

Bergin. A. E. (1991). Values and religious issues in psychotherapy and mental health. *American Psychologist, 46*, 394-403.

Bergin, A. E., & Jensen, J. P. (1990). Religiosity of psychotherapists: A national survey. *Psychotherapy, 27*, 3-7.

Coughlin. E. K. (1992. April 1). Social scientists again turn attention to religion's place in the world. *The Chronicle of Higher Education*, pp. 6, A7, A8.

Council for Accreditation of Counseling and Related Educational Programs. (1988). *Accreditation procedures manual and application*. Alexandria, VA: Author.

Council for Accreditation of Counseling and Related Educational Programs. (1991). *Second draft, standards revision proposal, June, 1991*. Alexandria, VA: Author.

Ellis, A. (1981). Science, religiosity, and rational emotive psychotherapy. *Psychotherapy: Theory, Research and Practice, 18*, 155-158.

Employment Division, Department of Human Resources of Oregon et al. v. Smith et al. 110 S. Ct. 1595 (1990).

Ibrahim, F. A. (1991). Contribution of cultural worldview to generic counseling and development. *Journal of Counseling & Development, 70*, 13-19.

Kroll, J., & Sheehan, W. (1989). Religious beliefs and practices among 52 psychiatric inpatients in Minnesota. *American Journal of Psychiatry, 146*, 67-72.

Lee, C. C. (1991). Cultural dynamics: Their importance in multicultural counseling. In C. C. Lee & B. L. Richardson (Eds.), *Multicultural issues in counseling: New approaches in diversity* (pp. 11-17). Alexandria, VA: AACD Press.

Locke, D. C. (1990). A not so provincial view of multicultural counseling. *Counselor Education and Supervision, 30*, 18-25.

McWhirter, J. J. (1989). Religion and the practice of counseling psychology. *The Counseling Psychologist, 17*, 613-616.

National Board for Certified Counselors. (1987). *Code of ethics*. Alexandria. VA: Author.

Patterson, C. H. (1992). Values in counseling and psychotherapy. In M. T. Burke & J. G. Miranti (Eds.), *Ethical and spiritual values in counseling* (pp. 107-109). Alexandria, VA: AACD Press.

Pedersen, P. (1990). The multicultural perspective as a fourth force in counseling. *Journal of Mental Health Counseling, 12*, 93-95.

Pedersen, P. (Ed.). (1991). Multiculturalism as a fourth force in counseling [Special Issue]. *Journal of Counseling & Development, 70*(1).

Richardson, B. L. (1991). Utilizing the resources of the African American church: Strategies for counseling professionals. In C. C. Lee & B. L. Richardson (Eds.), *Multicultural issues in counseling: New approaches in diversity* (pp. 65-75). Alexandria. VA: AACD Press.

Snead, B. (1991, September 15). For heaven's snakes. *Washington Post*, pp. F1, F4.

U.S. Bureau of the Census. (1990). *Statistical abstract of the United States: 1990* (110th ed.). Washington, DC: Author.

Wesner, D., Patel, C., & Allen, J. (1991). A study of explosive rage in male spouses counseled in an Appalachian mental health clinic. *Journal of Counseling & Development, 70,* 235-241.

Worthington, E. L., Jr. (1989). Religious faith across the life span: Implications for counseling and research. *The Counseling Psychologist, 17,* 555-612.

Exploring the Religious-Spiritual Needs of the Dying

DOUGLAS C. SMITH

IN 1990, A survey was circulated among directors of hospice programs asking them to describe patients achieving a "healthy" death, a death in which there were psychological benefits to the dying person and the dying person's family (Smith, 1990; Smith & Maher, 1991). In that survey, there was dramatic agreement among those surveyed concerning the need to explore religious-spiritual issues: 79% of the descriptions of people attaining a "healthy" death had references to the dying person's need for some form of religious-spiritual dialogue. Of even more significance was the finding that over 50% of those dying people who were identified as "not involved in organized religion" also had a need to talk about religious-spiritual matters. The survey also revealed that this need and interest in religious-spiritual matters became extremely heightened as death became imminent, a finding that has been supported by several other sources (Andersen & MacElveen-Hoehn, 1988; Hinton, 1963; Leviton, 1986).

THE PATIENT'S SITUATION

This heightened interest among the dying in religious and spiritual issues should not be too surprising to any student of theology because much of the literature of the world's religions is immersed in the vocabulary and metaphor of dying (Kramer, 1988). Watts (1961) and Axelrod (1986) have even suggested that a great amount of incentive for creating and perpetuating religious and spiritual systems is precisely to serve people's involvement in some form of anticipatory grief. In other words, much of the purpose of religious and spiritual explorations is precisely to aid those who have decided to face the fact that they are going to die. Religious and spiritual issues are designed for the explorations of the living who know that they are also among the dying.

From "Exploring the Religious-Spiritual Needs of the Dying," by D. C. Smith, 1993, *Counseling and Values, 37,* 71–77.

The Counselor's Approach

The counselor may have difficulty accurately assessing patients' positions on religious-spiritual issues. According to Jarvis and Northcott (1987), religious membership often can be confused with religious involvement, and both of them can be mistaken for religiosity and spirituality (e.g., beliefs, devotion, moral philosophy). What is openly professed by the patient might, in fact, be entirely different from what is believed in actuality. So, when the counselor is assessing a client's belief system, the counselor is likely to be very confused.

Yet, in spite of this confusion, Rogers (1986) felt that the counselor's attitude toward the patient must always be the same: a "nonjudgmental, acceptant attitude toward whatever the client is" (p. 198). Consequently, Mauritzen (1988) has written that patients "have the right to expect total acceptance of all they stand for as persons. This applies especially to everyone's spiritual beliefs and preferences" (p. 119). Therefore, the counselor must exercise restraint so as not to impose his or her own theology on the patient, and the counselor must strive to totally accept the patient's belief system, whatever that belief system might be.

Rando (1984) has said that imposing theology on any client is certainly inappropriate, but it is most inappropriate on the person who is dying. Mauritzen (1988) echoed that sentiment in saying that "there is no excuse for imposing on a dying patient" (p. 120). No matter how nourishing a counselor's theology might be for the counselor, there is no guarantee that that same theology might not be very toxic for the patient. It is not the role of the counselor to proselytize under any circumstances.

Not only does a counselor not give a theology to a client, but just the opposite is to be the case: The counselor is to receive the theology of the client in a nonjudgmental attitude of acceptance. After all, the dying patient's theology "may be the glue that holds their world together" (Anderson, 1989, p. 142). It is the counselor's work to focus on this "glue" that the patient presents so that the counselor might reveal to the patient the patient's own resources, resources that can be used in traveling the journey of anticipatory grief. Therefore, Propst (1980) has claimed that it is the counselor's role to "make maximum use of the assumptive world of the client" (p. 176).

EXERCISES FOR ASSESSING AND EXPLORING THE SPIRITUAL

Based on the foregoing, the following tools are being presented for counselors to use in assessing and exploring religious-spiritual issues with the dying. These tools are being suggested as ways of bringing forth a patient's own resources. The counselor's role is to help the client identify these resources and then help the client learn how to rely on these resources. The tools being suggested view religious-spiritual resources from a nonjudgmental, nonparochial perspective.

Much awkwardness can be felt for both the counselor and the client concerning when and how these exercises are introduced. The following straightforward introduction could be used during the third or fourth session with the client: "In working with people who have been told that they are terminally ill, I have found that they often do not just have physical needs. I have found that clients also have emotional and spiritual issues that they would like to discuss, but they often feel awkward in initiating those discussions. I also feel awkward sometimes in talking about emotional and spiritual things. Yet, I have found that we can both benefit by getting over that awkwardness. Would you mind if I introduce you to a technique I use in helping to eliminate some of that awkwardness? I feel it will be helpful."

Seven Questions

Counselor: "There are some questions that I would like you to answer."

1. What are your three greatest sources of strength?
2. When you want to feel comforted, where do you go, or whom do you see?
3. In one sentence, how would you describe the purpose of your life?
4. What one goal do you have that is most important to you right now?
5. How would you respond to someone who said, "Do you believe in God?"
6. How would you respond to someone who said, "Are you ready for your life to come to an end?"
7. Do you believe in any kind of existence after this life?

The Journey Analogy

Counselor: "Sometimes people use the analogy that life is like a journey. If you were to describe your time now as coming toward the end of a journey, how would you describe this last part of the journey: for example, a walk across a desert, a climb up a mountain, an ocean voyage? What do you believe will happen at the end of your journey? What one thing do you feel you most need to do before your journey is over? To what extent do you sense God's presence with you on this journey? What kinds of thoughts and beliefs are you having at this time in your life? What worries you the most? What helps you feel relaxed and peaceful? Whom do you most want to be close to you during this time? What do you most want from that person? What can I personally do for you?" (End with a reference to the client's own imagery, explaining how you will help.)

Counselor's follow-up: (a) "_____, you have described your journey as a walk through a desert. Let's put something in that desert to refresh you, an oasis in the desert. What would that refreshing oasis be like? What would be comforting and refreshing to you in your dying? How might I help you create that oasis?" (b) "_____, I see that the end of your journey is very terrifying to you. Is there another possibility for the end of your journey? If you were to imagine the best possible end to your journey, what would it be like? How might we explore that as a possibility?"

Three Views of Dying

Counselor: "I will read three statements to you that I would like you to comment on."

1. Chief Crazy Horse, the Sioux Indian, before entering into a battle would always say, "Ho Ka Hey," which means "Today is a good day to die" (LaPointe, 1976, p. 160). For you, how is today a good day to die? How is today a bad day to die?
2. As he was about to die, Socrates said, "Now the time has come, and we must go away—I to die, and you to live. Which is better is known to god alone" (Plato, 1956, p. 49). How is death perhaps better than living? How is living perhaps better than dying?
3. A philosopher of death has related the following short parable: "A Christian died one day, and he awoke to find himself before the big Buddha. And the big Buddha did not smile" (Amato, 1985, p. 15). In what sense does that parable discourage you? In what sense does that parable encourage you?

The Sacred Shrine

Counselor: "Many people believe in powerful forces beyond what can be seen or touched. Some people believe in a personal Higher Power, some in a Christian God, some in a Hindu God, some in a Divine Force that is inside everyone, some in a Divine Nature, some in Divine Energy. There are many names and descriptions of how people perceive powerful forces beyond what can be seen or touched. I would like to learn about how you view what many people label as Divine. Between now and the next time I visit, I would like for you to construct a Sacred Shrine that expresses what you label as Divine. Choose someplace in your house (a bookshelf, an end table, on top of a dresser) where you can build a Sacred Shrine. At this Sacred Shrine, I would like you to put various items: pictures, mementos, special objects, certain books or words—items that somehow symbolize your conception of the Divine. Then, when I visit next time, I would like for you to explain to me what is at your Sacred Shrine."

EXERCISES FOR EXPANDING ON SPIRITUAL EXPLORATIONS

The Spiritual Journal

Counselor: "I believe that it would be helpful to you and me if, starting today, you were to keep a spiritual journal. In this spiritual journal, you will write down any thoughts or feelings that you have about God, afterlife, religion, or spirituality. Whenever you write things down in this journal, label your entry with a date, time, and occasion. Then, whenever we next meet, you can share with me some of the things that you have written. You won't have to share anything that you do not want to share. I would, however, like you to share some of what you write. That way we can have some discussions and we can possibly both benefit from those discussions."

Picturing the Divine

Counselor: "Many people have different impressions of the Divine. Some think of the Divine as a creative force, some as an angry person, some as a loving person. Some people do not believe the universe has a Divine aspect at all. I would like you to draw your impressions of the Divine. However you see the Divine, draw that impression. Try to be very creative, drawing a picture different from any picture that you have ever seen: a picture that captures all your feelings and thoughts about what is Divine."

Healthy Death Story

Counselor: "There is an assignment that I would like to give to you. I would like for you in the next week to write what I call a 'healthy death story.' In this story I want you to imagine the best possible death that can happen to you. It has to have only elements that are actually possible, but it will be the best possible death for you. In your story, mention how you die, where you die, what you look like, who is with you, what your thoughts are like, and what you are doing as you die. Go into a lot of details and let your imagination really take over as you portray this ideal death that is also a possible death. The next time that we are together, we will spend some time reviewing the story. If you prefer to draw a picture of your death scenario rather than write a story, go ahead and draw, and we can discuss that when I next see you. Then each time we meet in the future, we will explore ways in which we might make part of that story closer to reality."

SUMMARY

Because religious-spiritual issues have been shown to be of great importance to the dying person, several tools have been presented for the counselor to use in helping clients explore their own religious-spiritual struggles, concerns, and resources. All of these tools have been presented in such a way as to convey the message that the counselor is completely open to the client's religious-spiritual preferences. Through these tools, clients can feel free to express their thoughts and emotions without fear of being influenced or proselytized by the counselor. To the counselor and to the client: May your explorations be enjoyable and profitable.

REFERENCES

Amato, J. A. (1985). *Death book.* Peoria, IL: Ellis Press.

Andersen, H., & MacElveen-Hoehn, P. (1988). Gay clients with AIDS: New challenges for hospice programs. *Hospice Journal, 4*(2), 37-54.

Anderson, H. (1989). After the diagnosis: An operational theology for the terminally ill. *Journal of Pastoral Care, 40*(2), 141-150.

Axelrod, C. D. (1986). Reflections on the fear of death. *Omega: Journal of Death & Dying, 17*(1), 51-64.

Hinton, J. M. (1963). The physical and mental distress of the dying. *Quarterly Journal of Medicine, 32*, 1-21.

Jarvis, G. K., & Northcott, H. C. (1987). Religion and differences in morbidity and mortality. *Social Science & Medicine, 25*(7), 813-824.

Kramer, K. (1988). *The sacred art of dying.* New York: Paulist Press.

LaPointe, J. (1976). *Legends of the Lakota.* San Francisco: Indian Historical Press.

Leviton, D. (1986). Thanatological theory and my dying father. *Journal of Death & Dying, 17*(2), 127-144.

Mauritzen, J. (1988). Pastoral care for the dying and bereaved. *Death Studies, 12*, 111-122.

Plato. (1956). *Euthyphro, apology, crito* (revised ed., F. J. Church, Trans.). Indianapolis: Bobbs-Merrill.

Propst, L. R. (1980). The comparative efficacy of religious and nonreligious imagery for the treatment of mild depression in religious individuals. *Cognitive Therapy and Research, 4*, 167-178.

Rando, T. A. (1984). *Grief, dying, and death.* Champaign, IL: Research Press.

Rogers, C. R. (1986). Client-centered therapy In I. L. Kutash & A. Wolf (Eds.), *Psychotherapist's casebook: Therapy and technique in practice* (pp. 197-208). San Francisco: Jossey-Bass.

Smith, D. C. (1990). *Achieving a "healthy" death: The dying person's attitudinal contributions.* Unpublished master's thesis. Bradley University, Peoria, IL.

Smith, D. C., & Maher, M. F. (1991). Healthy death. *Counseling and Values, 36*(1), 42-48.

Watts, A. W. (1961). *Psychotherapy east and west.* New York: Random House.

Exploring the Counselor's Role in "Right to Die" Decisions

DAVID FARRUGIA

Rather than sudden and rapid death following a lifetime of enjoyment and meaning, most people die after an extended period of gradually deteriorating health (Nelson & Bernat, 1989). There is almost always a therapy available that could prolong life. In fact, Nelson and Bernat (1989) stated that most hospital deaths require someone to decide how long life will be prolonged and at what quality. Advances in medicine and technology that prolong life without providing a cure have outpaced the development of a social and legal consensus regarding the use or the discontinuation of such procedures (Abbing, 1988; Keilitz, Bilzor, Hafemeister, Brown, & Dudyshyn, 1989). Ever since the New Jersey Supreme Court handed down the first "right to die" opinion in 1976 in the Karen Ann Quinlan case, medical, ethical, legal, and social issues have become more central to discussions regarding the conditions under which medical treatment that can prolong life should be withdrawn or withheld (Bosmann, Kay, & Conter, 1987).

New legislation is beginning to require specific procedures regarding patients' rights to refuse medical treatment. For example, Congress recently passed the Patient Self-Determination Act, which requires all hospitals and nursing homes to develop and implement a procedure for advising patients of their rights to accept or refuse treatments and to make advanced directives (Rubin, 1991). Unfortunately, there are a number of situations where current procedures and practices continue to fall short of a satisfactory application of the principles related to the right to die. The estimated 10,000 patients who are comatose or in a persistent vegetative state (PVS) add a significant element in right-to-die discussions. Also, it is important to recognize that the advent and growing problem of AIDS indicates that concern with issues regarding the right to die will continue and grow in the foreseeable future (Abbing, 1988).

In many cases, death-related decisions are not just a matter of medical expertise and procedure; rather, they are experienced as strongly felt emotional value judgments requiring ethical and personal consideration. Increasingly, counselors in and out of medical settings will be asked to assist both afflicted individuals as well as close family members in making decisions regarding right to die issues. The purpose of this article is to provide coun-

From "Exploring the Counselor's Role in 'Right to Die' Decisions," by D. Farrugia, 1993, *Counseling and Values, 37*, 61–69.

selors with a background of historical, religious, philosophical, and legal concepts that relate to decisions on terminating or withholding treatment from terminally ill patients.

HISTORICAL PERSPECTIVE

Actually, the term *right to die* is a popular misnomer. As Weber (1938) pointed out, if society truly believed that there is a right to die, that "right" would extend to a number of circumstances including suicide. Although suicide is generally not unlawful, it is certainly not sanctioned by Western society. Assisted suicide, even in cases of mercy killing, is not accepted by most Western societies; however, the law in America has recognized the right to refuse treatment, even when such treatment may be necessary to preserve life. Although the courts and writers who support the right to refuse treatment often make a distinction between euthanasia and refusal of treatment (even if it will lead to death), Fletcher (1988) suggested there is actually little distinction, because in both cases the intention is to bring about death.

In our society *euthanasia* is an emotional and value-laden term. The word euthanasia derives from Greek and originally meant a "good death," referring to the spiritual state of the dying person just prior to death (Carrick, 1985). In modern times active euthanasia has come to mean direct assistance in bringing about death such as in the administration of a lethal injection. Passive euthanasia means the withdrawal of life-prolonging measures in order to bring about death, such as the removal of a patient from a respirator. The terms *voluntary* and *involuntary* are used to denote consent or lack of consent by the dying individual (Goldberg, 1987).

Plato, Aristotle, and the Greek and Roman stoics all supported voluntary euthanasia when conditions were evident that would justify suicide, such as in the case of incurable physical or mental illness. Only the Pythagoreans adhered to a strict respect for life (Goldberg, 1987). Jewish law requires that life should be preserved at all costs, and active euthanasia is prohibited. Because Jewish law does not encourage the artificial prolongation of life, however, a number of writers have not ruled out passive euthanasia (Jakobovitz, 1959). The Roman Catholic position is like the Jewish tradition in recognizing the inviolability of human life. Roman Catholic ethics are, however, more liberal in the case of terminally ill people. Direct euthanasia is thought to be wrong because it entails a direct intention to end a person's life. Indirect euthanasia may be acceptable under the principle of double effect (doing good but bringing about a bad result without intent). An example might be the provision of lethal doses of medication to alleviate pain and not to bring about death directly (Paul II, 1980).

Most Protestant ethicists have treated questions of indirect euthanasia according to the specific situations that arise from an individual case (Goldberg, 1987). Fletcher (1974) supported some forms of euthanasia based on four considerations. The first consideration is on the quality of life for a person rather than on simple biological existence. The second consideration is on death's meaning for a person, when it may be desired as the only relief from a debilitating illness. The third consideration is the recognition that medical intervention at death may be considered against "nature." Finally, Fletcher (1975) stated that extraordinary means, special equipment, and surgery are not morally required for a person who is terminally ill.

According to Fletcher (1974), most Roman Catholic and Protestant moralists have a fairly extensive consensus on right to die issues. They agree that (a) a patient may be allowed to die when there is no reasonable prognosis and that (b) pain killers may be administered even though they may result secondarily in a patient's death (Fletcher, 1975). Despite general agreement, the literature does reflect contrary ethical opinion within these perspectives. For example, Barry (1986) suggested that death by omission (such as removal of life-prolonging equipment) and commission (such as a lethal injection) are equally wrong, and Connery (1982) stated that life-prolonging equipment could become overly burdensome and could be discontinued with incurable patients.

COURTS AND PHILOSOPHY

Over the last 15 years the courts have begun to address a number of cases related to the right to refuse treatment. The courts are generally considered to be circumspect, setting broad boundaries within which deliberations are usually left to doctor, patient, and family (Nevins, 1988). Fletcher (1988) has observed that the courts have tended to avoid the broader debate regarding euthanasia by employing illogical and semantic maneuvers, while building case precedent for voluntary indirect euthanasia. As an example, Fletcher (1988) pointed out that an essential part of the courts' efforts has been to ensure that a patient understands that death will come as a consequence of discontinuing a treatment, while at the same time stating that the death occurring after the removal of life support systems is from natural causes and not intended by the patient. In such rulings the courts have avoided questions regarding suicide or physician assistance in the patient's death. The courts have treated procedural and practical issues in handling right to refuse treatment cases by focusing on the following: (a) determining the competence of the terminally ill patient, (b) exploring the existence and significance of prior documentation of the patient's wishes (such as the existence of a living will), (c) determining what is and is not life-sustaining medical treatment, (d) identifying appropriate family or other surrogate decision makers when a patient is incompetent, and (e) defining the role of institutional ethics committees (Keilitz et al., 1989). Although by no means uniform and consistent, several legal directions are becoming evident. From a legal perspective, Fletcher (1988) found the right to refuse treatment was based on the common-law right to be free from nonconsensual bodily intrusion and the constitutional right to privacy.

Regarding the question of what is considered extraordinary means to prolong life, the courts have generally focused on the likely prognosis of the patient rather than on the means of prolonging life. Therefore, courts have allowed for the removal of the more obvious technological interventions such as respirators and dialysis machines, as well as the discontinuation of more basic interventions such as intravenous hydration and feeding tubes (Keilitz et al., 1989).

Second, the courts have sought to ensure that the terminally ill person has competently chosen to decline treatment. Generally, the courts have upheld the right to refuse treatment when competence can be shown. The three situations where the competency question has arisen include a conscious terminally ill patient, an incompetent patient in a prolonged coma or permanent vegetative state (PVS), and an incompetent patient who is severely and permanently debilitated but has some limited contact with the environment (Nevins, 1988). The courts have recognized that life expectancy is not an important criterion. A prognosis, including the reasonable possibility of returning to a cognitive and sapient life, is the most essential criterion. Cases involving an incompetent person in a PVS or in limited contact with reality are the most troublesome. If prior documentation exists stating the patient's wishes, that documentation is generally followed. Even when no documentation exists, however, if it can be shown that the patient verbally expressed the desire not to have life unduly prolonged, the courts have upheld the right of proxy decision makers to withhold treatment (Keilitz et al., 1989; Nevins, 1988). In cases where the prior wishes of the incompetent person with limited contact with reality cannot be shown, the courts have been the most reluctant to allow the withholding of treatment.

As an important side note in a study of 22 legal decisions in 14 states, Miles and August (1990) have noticed that the courts have been more likely to allow men (rather than women) who have become incompetent to discontinue treatment when no documentation of prior wishes have existed. In women's cases prior statements made to friends or relatives have not carried the same recognition of competence as prior statements made by men. Instead, the decision to maintain medical treatment was more likely to be given to a relative or the institution of care. Miles and August (1990) suggested that jurisprudential practice has undervalued the "communal" moral reasoning pattern observed in the cases involving women. They suggested the need for appropriate reforms. Despite significant avoidance of a number of issues in cases regarding the right to refuse treatment, there have been a number of legal developments through the courts and state legislatures. The vast majority of states now have statutes that establish procedures for forgoing life-sustaining treatments (Keilitz et al., 1989). Such mechanisms as "do-not-resuscitate" orders, living wills, and durable power of attorney for health care have been established as part of our current medical and legal systems. Beyond the legal developments over the last 15 years regarding the right to refuse treatment, the importance of the personal, emotional, and ethical experiences of the affected patient, family, and helping professionals cannot be understated. A number of writers, including Nelson and Bernat (1989), Goldberg (1987), and Powell (1982), have addressed these concerns. There are a number of ethical principles that are relevant to the issue of terminating or withholding treatment. The first is the principle of autonomy, or the right of persons to make decisions for themselves, which others must respect. Clearly, the Western tradition of respect for autonomy is central in right-to-die cases. In medicine, valid consent and refusal provides that competent adults can accept or refuse all treatments (Nelson & Bernat, 1989). Powell (1982) pointed out that age must also be considered when exploring ethical questions related to indirect euthanasia. If the patient in question is an adolescent or younger, competence and therefore the right to autonomous decisions cannot be presumed, even in the case of a conscious patient (Powell, 1984). As a result, family and related decision makers are likely to become the focus of decision making.

A second critical ethical principle is that of nonmaleficence, which is included in the oath of Hippocrates where the physician is enjoined to do no harm. Nonmaleficence can apply when medical intervention is sustaining life without any hope of medical recovery. The typical result of such treatment is prolonged suffering for the patient and family. In the case of patients in PVS or with severely limited contact with reality, suffering may be more difficult to demonstrate. Significant people in the patient's life, however, often bear a special pain because of the subsistence of the afflicted person.

The related principle of beneficence is also central to questions surrounding the discontinuation or withholding of medical treatment. Beneficence is the moral duty to promote good. Proponents of the right to discontinue treatment have pointed out that prolonging life in cases where a reasonable recovery was not possible was really a matter of prolonging death (Goldberg, 1987). Thus in order to promote good we may be impelled by the principle of beneficence to withhold or discontinue treatment. The ethical principles discussed above are imbedded in other philosophical beliefs for those who believe in indirect euthanasia. These include the position that quality of life is more important than quantity. Essentially, sheer biological life is not considered worth living. In addition there is a moral distinction between active and passive euthanasia. Finally there is a belief that some limits should be placed on human suffering. As Fletcher (1988) asked, if animals can be put to death, why can't humans be given the same humane treatment?

Writers who have opposed euthanasia in any form (Cole, 1989), as well as some writers who are less categoric (Weber, 1988), have raised concerns that individuals and society in general may abuse the use of indirect euthanasia and discontinue medical treatment for congenitally cognitively disabled persons, poor persons, persons who have not given their consent, and others. There are a number of reasons why this kind of scenario is very unlikely. First, hospice care in our society has shown that dying people can be treated as individuals (Magno, 1990). Care is provided on an individual basis and is sensitive to the particular needs and concerns of each case. In addition, research by Wade and Anglin (1987) showed that attitudes toward euthanasia are not governed by categorical support of euthanasia but rather by situational consideration of physical condition and pain, by the lack of expectation of recovery, and by the mental alertness of the patient. Perhaps most importantly, even when euthanasia is sanctioned and allowed by a society as in the Netherlands, Abbing (1988) observed that abuses could not occur when euthanasia was clearly regulated and properly governed by law.

THE ROLE OF THE COUNSELOR

Only recently have the fields of counseling and psychology begun to address questions of death. Feifel (1990) described his early efforts to research psychological questions related to death in the mid 1950s. During those years Feifel reported experiences tantamount to being "blackballed" by other psychologists and health-care professionals. It seems curious to observe these attitudes in the helping professions, especially when it is noted that Sigmund Freud ended his life through an agreement with his physician, who gave him repeated doses of two centigrams of morphine after a long period of painful cancer of the jaw (Schur, 1972). What is most important is that over a 15-year period between 1965 and 1980, the number of publications related to death and dying increased over 1000% (Barnard, 1980).

Despite the increase of professional interest in issues related to death and dying, there do not seem to be any standard guidelines for counselors when working with terminally ill persons where the question of the right to refuse treatment is evident. In an attempt to suggest tentative directions, attitudes of counselors and health care workers will be discussed, related professionals' positions will be examined, and suggestions for counselors dealing with these issues will be developed.

In a study of 130 counselors, Sullivan (1983) found that the majority supported a terminally ill patient's right to die, with even stronger support shown for indirect euthanasia. Those counselors who had experiences with a terminally ill relative tended to be more open and direct with patients and families regarding questions of euthanasia. In related research Bosmann, Kay, and Conter (1987) studied 190 health care professionals, three fourths of whom were associated with long-term care facilities. The majority, 83%, recognized the appropriateness of indirect euthanasia, whereas only 21% believed that direct euthanasia could be justified. It is curious that the majority felt the family should not be involved in questions of euthanasia despite the fact that family involvement was part of the policy of most facilities, and that courts have supported the need for family involvement. The authors noted that these results may be because of the complexity and emotion involved in euthanasia cases. In another study on attitudes toward death, Howard (1974) found that nurse's aides who had witnessed a death in a nursing home tended to avoid talking about death in general with other nursing home patients.

In a special article in the *New England Journal of Medicine,* 12 medical doctors supported the importance of providing flexible care to terminally ill patients, including do-not-resuscitate orders and the implementation of withdrawing life-prolonging interventions, and including intravenous hydration and tube feeding (Wanzer et al., 1989). Their position included the beliefs that patients' wishes should be respected in such cases and should be solicited in advance of critical stages of the disease or condition. Furthermore, patients should be able to anticipate being allowed to die in hospitals or nursing homes. All but two of the physicians did not feel it was morally wrong to assist in the rational suicide of a terminally ill patient. Finally, the physicians emphasized the need to maintain high quality palliative care until the patient's actual death (Wanzer et al., 1989).

In a statement prepared for a symposium for The Group for the Advancement of Psychiatry, Butler (1973) stated that psychiatrists should support the right of patients to refuse treatment. Butler also said that there was no reason to extend life if there was not an ability to extend quality. Finally, the statement suggested that the goal of treatment in these cases was similar to the goal of psychiatry in general, namely to preserve the identity and dignity of the patient.

Lynn (1988) stated that the role of health care services was to ensure that each patient had the best possible life from that patient's perspective. Lynn suggested decisions regarding requests to terminate treatment should be delayed in order to give the patient time to consider the finality of the request. All of the alternatives should be discussed with the patient. If the patient reasonably preferred to discontinue treatment, that choice should be allowed. Lynn strongly condemned any role of health care workers in direct euthanasia, however.

Bernstein (1980) suggested that the social worker's role for the terminally ill should include discussing the whole range of concerns that confront a person who is terminally ill. These concerns would include the right to a natural death, living wills, and do-not-resuscitate orders, anatomical gifts, power of attorney, joint bank accounts and wills, and insurance and estate questions. According to Bernstein (1980), the social worker should act as part of an interdisciplinary team often acting as an information and referral source for many of the previously mentioned concerns, especially in monetary and estate matters.

A number of suggested directions would seem appropriate for counselors based on a review of the preceding studies. In addition, Smith and Maher (1991) made an important fundamental observation that writers who have addressed concerns related to death and dying seem to ensure that there is a "healthy" death. Smith and Maher (1991) defined a healthy death as one that involves the dying person's attitudes and decisions about his or her death as well as the experience of dying. This definition implies that the dying person's family and their caregivers will act in a manner that will create a mutual, psychological relationship. For such a mutual relationship to develop, right to die issues and subsequent decisions by the dying person, family members, counselors, and other health care providers would seem to be a necessary part of a "healthy death." Like most matters in counseling, the counselor should respect and help clarify the client's concerns. Should the patient or a member of the patient's family raise the issue of the patient's right to die, the counselor should objectively assist the client to explore the relevant issues. In most cases, exploration of religious and ethical perspectives would probably be part of the client's exploration. Focus on patient control of the decision-making process would be appropriate. Taking a cue from Bernstein (1980), it might also be appropriate to discuss with the patients or family members the issue of the right to refuse or discontinue treatment. Care should be taken not to imply any direction regarding the question. It may be appropriate to approach the issue by inquiring if information is desired by the patient or family on the topic. Regular intake procedure and subsequent patient contact should include this vital concern. The counselor's role is not going to be limited to questions regarding decision making in right-to-die situations. The emotional pain of implementing a decision and the aftermath of grief in any death may also be issues where the counselor can directly assist family members. In cases of disagreement among family members, the counselor may become involved in resolution efforts. Finally, as indicated by the research, counselors may also work with other professionals regarding their reactions to patients' wishes and deaths in cases of indirect euthanasia. In short, counselors should be both proactive and reactive to the needs of clients, families, and other professionals according to the circumstances of each individual case.

As current social factors continue to influence our experience in life, including the advancement of medical technology, the aging of the population, and the growing problem of AIDS, counselors will increasingly be called on to assist in helping answer questions related to the right to die. Further consideration by the counseling profession of right to die issues remains an unmet challenge, a challenge that should be met with the development of ethical and procedural guidelines by the counseling profession addressing right to die issues.

REFERENCES

Abbing, H. (1988). Dying with dignity and euthanasia: A view from the Netherlands. *Journal of Palliative Care, 4*(4), 70-74.

Barnard, C. (1980). *Good life good death: A doctor's case for euthanasia and suicide.* Englewood Cliffs, NJ: Prentice-Hall.

Barry, R. (1986). Facing hard cases: The ethics of assisted feeding. *Issues in law and medicine, 2*(2), 99-115.

Bernstein, B. (1980). Legal needs of the ill: The social workers' role on an interdisciplinary team. *Health and Social Work, 5*(3) 68-72.

Bosmann, H., Kay, J., & Conter, E. (1987). Geriatric euthanasia: Attitudes and experience of health professionals. *Social Psychiatry, 22*(14), 1–4.

Butler, R. (1973). *The right to die: Decision and decision makers.* Topeka, KS: Group for the Advancement of Psychiatry.

Carrick, P. (1985). *Medical ethics in antiquity: Philosophy perspective on abortion and euthanasia.* Hingham, MA: Reidel and Kluwer.

Cole, J. (1989). Moral dilemma: To kill or allow to die? *Death Studies, 13,* 393-406.

Connery, J. (1982). In the matter of Claire Conroy. *Linacre Q., 52,* 325-326.

Feifel, H. (1990). Psychology and death: Meaningful rediscovery. *American Psychologist, 48*(4), 537-543.

Fletcher, J. (1974). Anti-Dysthanasia: The problem of prolonging death. In R. Reeves, R. Neale, & A. Kutscher (Eds.), *Pastoral care of the dying and bereaved: Selected readings.* Washington, DC: American Psychological Association.

Fletcher, J. (1975). The right to live and the right to die. In M. Kohl (Ed.), *Beneficent euthanasia.* Buffalo, NY: Prometheus.

Fletcher, I. (1988). The courts and euthanasia. *Law, Medicine and Health Care, 15*(4), 223-230.

Goldberg, R. (1987). The right to die: The case for and against voluntary passive euthanasia. *Disability, Handicap & Society, 2*(1), 21-39.

Howard, E. (1974). The effect of work experience in a nursing home on the attitudes held by nurse aides toward death. *The Gerontologist, 14*(1), 54-56.

Jakobovitz, I. (1959). *Jewish medical ethics.* New York: Philosophical Library.

Keilitz, I., Bilzor, J., Hafemeister, T., Brown, V., & Dudyshyn, D. (1989). Decision making in authorizing and withholding life sustaining medicine: From Quinlan to Cruzan. *Mental and Physical Disability Law Reporter, 13*(5), 482–493.